17 to Life:
A Black Boy Memoir

Available at:

www.lulu.com/orondeash

www.orondeash.com

www.amazon.com

www.youtube.com/bygincpresents

17 to Life: A Black Boy Memoir

On Becoming a Human... Being in America

by

oronde ash

bygINCpublishing
PO Box 33332, Raleigh, NC 27636
919-600-3210
bygINCpresents@live.com

Published by bygINCpublishing, Raleigh, NC

bygINCpresents@live.com

www.orondeash.com

ISBN 978-0-578-03675-5

Printed in the United States of America

Cover photo of author: © 1998

Photographer: Koren Atwater

Photo Editing: Jason Martin

To My Mother

For deciding I was worth the pain of
childbirth
And the faults of men

For putting up with my adolescent
withdrawal

For showing me strength and
understanding that all will be better

bygINCpublishing titles coming soon

<u>The Adolescent Philosopher</u>

<u>james, mos def, MY BROTHA and me: resampling</u>
<u>conscience in the b-boy rawkus</u>

<u>Letters to James Baldwin</u>

TABLE OF CONTENTS

INTRODUCTION

I began writing **17 to Life: A Black Boy Memoir** during my four years at Brooklyn Technical High School, 1990-94. The story had to be written then while possibility was still fresh in me. I saw how the working world lay waste to adolescent dreams and so I began recording my innocence before it was corrupted. I kept a journal noting what I understood about the changes in me physically, intellectually, spiritually. Adolescence was constant flux so I tried to keep pace by recording and studying my life the same way I would any subject in school.

High school was to be a new chapter in my development as a human being, the way I felt about my self, my family, my relationship to people and to the world. But after one year, I was still the same introverted, self-absorbed, timid soul trapped in a life I didn't want. I was too afraid to change my situation but knew I had to. I began seeing glimpses of the personality I wanted to showcase, and he was actually a smiling, happy, funny guy. No more sulking away, cursing the world for not figuring out my pain. No more dismissing happiness as fake and unattainable. No more wishing to be something yet never fully making it happen.

I made the decision to change and began pursuing the life I wanted, the way I wanted. And I've been better for it. That's the happy part. But before all that, I had to deal with the other stuff. Fear, angst, confusion, doubt, envy and hate among others.

During middle and elementary school, too much was happening in my life inside and out. I lacked the capacity to fully understand it all but that didn't stop me from thinking about my circumstance all the time. I had to deal with that history before anything good could happen to me. I saw too many miserable adults still stuck in their childhood memories. I refused to be one of them.

What you will read in the pages to follow are my recollections of coming into my own as a human being, as a brother, a son, as a man. You will see me take baby steps towards the *self* I am today --a man who understands and accepts his history enough to share it with you. **17 to Life** follows me from fourth grade to high school graduation, from my first day in America, off the plane in Newark airport, 1985, to me riding a Greyhound bus to Canada, deported from an America I had slowly accepted was not so much the troubling life I had lived, but a means to achieve the life I wanted. Those eight years had earned me liberty beyond measure.

Seventeen is a tough age for young men. For some, *seventeen to life* is the death knell handed down from a judge. Those boys will be locked away from the life they once dreamed of.

For others, *seventeen to life* is the promise of what's ahead. Those boys have studied and worked, learned and experienced, reflected and grown. College, a job or some other prospect is waiting and they feel ready for and excited by the challenge.

I hope that sharing my story will help someone get ready for their journey to life by understanding, overcoming and accepting who they are. Any journey begins with an honest look in the mirror and assessment of who is staring back.

17 to Life: A Black Boy Memoir chronicles that look back to self-hood. Perhaps there is something in the tale about you, for you or someone you know.

I.

THE NEW

IMMIGRANT

"I'm cold," a whimper inside would foretell. Winter was approaching. I had heard the voice before in St. Vincent, the island where I was born. He sounded happier then. In America, the voice wanted to speak but his will was weak. "I'm not dumb," the voice assured me. "You're not dumb. You have to say something." One day the voice did.

Maybe I had enough of the classroom walls at Evergreen Elementary. In St. Vincent, my school didn't have inner walls. The building was one open space like a warehouse. I could look around and see my friends in the next class or hear them when they talked. There was a collective energy feeding me back home.

Perhaps I was longing for island warmth. Every day I woke up in this new state and it got colder and colder. The leaves outside, alive and green when I arrived, like leaves are supposed to be, were turning orange and brown and red. The trees were dying, blood rushing to the leaves before they fell and got trampled on the ground. The kids at Evergreen stomped on the leaves and laughed as they squashed the life out of them. Then the snow fell and covered up all the death.

It was early winter before I wrote to anyone back home. I cut off my father and all his friends because television told me they were inconsiderate fools. In 1985, Nancy Reagan's "Just Say No" to drugs campaign opened my eyes to the idiots my father had surrounded me with.

On the island, I saw my father's friends and him smoking marijuana when they hung out. My father was in his mid twenties when I was born and a Rastafarian who believed, among other things, that smoking marijuana was natural. All his friends were the same age and into Rastafarianism as well. From age five or six, they would let me roll joints and smoke with them. Accepted in their company, I felt big, important, special. Surely, my father and his friends must have known what was best for me.

But TV warned that smoking marijuana killed brain cells. I figured the reason I was getting C's and D's on my fourth grade report card was because my father had killed my brain cells. Marijuana was the reason I was forgetting my island friends and the things we used to do, the reason I felt alone and confused, the reason my brain refused to work as well as it used to.

I never reasoned that island memories were falling away as I adjusted to a completely different culture. Old St. Vincent had to make way for new America. The summer comforts of my life were changing, falling, swept over, under and melting away. I blamed my father, his smoking, all who lived on the island and their stupid island ways for my psychic limbo. I cut him and all of St. Vincent out of my life.

It's sad to think about the sudden, sureness of my decision. In only six months, I had turned against the one person I loved above all else; the man who spent hours teaching me soccer; the man I ran to when my mother and her boyfriend, Mudd, tried to hurt each other in front of the town and only succeeded in embarrassing me. My father bought me my first Bible when I was six and talked to me about God in a human way and not the fire and brimstone terror of the Anglican pastors. (I didn't speak to my father until eight years later. "He can't be the one who made you dumb," I'd hear a careless whisper in my heart. But I didn't listen. I was losing the connection.)

Maybe it was all this uncertainty that caused me to erupt that Wednesday afternoon in school. Maybe I was a brat who didn't get his way one day and threw a tantrum. Whatever the reason, I snapped.

My teacher, Mrs. DiPeppi, had just returned from lunch and the class had our usual fifteen minutes of free time to draw, read or write. I wanted to practice typing on the computer but somebody beat me to it. I was upset, wandered over to the window and stared outside, not thinking of anything in particular. Soon I began feeling sad and kept my gaze out the window even after Mrs. DiPeppi called me back to my seat.

That day, I hated… I hated life. I hated the snow, the fall, hated my family, hated the skin I was in. I hated America for being cold and damp and not being anything close to the land of my dreams. I hated not knowing enough or having enough. I hated New Jersey; hated the state I was in.

I didn't laugh the way I used to on the island. I was special there. I missed being a special boy, nurtured by a town that always looked out for me. I missed me.

That Wednesday afternoon, I decided to end the hours holding anxiety and frustration inside like a disciplined immigrant child. Someone had to feel the wrath of a boy slowly going wrong.

"If you're good, we'll watch Slim Goodbody today instead of Friday," Mrs. DiPeppi said. I didn't give a damn about Slim Goodbody. He was a character in a series of videos we watched in Health class. Slim wore a tight body suit with a painting of the human organs all over so that if he talked about the heart, lungs or stomach, he would point to where the organ was. I didn't know what was inside me. At least Slim could remove his body suit when the camera turned off. I had to live in my crazy, confused, black boy skin every minute of the day. I was a slim nobody from nowhere anybody cared about. I didn't wear my self on the outside like the American kids seemed to do with ease. I couldn't. I didn't know how to do so in this new place.

Nobody saw the real me. No one heard the rumbling volcano or felt the hot magma burning away my insides. But they would… They would.

"I HATE YOU ALL. I HATE YOU ALL."

I wrote those words on a blackboard at the back of the classroom. Below it I wrote the names of all the kids in the class. The kids were shocked by what I did. Mrs. DiPeppi calmed the class down quickly and walked back to where I was.

"What's wrong, Oronde?" she asked. Hadn't she seen?

"I hate you all. I hate you all," I screamed at her.

Mrs. DiPeppi tried to get me to return to my seat at the front of the room. But that day, I would not be moved. It wasn't her day. The day was for me to be with the voice I was hearing inside. The day was for me to listen to his cry again and again and again. I sat at the back of the room reflecting on the dying world outside. I was cold and I wanted to go home.

I wanted to play with GI Joe action figures, a He-Man sword, Transformers, an orange Nerf football. I wanted to eat potato chips, hamburgers, Domino's pizza or grilled hot dogs with the black lines on them like in the television commercials. I wanted a lot of the things I began to see in America. I wanted the junk.

My grandmother wasn't crazy about junk. Me, my sister Annie and my two cousins, Gerry and Carla, ate as healthy as the doctor said Grandma had to. The broccoli and cauliflower on my dinner plate didn't have the tastes I was used to. Those were new vegetables to me. Even the yams, carrots and potatoes I was accustomed to eating in St. Vincent, soon lost their taste. America seemed to rob the flavor in them. I resented Grandma for force-feeding me her healthy, green crap, especially when it looked like American kids ate junk all the time.

Once school began in Fall 1985 and the lunchroom at Evergreen Elementary in Scotch Plains, New Jersey was ripe with cookies, jellybeans, candy bars, lollipops, fruit roll-ups and talk of lobster and steak for dinner, I had issues with my grandmother's menu. She never cooked anything like that. Couldn't there be some variety in my diet? Didn't she notice how skinny I was compared to every other kid in America? Pizza made people bigger. I heard something on TV about complex starches and carbohydrates that were supposed to be healthy. Hadn't she heard?

Television was teaching me much more than American style nutrition. We didn't have TV in Barrouallie *(barrow-LEE)*, my island hometown. The older people told us the mountains surrounding the town blocked the TV waves. Still, Barrouallie offered a lot to gaze upon.

In America, the TV set became my window to a world my grandmother could never afford. The pictures moved me, took me places. Four TVs were in the house. The biggest was in the family room, but nobody ever went in the family room. Hard plastic covered the velvet sofas making them uncomfortable to sit on. The minute I set foot inside the family room, I was asked to leave lest I break a vase or spill food on something. There was never any family-ing in that room... ever.

A twelve-inch TV set was in the kitchen. Grandma watched that one all day. Another set was in Auntie Sonja's room and a nine-inch, black and white set with rabbit ears was in the basement. After school, Gerry controlled the set in Auntie Sonja's room. He watched *Good Times* and *Video Music Box* for an hour and a half, never the cartoons I liked. I usually ran to the basement as soon as I got home from school, that is, if cousin Carla or my sister Annie hadn't beaten me down there.

The basement was dark, dank and dusty, with water pipes exposed along the walls and the ceiling. The tiled floor had no rugs or carpets and got miserably cold in early fall. The changing season was something to get used to. I had arrived in the heat and sunshine of summer. America was green then, gardens growing, the Lord's sun shining down on me. My mother, my sisters and I were joining the bigger Ash clan. I finally met the grandmother who had sent me money at Christmas and birthdays, the cousins who had lovingly packed their children's books and spare clothes to make me the envy of all my island friends.

When fall came, the temperature grew more chilled and that only compounded the anxiety of fitting into a new school. My mother was gone from the house all week working as a nanny a few towns away. I had to get used to that separation. My sister Annie was the same age as cousin Carla so the were always playing together. In St. Vincent Annie and I were always together... Not anymore.

My cousin Gerry was four years older than me and spent afternoons with his school buddies, leaving me alone in the cold basement with the rabbit ear TV set and the water dripping from the ceiling pipes. Even the heat didn't want to stay down there. Add to that my gnawing fear of being alone in the dark and I swear I'd hear voices talking to me.

It took a lot of my nine year-old nerves to stay in the basement but the reward was worth it. I watched all the TV shows I wanted without interruption. *GI Joe, Transformers, Diff'rent Strokes, Benson, Gimme a Break, The Jeffersons.* All I had to do was put up with minor discomforts like cold feet and fear.

When I didn't feel like staying in the basement I'd shuffle back and forth between Gerry's TV and Grandma's. There wasn't much variety in her viewing. Grandma watched one network from breakfast to bedtime: ABC. One of the few exceptions was Thursday nights when she watched *The Cosby Show* at 8 o'clock on NBC.

Monday Night Football was another blessing. Grandma didn't know anything about football but she was loyal to the ABC network and MNF was on ABC. I had fallen in love with American football, especially the college game. I never heard voices in the basement on Saturday afternoons nor was I scared or even hungry between the double and triple-headers. Something else was going on down there: I was learning.

Football taught me American geography and a bit of the country's personality. Oklahoma and Barry Switzer were in the Southwest Conference, next to, but not in the same league as Louisiana State University. The Alabama Crimson Tide hated their South Eastern Conference (SEC) rivals the Auburn Tigers even though Auburn had an incredible runner named Bo Jackson who I kept hearing about over and over again. Army vs. Navy was the biggest game of the year except any time Notre Dame played a ranked opponent.

At Penn State, Michigan, Ohio and other Northern schools, coaches ran the ball straight ahead because the fields got hard and slick for running backs to cut and change directions in late fall and early winter. The announcers also kept saying something about a Mid-western work ethic that, I assumed, made it easier for the players to survive three hours in freezing fall temperatures and brutal contact.

In the Southwest Conference and SEC, teams used the option running attack, while in the Western Athletic Conference (WAC) and Pacific Athletic Conference (PAC -10) teams threw the ball down the field more because Saturday afternoon weather was always nice in California.

To be a quarterback you had to be at least six feet two inches, 180-200 pounds, and white. Running backs and wide receivers were black. Tight ends and offensive linemen --usually the smartest guys on the team, according to the Chevrolet Scholar-Athlete Award announced at halftime-- were always white. Linebackers were black, except for middle linebackers, who were usually white, along with their head coaches.

Saturday afternoon football, specifically Notre Dame football, made me want to go to college and experience the excitement in the stadiums. South Bend sounded so much like its own glorious country it would be another year until I accepted that it was an actual town in Indiana and not some mythical Shangri-La.

"All you have to do is get a soccer scholarship," a faint voice in my head would offer. That's the way all the black boys did it in the movies.

On TV, the black boy was rarely the quarterback. Instead, he was the go-to receiver or running back. He never got the blond-haired, blue-eyed head cheerleader or even said much on screen but it was obvious the boy was going to college on a scholarship. The boy was always the first in his family to advance beyond high school and carried the hopes of a generation, of his neighborhood, of black people. A lot was expected of the boy.

I saw my tract before me. Scotch Plains was a soccer-obsessed town. I was shocked to see the level of interest for my island game. Maybe God was looking out for me. Why bless me with soccer skills and a competitive nature? Why send me to a town where the high school soccer team had been New Jersey State champs two years running? God had a plan for me and it had to do with Scotch Plains and soccer. I had prayed to God every night I could remember. My first ambition in life was to pastor in my town's Anglican Church. Even though I didn't think about God as much in America, I still had faith He worked miracles for those who abided by His rules.

Bob Ross, the gym teacher at Evergreen saw me play kickball one day and immediately called one of his buddies, Joe McEvoy. Mr. McEvoy called Grandma one evening in mid-October and the following Saturday morning, cousin Gerry walked me to the middle school fields.

There were five or ten soccer games going on at once, parents clapping and yelling, balls flying all over the place. The fields were actually green grass instead of dirt patches full of goat droppings, glass or rocks like in St. Vincent. There were no youth teams back home. Kids played in the streets, on the beach or in the park after the older guys were done. In Scotch Plains, however, youth soccer was organized. The games mattered. Every kid at school played. Gerry found Mr. McEvoy who gave me an orange shirt and sent me off to kick the ball around with the other boys in orange shirts. The orange team won that day.

Saturdays with the McEvoy family introduced me to the pleasures of the American spirit. I got to know them well during the course of our undefeated, championship run in fall 1985. There was Joe, who was on the team with me, his sister Jennifer, three years older, and mom and dad --the perfect American family. They had a pool, cable TV, a basketball hoop and all kinds of balls and toys in the garage. Joe's room was full of posters of athletes, actors, comic book heroes. His carpet, in his room, was strewn with his baseball cards, his action figures, his clothes. Joe even had his own TV set.

Mrs. McEvoy asked Joe what he wanted to eat and she made it. When they went grocery shopping, Joe picked out his favorite candy bars and soda, not broccoli or cauliflower. Most important to me, Joe talked to his parents and they seemed to listen to him. Mrs. McEvoy hugged him and told him she loved him. We never did that where I lived.

Whenever I was around the McEvoys there was never a raised voice. Of course, that could have all been for show, but I didn't care to know reality then. Just like on TV, I was with the perfect American family and felt accepted by them. Mrs. McEvoy spoke to me softly, listened to me and catered to my needs. For once, I felt like an American child, alive with the warmth and material excess island lore promised me was commonplace there.

The teammates I interacted with on the weekends could talk to their parents and get what they wanted. Their lives were not defined by the idea that kids should be seen and not heard. At nine or ten years old, my teammates were being prepared for an America that needed people who knew what they wanted. They were being prepared to participate in a society of independent thinkers, movers and shakers. What did island life prepare me for except to be thankful for what little hand-me-downs I got? And as for independent thinking, island kids were told to be quiet and then slapped quiet if they said anything. In America, kids talked. I wanted to talk the same way but couldn't fashion the words. I had never practiced this new, American way of engaging the world.

There were issues on my mind. New people, new situations, new observations flashed questions and comments across my senses but it seemed impolite for a fourth grader to bring things up in the house so I never opened up to anyone there. Instead of coming out, my crude notions dove deep and implanted themselves on my stomach walls. It was frustrating not to explore or articulate my own ideas. I knew I had thoughts and feelings but I could not access them like the American kids did. Every now and then, I would feel my stomach grumbling and knew some pent up emotion was aching to come out.

One day, about three months into fourth grade, I playfully slapped a boy named Chuck across the face. I don't know if there is such a thing as a playful slap, but that's what I thought I did. Chuck and I had been pushing each other on the football field because he was kicking and tripping instead of playing two-hand touch. That wasn't fair. Rules were rules. We had all agreed to play by them.

On the steps leading into the building Chuck and I began tugging at each other again and soon were swinging wildly. We were both sent to the principal's office. My grandmother gave me a whipping when I got home that afternoon. I was convinced she didn't like me.

There were other incidents where it seemed I was letting out some pent up frustration.

One Sunday morning, I didn't feel like going to church. It was already a hot day and I knew I would pass out before the two-hour service was up. Grandma was standing in the front doorway ushering my sister Annie, cousin Carla and me out the door. My shirt and tie, both hand-me-downs from Gerry, were too big and too tight. I was sick of being buttoned up and formal. My teammates wore comfortable jeans and sneakers to their Sunday morning church services. Why did I have to dress up to talk to the same God? It wasn't fair.

"I don't want to go to church," I mumbled as I walked out the front door. Thinking my grandmother was out of earshot, I turned to my sister Annie and said, "I hate her." Mistake.

Grandma opened the door, walked down the three front steps, pulled me by the arm and slapped me across the face.

"You must learn some manners," she said. "Now go to church."

Other signs of an inner discomfort began appearing.

The neighbor's apple tree hung into the front yard. In late fall, apples would fall onto the driveway and rot. Every day I saw worms crawling out of the rotten cores. My sister Annie and I swore we tasted blood in the apple juice Grandma would buy. We were the only ones in the house who tasted the blood. Everyone else drank it up without question. I figured the rest were just used to the peculiar taste.

To this day, I don't know why my sister and I both tasted blood in the apple juice, but we did. She and I would dump our half empty glasses into the sink when Grandma wasn't looking. The apple juice tasted fine at my teammates' houses. I wondered why?

For the most part, I kept calm in the house. Playing soccer and spending Saturday afternoons or entire weekends with the McEvoy

10

family provided needed respite. No matter how much I smiled, even after Mr. McEvoy took Joe and me to the Meadowlands to watch Kareem, Magic and the Los Angeles Lakers play NBA basketball against the New Jersey Nets, I could not shake the discomfort in my stomach.

Happiness used to be so simple. Back home, if my father gave me a quarter, I was giddy. If my mother said I could go to the beach in the morning with my neighbor, Jerry, I was pleased. If I ate a mango, bought roasted peanuts, licked an emptying jar of peanut butter, watched a kung-fu movie at the theater, rode a bicycle, ate two spoonfuls of Klim powdered milk and Milo chocolate powder, I was satisfied.

The price for happiness had gone up in America and the Ashes were too poor to go anywhere, to do anything, and sought no means to find, to buy, to eat up the freedom and happiness my teammates stuffed themselves with.

MUSICAL INTERLUDE

Song title: Living in America
Artist: James Brown

II.

<u>TALES OF A FOURTH</u>

<u>GRADE NOTHING</u>

In St. Vincent, I felt encouraged enough to think I was an above-average student. My mother said I began talking at eight months and could say whole sentences by the time I was a year old. I knew lots of stuff to repeat too. The multiplication tables always impressed people, so did saying the ABC's --*Zed, Why, Ex, Dub-u, Vee, You, Tee...* --backwards. My mother tried enrolling me in the Barrouallie primary school but I was denied entrance. She said I was ready but teachers thought my age would pose a problem. I was three years old. My mother ended up paying twenty-five dollars from her teacher's salary to send my sister Annie and me to the Seventh-Day Adventist School in Barrouallie.

Along with math and reading, the Adventists schooled me to the Holy Bible. Before age four, I could recite the first two pages of Genesis with the same proficiency as the one times tables. (I found all this personal history out years later when I had a brief conversation with my mother. In fourth grade, a wall was forming between memory and me. Whoever I was in my island days, I was no more. "Remember the Anansi the Spider stories," a voice would plead in the middle of American History class. I used to recite Anansi stories to my friends when the power went out in town and kids came outside to talk. I was no longer sure about the moral fables or if they mattered in my new world.)

At 10:30 AM each day, Mrs. DiPeppi's fourth grade class would split up for Reading Comprehension. Half the smart kids and half the retards would go next door to Mrs. Franco's room. I was with the retard group, otherwise labeled, Group B.

Group B wasn't just the stupid kids; the geek population was fully represented too. One kid, Ben, had asthma, which in fourth grade meant, geek. He would gasp for air in the middle of a sentence and put a gun to his mouth before continuing. Some kids would snicker while he struggled to regain his breath. Another guy, Greg, would eat anything in the schoolyard. I saw him chew on a green and purple grasshopper once. Disgusting. The lone girl in Group B, Amy, was a pudgy, white-haired girl with oversized red glasses. She cried easily and never said anything to anybody.

All the cool kids from Mrs. Dipeppi's class, the ones who rode their BMX and Mongoose bikes to school, ate Fruit Roll-ups and Snickers for lunch and talked about their weekend trips, those kids were in Group A. Many of them were blonde, blue-eyed and if they didn't have bikes, got picked up by their moms or dads in luxury cars after school. Annie, Carla, me and the other seven or eight black kids at Evergreen rode the same yellow and brown fifteen-passenger, commercial van to and from school each day. We all lived close to each other, away from our white schoolmates.

I wasn't separated from the white kids by reading level and address alone. Their lives sounded so much more exciting than mine. At lunch, I'd hear them go on about a movie they saw on HBO, ski trips to the Pocono mountains, excursions to Six Flags Great Adventures theme park or their cottages at the Jersey shore.

The Ash clan had no cable TV, didn't order Chinese take-out, took no family vacations. For entertainment, relaxation or to get away from it all, I watched a black and white TV set in the basement. Even when I was supposed to be doing something else, I was watching TV in the basement.

Every Friday, the school librarian gave students a blue note card to record the titles of the books we'd read the following week. Even though the basement had extensive shelves of books my Auntie Sonja had forgotten to return to the Scotch Plains library, I didn't do a lot of reading in fourth grade.

Auntie Sonja used to send *Dick and Jane* books, *Hardy Boys, Nancy Drew*, as well as coloring and reading workbooks to St. Vincent. My favorite was a *Huck Finn* book. I used to repeat a famous line from it wherever I went, something about a murderer jumping out a courtroom window and running away. But I was forgetting the line.

In America, there were new lines to remember. From the *A-Team* there was, "I pity the fool." *Diff'rent Strokes* offered, "Wha'chu talkin' 'bout Willis?" *Knight Rider* had, "Turbo boost, KITT." How could I turn my eyes from a talking car with turbo power and space age gadgets to static words on a page?

The librarian must have thought I was a genius. According to my blue cards, I read Auntie Sonja's medical books on human endocrinology, physiology, cell biology. I also read medical journals and nursing magazines. The Librarian had to believe me because Grandma signed my blue card every Friday morning without question.

My classmates were big into author Judy Blume and Beverly Cleary's Ramona books. I detested Ramona and hated her sisters even more. I thought the guys in my class were sissies for reading girl stuff. The only books I remember reading in fourth grade were thin biographies of Ray Charles, Jim Brown, Charlie Pride and Stevie Wonder. I chose those books because they were only forty pages and had pictures on every other page.

The other guys may have been sissies but they seemed worldlier than me. They knew things like how to throw up on a roller coaster without getting their shirt dirty, knew the best way to eat a hot slice of pizza without getting burned, or how to change a flat bike tire. They all dined at the best restaurants in Scotch Plains, had arguments about the quickest shortcuts home, knew all the dinosaurs by name and feeding patterns. The guys drew in colors I hadn't seen (fuchsia), ate foods I'd never heard of (radishes), and estimated distances with no problem.

When I first got to Scotch Plains, I had the hardest time figuring out distances. Someone would say, "Oh yeah, that's about a mile and a half away" or "That tree is fifty yards from here." How did they know? Everything I knew in Barrouallie was within walking distance so I never had to think about miles or yards, I just started walking. In Scotch Plains, everyone else drove cars or rode their bikes. I didn't have a bike or a car so where was I going? And if I was struggling with distances, how would I know when I got there?

The people at school couldn't understand me, literally. "Enunciate," Mrs. DiPeppi would insist when I tried answering a question. Her mouth would be exaggerated and slow moving as if talking to an infant. "You've got to enunciate, Oronde." I didn't know what the word meant until school officials made me attend speech therapy for thirty minutes every Tuesday afternoon. The therapist told me I was rushing my words. "You should slow down and speak more clearly," he said. "Eee-NUN-c-ate." I got it. By January 1986, six months in America, my St. Vincent accent, the last vestige of my island boyhood, was gone.

Speaking slower and clearer wasn't helping my grades though. Where I used to get A's and B's in St. Vincent, at Evergreen Elementary, I got C's. Before I left the island, my friends and I were just starting to learn the national anthem. I didn't even know my country's song yet I knew the Star Spangled Banner and stood up every morning, right hand over heart, to recite the Pledge of Allegiance without stumbling or stopping once. I was the first in Mrs. DiPeppi's class to learn the pledge.

"See, you're not dumb," the little voice inside reassured me. Mrs. DiPeppi soon stopped telling me to enunciate. I was even adjusting to being put back to fourth grade.

In the Barrouallie Middle School, I was promoted to the first class in fifth grade, the youngest student in the whole level. (I would have been younger if the system hadn't kept me back so many times). At Evergreen, I was supposed to be in the fifth grade but as it was, fourth grade was kicking my butt. I figured the teachers knew what was best for me.

Every Thursday in Social Studies class we watched a film on one of the fifty states. I was learning all the capitals, state birds, nicknames, flags, state mottoes. I was getting my fill of the Garden State, the Delaware River, Pine Barrens, The Revolutionary War, Paul Revere, Payne and *Common Sense*. I was learning things but my report cards still showed C's and D's. "See, I am dumb," I would beat into my brain.

In art and music I got B's, but so did everybody else. In the core subjects, where I knew intelligence really mattered, I wasn't doing well. The only class I excelled at was PE. There I got A's all the time.

In the gym or on the playing fields, I was the man and everybody knew it. The other kids wanted me on their team or wanted to be on mine. On the four square court I was king and rarely left the top spot at recess. Because I could throw the football the farthest, I was even the quarterback at lunch. A black quarterback? Who knew?

I began to see sports as my ticket to success in America but I never enunciated my dream to anyone in Auntie Sonja's house. What could they do? The kids never had a say in what was going on in the house so my dreams, my input --my life didn't matter. Everyone except me seemed to have choices into his or her life in America.

Gerry and Carla had choices, had friends around the corner to go out with and Grandma in the house to return home to. They hugged her when they got home from school and she always seemed happy to see them. The three had their own history. Grandma had raised them from birth while Auntie Sonja worked to afford life in the suburbs for two kids.

My sister Annie and I hadn't established anything with Grandma yet. She seemed to talk to us only when giving a command or asking a favor. I wished she hugged me, said how much she loved me, wished Grandma sat me down and told me stories about her past like grandmas on TV did with their grandkids. But she didn't have time for anything except her rules.

There were restrictions on everything. I couldn't go too far up or down the street for fear of child molesters or kidnappers. I never had those fears in St. Vincent. At five or six years old, I was free to walk all over town as long as I came home for supper. Nobody was going to hurt me. If they did, where would that person hide? All of us were stuck on the same rock in the Caribbean Sea.

All through my stay in Scotch Plains, I was terrified of dingy-looking commercial vans because that's what kidnappers on TV used to snatch unsuspecting kids off the street.

Annie and I watched how we acted in public as well. Caribbean children stay quiet if they know what's good for them. I must admit jealousy of my white schoolmates who rode around in the supermarket shopping carts or threw a tantrum and got what they wanted. Caribbean kids didn't do that. No crying, no outbursts, no scenes. In a way, it made us grow up faster. Adults must show restraint. I noticed that black kids in America were also being asked to show the same restraint island kids were.

For most people in St. Vincent, there wasn't the luxury of childhood. Life was birth, duty, death and all of it was communal. Everybody had to do his or her share for the good of the whole.

When they were kids, my mother and her siblings had to clean inside and around her father's store and work the cash register before going to school each morning. There was no hiding from responsibility. Duties were handed out the minute the midwife slapped the baby on its bottom. The child's first job was not to choke and drown. Then came household chores like taking the sheep, goat or donkey out to pasture before school, fetching a pail of water to make tea for breakfast, buying fresh eggs from the guy with the chickens or bread from the baker.

"As a black, you have to work twice as hard to get even wid-deese people," I overheard Grandma and Auntie Sonja tell my mother. "Deese people" meant white people, although negligent blacks were also scorned when not taking responsibility for their failures in a land where Caribbean folk knowing nothing but hard *wuk*, had always made good for themselves. All my aunts and uncles owned their own houses, had jobs, supported families. They weren't as rich as my teammates, but they weren't struggling either.

Life as a black person in America and racism was mentioned ever so often in the house. I didn't know exactly what racism meant but I understood enough to have some pride in what being black meant in America. I heard names like Michael Jackson, Lawrence Taylor, Eddie Murphy, OJ Simpson, Nell Carter, Ben Vareen, Jesse Jackson. Blacks sang, acted, danced, boxed, played sports. We entertained America. Blacks did some other things too, like marches and Civil Rights, but I couldn't grasp those ideas at the time. The ladies in the house were too busy earning a living to explain blackness in-depth and I was too busy playing American to stop and think about it for too long. But little by little, I was becoming ever more aware of my color. I was a fourth grade nothing.

Annie, Carla and I were among the ten black students in school. My sister and I were by far the darkest. Carla and Gerry will never pass for white, but they were among the lightest Ashes in the family, skins the color of paper bags.

Growing up on an island where the only white faces I saw were occasional European tourists passing through in jeeps, wanting to take pictures of the women standing in the river washing their family's clothes, I had taken my color for granted. Nine years old and wanting so badly to fit into America, being black was yet another thing to jam into my already overcrowded head.

When the fall soccer season was over with the McEvoys, Grandma, Annie and I walked to Westfield --the next town-- just about every Saturday to go grocery shopping. The three of us would visit the stores and supermarkets Grandma had coupons for, fill the folding, four-wheeled shopping cart she brought, and walk the two or three miles back to the house, Annie and me carrying the extra bags. Sometimes, we were lucky enough to take the bus, but that was a rarity. After a few trips, I got used to the fatigue. I even began thinking of it as training for soccer. All the walking would make my legs stronger than my opponents'.

Shopping with Grandma was draining and a bit embarrassing. In the checkout aisle, she would fumble through her coupons looking for deals on the discount items. My sister and I watched as she inevitably held the line up. I wasn't even allowed to walk around most stores with her. While Grandma picked out food I did not want to eat, I sat behind the cashiers or next to the store windows on display like meat.

Young, strong, West Indian buck. Just arrived.

Can carry bags of groceries up to three miles.

$0.59/lb.

I would see schoolmates ride into the *A&P* or *Food Town* grocery stores bouncing on the sides of the shopping carts or if they were small enough, sitting in one. That was cool. Once, I went shopping with the McEvoys and could finally see what was up and down the grocery store aisles. Mrs. McEvoy didn't mind a bit when Joe and I jumped on and off the cart. I even got to steer it.

We were in the cereal aisle when Mrs. McEvoy asked, "What cereal would you like, Oronde?" I was dumbfounded.

"Excuse me?" I asked. "You mean I can get any of them?"

"Do you want Cocoa Puffs or Count Chocula?" Joe followed. "I'm gonna have Cap'n Crunch. Can I, mom? Can I?"

"Yes," Mrs. McEvoy said. "What do you want, Oronde?" she repeated.

I looked at my options. All the commercial jingles played in my head.

Snack, crackle, pop, Rice Krispies.

I'm cuckoo for *Cocoa Puffs*... part of a healthy breakfast.

"What do you want, Oronde?" Joe asked again.

Finally, I stumbled out, "Corn Flakes."

"That's all you want. Cornflakes?"

"Yeah," I answered.

"OK."

At that moment, Mrs. McEvoy, Joe and I recognized there was something wrong with me. I took too long to make up my mind. Joe knew exactly what he wanted before he even entered the store. American kids knew their wants right away. Corn Flakes? What American kid chooses Corn Flakes when there is all the sugar and artificial flavors before him? Corn Flakes was too plain, too safe, no pizzazz, nothing extra. I wasn't an American. There was nothing extra, no pizzazz in me. In fact, there was something definitely wrong with my family and something extra wrong with me.

III.

CRY

[THE BELOVED COUNTRY]

At the back of my fourth grade class that cold Wednesday afternoon, I was hungry for something I hadn't developed a taste for yet. Mrs. DiPeppi tried to persuade me otherwise but I refused to budge. She let me be and went on with her lesson that day, figuring I would integrate with the others soon enough. I didn't that day. I think I was making my first stand, against a force I was too young to fully comprehend.

I didn't hate my classmates. I was just jealous. When Mrs. DiPeppi asked questions, the fourth graders had answers. In St. Vincent learning was about repetition and regurgitation. The kids at Evergreen were actively thinking and giving responses that included bits of their individual personality. I could never jump into the conversations they had. When they talked about Chuck-E Cheese, the new toys at Toys-R-Us or the latest *Nightmare on Elm Street* or *Friday the 13th* horror movie, I listened in envious contempt. I'm sure I could have added a few of my island *jumbee* --ghost-- stories to the lunchroom stew, but what would it garner. The other kids had no idea where I was coming from.

On the island, I never questioned what we had, what the place smelled or felt like. Like my country's national anthem, St. Vincent hadn't resonated in me. For nine years I woke up every morning and enjoyed my days. Other than that I didn't think about things.

At Evergreen I was thinking about things all the time and none of it added up. I thought about Kathy O'Connor. Why did the other boys like her blond hair and blue eyes? Why, after only a few months in America, did I understand there was something special about that combination? I had no experience around white women yet why did this white girl tug at my heartstrings? Why did all the white girls make me ache? I knew I couldn't have any of them, not after the St. Valentines Day Massacre of 1986.

February 14. Two days before my tenth birthday. I had never heard of a day devoted to love. In St. Vincent, we loved but didn't make a ceremony of it. I had a girlfriend when I was in the third grade. And even though I would have been the youngest student in the fifth grade, my friends told me there was a girl who already wanted to be mine. I didn't have to do much back home and girls wanted to be with me. My family name, our place in town lore, my social status had made that possible. Cupid didn't make that happen. But on Valentine's Day, I found out about this Cupid because he put ten bullets in me.

When I came back from lunch there were ten cards on my desk. Some asked, "Would you be my Valentine?" Others had pink hearts, riddles or jokes on the front. The cards were from all the girls in class. Even Kathy, the blond-haired, blue-eyed nymph, professed her love for me.

At home on cousin Gerry's bed, I counted the cards over and over again: ten. I laid them out and flipped them: ten. I memorized what each card said: Ten American girls loved me. I felt special.

"See. You're just as handsome as the white boys."

It was on Gerry's bed where I realized I had cards from the boys in class as well. Snoopy or Garfield was on the front of those. I tore those cards up and kept the ones that said, "Be my Valentine." All ten.

The following day, my head was up in Mrs. DiPeppi's class, eyes darting around like a desert mole. I smiled at all the girls, especially the blond-haired, blue-eyed nymph Kathy. She smiled back once. "See. She loves you. They all love you."

Why would the girls have given me the love notes if they didn't love me? Didn't they see me winning the foursquare games or running punts back for touchdowns in PE? For weeks I stole glances at the girls hoping one would acknowledge her feelings. I waited and waited and still none of the girls talked to me. We didn't have this Cupid in St. Vincent but we had love. People didn't play with love back home.

Maybe it was all a big joke, like the time the boys told me to stick my middle finger up while Mrs. DiPeppi's back was turned. They all giggled and snickered. I didn't know what the gesture meant. I was the new boy.

Maybe I was ugly? Maybe I was black and ugly? How else to explain why none of the girls were looking at me?

At Auntie Sonja's house, I'd stare into the bathroom mirror, stand profile and pinch the bridge of my nose to make it straighter. I got clothespins and clamped my nostrils or bit my upper lip with my lower teeth to make it thin like the white boy's. Nothing worked. My nose was too big, my lips too full. I was ugly and no good.

I hated looking in the full-length mirror at the bottom of Auntie Sonja's stairs. It mocked me every morning. Why couldn't I have the Roman nose, the long straight hair, the thin lips that made everybody else handsome? Why did I have to think all this new stuff and feel this new way? What was this voice in my head all the time? Didn't anybody hear me?

I was tapping the chalk loud enough so the rest of the class would hear it. They all had their backs to me. Mrs. DiPeppi did all she could to keep the students focused on her lesson. She was facing me but she wasn't addressing me.

I sat down and blankly stared out the window until the bell rang at three. Must have been two hours that passed with my eyes focused on the outside. I wasn't angry at any one person or any one thing, just pissed off at life for not providing me the same niceties my classmates had. Months of keeping frustration bottled up had punctured tiny cracks where pain, anger, dread, despair, confusion and hate were beginning to seep out.

I wanted my own bike to ride around the neighborhood. I wanted cold, crisp cereal instead of hot, soggy oatmeal before school. I wanted to go to the movies once, wanted somebody to be able to drive the Chevy Nova sitting in the driveway so I wouldn't have to walk three miles lugging food I didn't want to eat. I didn't want broccoli or cauliflower, no iron or vitamins. I wanted empty calories and processed sugar.

When school was out, I didn't want to watch ABC soap operas like One Life to Live and General Hospital. Who cared about Llanview, Pennsylvania or Port Charles, New York? Cartoons started at two o'clock on WPIX, channel 11 and I wanted to watch them. I wanted to go places, see the other side of the town I lived in. I wanted a lot but it was what I thought every American kid had. And I wanted to be American more than anything.

America wasn't about sitting around in a basement. It was about moving on up. America was about Thomas Jefferson, who I learned in fourth grade, was the man who stood up and wrote the Declaration of Independence guaranteeing me life, liberty and the pursuit of happiness. America was about Ben Franklin walking into a rainstorm and finding out for himself how the forces of nature acted on life. It was about the plains I lived on, battlefields for the American Revolution, the most important war in the history of the world. It was about the wide-open spaces I saw in the thirty-minute movies about each of the fifty states.

Iowa had the widest, most amber waves of grain. The world's longest pipeline ran from Alaska to the lower forty-eight states. Arizona and Colorado had to share the Grand Canyon because it was too big for one state alone. In America, big things were possible and even more were probable if a person just got up and did something.

Go to college. Mr. McEvoy and the rest of the moms and dads I hung out with on weekends did.

Buy a house, a car, have two or three kids and provide them with the necessities TV said a kid needed to be happy, to be American. Live near a park where the kids could play basketball, tetherball, football or soccer with friends from the neighborhood. Give your son his own room so he could get used to the big spaces America was all about. The white parents were having no trouble doing all that.

Every time a car brought me back from a soccer game, I was struck by how little the Ash family had. No VCR, no movie club membership, no garage door that opened automatically with a basketball rim and its white net above it. We didn't play board games once each week, never did anything together once-in-a-while. All we did was sit down, watch TV and there was no democracy about that.

I began wanting options; all I got were orders. What was wrong with me? My classmates' clothes weren't after-thoughts. Each dress or pant was picked out with thought and care from a mall I never even got to visit.

The biggest difference between them and me was not the money, the clothes, their skin color; it was options and participation. Even in the fourth grade, the white parents wanted to know what their kids thought. My teammates were asked simple questions like, "What time will you be back, Chad?" or "What do you want for dinner, Jamie?" Nobody ever asked me that. Grandma cooked food and we ate it or got smacked for being rude. That's the way it was on the island too, except most folks there were grateful to eat anything at all.

In St. Vincent, I had options. My mother had a teaching job. E had money but We weren't wealthy. I mean, how rich can you be if you're going to the bathroom in the same style outdoor latrine everybody else has and your house is just as vulnerable as your neighbor's during hurricane season? But my mother could afford the extra bread or fish and be able to save the chicken an extra day in a refrigerator most families didn't have.

In America, I never got to practice the independence I read and dreamt about. What made it worse was that I had yet to develop the language to verbalize my frustration about all of it. But that's what my classmates were doing. They were being honest, open minded, opinionated, vocal, what my Grandmother may have called, "rude" Americans.

When somebody asked, "What would you like, Mikey?" or "Doesn't this taste good, Allison?" the child had to dig deep inside and find out what mood they were in, what flavor they wanted, what smell their body was sensing. Their answers were attempts to begin defining their many selves to the world.

The white kids were being prepared for a society awaiting that "rudeness". Thomas Jefferson, Ben Franklin, George Washington, Martin Luther King Jr. --he was mentioned a couple of times in February too-- those were the *rude boys* in America.

What was my family preparing me for if not to be a nice, withdrawn, compliant, insignificant, black tramp who deserved nothing but what he could borrow, beg for or get as a hand-me-down like a second-class citizen.

Even though my grades didn't reflect it, I had a first class brain that was running manic all the time. I had things to say but who would listen? Most of the questions I wanted to ask weren't subjects to be brought up anyway. Immigration, naturalization, deportation; I didn't want to go back to St. Vincent. On weekends, with my teammates and their excesses, America was starting to live up to its promise.

But I heard whispers about social security numbers, green cards, work permits and knew that my mother, Annie, nor I had any such documents. Everybody else in the Ash house was fine; they had options. We didn't. I slept nights waiting for Immigration and Naturalization Service (INS) officers to bang down the door and haul me away from all I was starting to enjoy in America.

After the incident in Mrs. DiPeppi's class, I couldn't wait until my mother got back from her nanny job that Friday night. I was sure she'd understand me. But when Ma heard Grandma's version of the story, I received an even harder whipping than I got that Wednesday afternoon. My mother scolded me in front of the whole family. She had never done that. On the island, she and I had never established a strong relationship. My father was the one I went to with questions, for answers, for change. Mothers didn't relate to kids back home. Mothers were practically preoccupied with making sure fathers provided the money to get the stuff --diapers, schoolbooks, powdered milk-- their kids needed.

But that was back in St. Vincent, a past I was forgetting or trying to forget. The present was pushing my mother away physically and emotionally. I'm convinced she disciplined me that night to assure Grandma my bad behavior wasn't a reflection of her rearing. My mother hit me with all the years and experience of the three Ash women in the house. When she was done she sent me upstairs crying. That was our bonding moment for the week. There was no joint, positive memory to counteract the beating.

My mother spent that Saturday like she spent most of her weekends, getting reacquainted with her mother and sister. It had been over ten years since she last saw them. Why didn't my mother try to get acquainted with me? Why didn't she see what I was going through? Couldn't she read a cry for help when it was written on a blackboard for her?

No, all the women thought I was being rude and disrespectful. That was the explanation for anything offhand from a child. Not even Auntie Sonja understood the transition I must have been going through, and she spent her days around doctors. Didn't some medical sense seep in?

After that week, I kept even more to myself. The soccer field became the place where I did all my talking. I spoke to the ball and it responded in kind, going where I directed, bringing recognition from parents and players all over Scotch Plains. Mr. McEvoy's orange team was all I had in life. I scored at least two goals every game and after the fall season, I had my first possession in America, a gold-plated trophy.

In the spring of 1986, Mr. McEvoy recommended me to the coach of a local team that traveled all over New Jersey representing Scotch Plains. Their scores and names even made the local paper. Mr. McEvoy thought I needed a new challenge. His son Joe would be on the team too, so I'd know someone. Why not something new?

When Mr. McEvoy told me the name of the new team, I couldn't believe it. In the spring, like Washington, Jefferson and Franklin, I would be playing for The Spirit of '76.

IV.

THE SPIRIT OF '76

C oach Len Ferraro and his wife were teachers. Mr. Roser was a Principal and his wife worked in real estate. Mr. Kellerher was a record executive at the company that helped launch the rock group, Bon Jovi. Mr. Krump was a bigwig for an aeronautics firm in North Jersey. He took his son Kevin and me to the building once. He had to swipe a plastic card to get in. It was just like the movie *War Games*. Real cool.

The Spirit of '76 drove BMW's, Mercedes Benzes, Audis, belonged to pool clubs, took tennis lessons. Theirs was the life. All the stuff I saw on the soap opera *Dynasty* was made real to me when I joined the team.

The families seemed patriotic. Many had American flags hanging above their front doors. Their sons didn't plop down in front of the TV like I did when I got to the house. Instead, the boys went to their rooms to play with their toys, read their comic books or listen to their music tapes. If they got bored indoors there were hockey sticks, basketballs, bikes and all sorts of other stuff to keep them occupied. They had choices. Me? I had begun cutting back on my choices before I even realized what they were. It was an unconscious determination. If going to the movies wasn't a reality, why bother thinking about it?

The only thing I craved more than choices in Scotch Plains were trophies. My new teammates had upwards of thirty or forty on their dressers, windowsills, bookshelves all over their rooms. I had one trophy that I polished once every week with Murphy's Oil Soap, Pledge or Windex. I was sure it was the beginning of a collection to rival my teammates'. My athletic skills were superior to theirs so I deserved more recognition. Trophies signified that recognition.

With that in mind, I learned to play basketball, tennis and even golf while I was with the Spirit of '76, but soccer... soccer became my obsession. Winning was the only thing. Every game was life and death because I had to build my trophy collection.

My first game with the Spirit, I scored five goals against the Colonia Raiders. One goal came directly off a corner kick and another from the midfield line. At age ten, a shot had to be a little higher than head-level to a goalkeeper and it was in. (My mother was at the game. It was the first and last time she saw me play for twelve years. On Sunday afternoons, she usually had to catch the train back to the family she worked for and didn't have time to travel to the towns where my Spirit went. That would have been impractical.)

No matter, there were other moms on the sidelines to take my mother's place. They brought oranges and paid for McDonalds Happy Meals after we won. All the team's moms and dads became my mom and dad. They were the ones who congratulated me when I did something good. Even when I messed up or we lost, in which case I was furious at my teammates because that meant less of a chance I'd get my coveted trophy, the other moms were there to console me. They paid my monthly dues to the Scotch Plains Fanwood Soccer Association, paid for tournaments and even paid when the team went to soccer camps. The Spirit became my family.

One day, dropping me off from practice, Coach Ferraro saw the neighborhood kids riding around on their bicycles popping wheelies and playing tag.

"Be careful not to get hurt when you ride with the kids," he said, "we have a big game on Sunday." I told Coach not to worry because I didn't have a bike. It couldn't have been more than a week later when he showed up at the house in his station wagon. Coach got out of the car, went to the back and pulled out a bike. "What do you think, huh?"

I looked at it. The body was black with yellow handlebars; there were two different colored rims on the tires and no hand brakes to bounce on the front tires like all the boys tried to do. The spokes were rusting and after riding the bike for one week, the handlebar would fall down onto the frame. I literally had to hold the bike in place when riding. But it was a bike. And it was mine.

Grandma came out of the house to see what was going on. Coach Ferraro introduced himself. That was the first time Grandma had seen him face-to-face. Even when he dropped me off from practice, she usually just peeked out the front door and waved.

"He said he didn't have a bike," Coach Ferraro told Grandma.

"I guess he got one now," she said. "Did you say, thank you?"

I thought I had. I said it again anyway. I was still ogling the bike in amazement. There it was on it's own kickstand. And it was mine.

"Aren't you gonna take it for a spin?" Coach Ferraro asked. My eyes lit up. I looked at him, mouth open, then at Grandma. "Be careful," she said. She probably didn't even know I could ride.

"Every kid should have a bike," I heard Coach Ferraro say just before I went for my first spin up and down the block. I thanked Coach again before he left. I will never forget what he gave me that day.

It wasn't just the bike. For once, I was feeling like I fit into the stars and stripes. I was one of them with the bikes and the trophies. I hung out with people who could do whatever they wanted whenever they chose. I saw the other side of my neighborhood, saw how hard those families worked to obtain and maintain their piece of America. Nothing was going to stop me from getting my piece.

Even after my mother, Annie and I moved to Brooklyn in fall 1986, one month into fifth grade at Evergreen Elementary, I carried that spirit with me.

****

(In Brooklyn, my Uncle Rudy would pick me up every Friday night from our apartment on East 34th Street and Church Ave. I would sit at the window watching all the cars pass, praying his van would be the next. Sometimes, he'd call to say he was ten or fifteen minutes away at a friend's house. An agonizing hour later, he would show up. During that wait, I would imagine my uncle had gotten into an accident or had forgotten and went ahead to New Jersey without me. Sometimes my mother would have to wake me because I had fallen asleep. It didn't matter if I was having a dream about money, a happier family or if I was tired and cranky, I woke up, walked outside into the cold night air and got into Uncle Rudy's car.

The trip to his house in Piscataway, New Jersey took about an hour and a half. We'd take the Manhattan Bridge to Canal Street, through the Holland Tunnel, drive across the Polaski Skyway, take Route 22 past the Autoland in Springfield, make a right after the Mazda dealership near Dunellen, across the street from the Midas repair shop, go up the hill and down the loop, past the stoplight and make the next right, drive to where the road formed a "T", make a left, drive to the next light and make a right at Union Bank, go pass the flashing yellow light, make a left and go all the way down, past the train tracks, make a right, go four blocks and make a left onto Desna Street. His house was the faded yellow one on the right, near the end of the block.

Saturday mornings, Uncle Rudy would drive me to practice in Scotch Plains. I'd spend the day with one of my teammates or if we had a tournament, I'd spend the weekend. Saturday night meant junk food, cable TV or a trip to the movies. That's how I saw the movie *Coming to America* with the Roeser family. It was also on one of those weekends that Mr. Krump taught me to play chess.

The Krumps were one of the wealthier families on the team. Mom drove a BMW while dad had a Mercedes. Their son, Kevin, was our goalkeeper. He was quick to express himself but otherwise harmless. I was the quiet one on the team. Coach once told me that although I never said much off the field, when I did, it had meaning. That's probably why I said nothing when Kevin asked the question, "Who's the ugliest kid on the team?"

We were playing whiffle ball in his backyard when one of the kids, rather blankly answered, "Oronde." It didn't bother me. It didn't hurt because I had come to accept the fact that I was black and ugly. When I asked the kid why was I the ugliest, his answer only confirmed what I had already been learning about America. "Because you're the only black guy," the kid said.

I guess I couldn't be angry with the people treating me to all the things I thought I was missing in life. If I made them angry, I would be cut off from the love and attention I was getting from my new family.

The issue of my skin color confronted me only one other time in my years with the Spirit of '76. I was eleven. We were playing a much weaker team. I stole the ball from an opponent and was dribbling around him. In frustration, the kid tripped me. The referee didn't see the foul.

"Take that, you nigger!" the eleven year-old boy scowled. He was standing over me, watching me struggle to rise up on the muddy field. I hadn't yet grasped the full weight behind the word *nigger*, but I knew it was two heavy syllables that, as a black person, I should take offense to.

I got up and started running after my offender. The boy didn't know what he had done. He wasn't just getting the scorn of my unrealized racial anger. That day the boy was gonna feel the brunt of all my misunderstandings about America, about Valentine's Day, about mothers, fairness, money, school, hate, home and equity. I was gonna go to work on his ass.

Luckily, the foul happened in front of our bench. Coach Ferraro heard what the boy said, saw what I was about to do and dashed onto the field to grab me.

"Did you hear what he called me," I protested, trying to wriggle free.

"Yes, I heard," Coach Ferraro said. "He's just ignorant." I was ready to fight, but Coach walked me to the cooler, put his arms around me and tried to calm me down.

That wasn't the first time I had gone nuts in a game. I was constantly screaming at my teammates to play better. If I was fouled, I immediately ran after the offender. The soccer field was the only place I felt bigger than any of the boys. The game was my show of dominance and power otherwise denied. On the field, I was the one two and three steps ahead of the others. I was the player opposing coaches always shook hands with saying "You're an amazing talent. Keep it up."

After our talk on the sidelines, Coach Ferraro put me back in the game. We won that day so the name-calling thing didn't bother me.

What bothered me more than anything was my teammates' lackadaisical play. They didn't have to win as badly as I needed to. They already had their trophies, had karate, baseball or swimming to put their energies into. Soccer was it for me.

In St. Vincent, my friends and I were lucky if we had a ball much less big, green fields to play on or cleats to wear on them. The only shin guards we could fashion were from pieces of cardboard tucked in our socks, but we played soccer and we loved it. Be it with a dried-out coconut, a tennis ball, rags tied together with string, we made a ball and played the game wherever and whenever. The kids on the Spirit of '76 were spoiled. They had everything and didn't know it.

I knew what I wanted on the soccer field and demanded perfection from everyone with me. If that meant cursing at the other ten and eleven year old boys because they missed a goal, I did so. If it meant calling the referee an idiot when he missed an obvious foul, I did that too. Other teams in the region knew about my short fuse and would try to foul me to get a reaction.

"Calm down, Oronde," Coach Ferraro would preach at half time, "they're just trying to get under your skin. We need your head in this game." I rarely listened. I probably got the most yellow card warnings on the team, but I never got a red card and thrown out of a game. Thank God news of my on-field behavior never made it to my grandmother.

Things were going well that first season with the Spirit. We won our division in spring 1986 and were dubbed one of the best youth teams in New Jersey. For that I got three plaques. In my years on the Spirit, we won fifteen tournaments. Finally, I had a trophy collection to be proud of.

In the spring of 1988, we were playing the first round of the New Jersey State Cup against a team from Kearny that we'd beaten 5-0 two weeks prior. By half time, however, Kearny was ahead 2-0. During the break, I didn't say a word. I just stared at my teammates real evil-like. Ten minutes into the second half, I scored on a shot from midfield. The goalie thought the ball was headed over the crossbar but it kept dropping and dropping 'til it hit the back of the net, over his outstretched hands.

"Now will you shut up, Oronde," one teammate said while the team was trying to congratulate me. "No," I returned, refusing to join in the joy of the moment. I wanted to grab the boy by his scrawny little neck and ring it off.

"This team is awful," I'd say while running up and down the field. "We stink for not beating them." The referee had heard enough. After one of my tirades, he gave me a yellow card warning for abusive language. One more offending word and I would be thrown out of the game.

Both teams were playing hard in the second half, but the Spirit was attacking more. I had chances to score but didn't. Once, I had a clear breakaway and got tripped or fell over the ball --I can't remember.

"Are you blind?" I yelled, running after the referee, who hadn't called the foul. "How can you not see that?" I wanted to know. I must have been louder than usual, because Coach told the referee he wanted to take me out of the game. Before Coach could remove me, I stormed off the field and headed away from the bench. Mr. Krump came after me.

"Don't worry about it, Oronde. You'll go back in just now. Coach just didn't want you to get another card. We need you out there, buddy. There's still a lot of time left. We beat these guys before, right?"

"I don't want to play anymore," I began, tears welling up in my eyes.

"Why not?" Mr. Krump asked. "We need you. You gotta go back in there. You don't wanna lose, do you?"

I don't care if we lose. I don't care anymore." I was crying.

I know that's not true," Mr. Krump said, putting his arms around me. As soon as he touched me, I walked away, looked at my teammates, and yelled as loud as I could, "I hope you guys lose. You stink!" With that, I headed for the nearby parking lot and sat on the curb.

"C'mon Oronde. Get back in the game," Coach said, coming over to me. By now, two of the moms were walking towards me. When they got ten yards from me I got up and ran even further away from the field. I didn't care. I just wanted uncle Rudy to pick me up.

The Spirit of '76 lost 3-1 that afternoon and got eliminated from the New Jersey State Championship. No trophy. No recognition for me. While I was in the parking lot, some of the parents had gotten together and asked Coach to levy some punishment against me. They thought I was setting a bad example for their boys. Coach suspended me for the next two games.

On the ride to uncle Rudy's house, he asked for my side of the story. I highlighted my teammates' lack of effort and inability to see how important the game was. Surprisingly, my uncle agreed with me.

"Soccer is just a game to them," he said. "It doesn't mean as much as it does for us." Finally, somebody who understood.

I never talked to my uncle much. He was basically my weekend ride to The Spirit. Even when we were alone in his van for nearly two hours on Friday nights, very little was ever said.

"But you shouldn't have said all the things Coach told me. That was rude. They've done a lot for you."

My uncle was right. I knew that but was too proud to admit my mistake. Instead, after I came back from my suspension and played the remaining games of the season, I told Coach I was quitting the team. I was tired of the commute, tired of the scene, tired of the way I was acting. I was tired of showing up to games and missing all the player interaction during the week. I was not really a part of the team. I was a soccer mercenary, a hired gun.

By then, I was in middle school in Brooklyn, NY. The life I saw everyday in my neighborhood and at school was so opposed to what I once knew in Scotch Plains. I wanted to concentrate on my Brooklyn life. I needed my energy to fight the wars going on there. I decided to not only quit the Spirit of '76, I also stopped playing soccer altogether.)

****

But all that was two years in the future. In the fourth grade, playing with the Spirit of '76 on the weekends, I had hold of my dreams of college and a better life in America. Notre Dame was still on the horizon. Mr. Kellerher, Coach Ferraro's assistant, was a Notre Dame alum who mentioned that he could talk to people in admissions when the time came.

"You could definitely get a scholarship," he told me. When I heard that, it only made me hungrier to do well on the field. My dreams were crushed one Friday night early in September 1986, one year after coming to America.

I was a few weeks into fifth grade and Coach Ferraro dropped me off from practice. From the road, I could hear my mother and aunt arguing. I was embarrassed and immediately thought the fight was because of me. All arguments were my fault. That's the mentality I was in at the time. I didn't see the tension already in the house. All I saw was the hole most children see the world through. When I heard my mother say, "No problem, I'll get my kids and get out of your damn house," I knew it was because of Annie and me.

That night, my mother packed our clothes, put the bags outside and called uncle Rudy. We moved forty-five minutes away to Piscataway to live with him, his wife and two young daughters. Annie and I were in a new place yet again.

Uncle Rudy drove us to Scotch Plains every morning to attend Evergreen Elementary. My sister and I would spend after school with Grandma until we got picked up in the evening. This went on for a month until my mother decided to move in with her boyfriend Mudd. He came to America a few months after us and had an apartment in Brooklyn, New York.

MUSICAL INTERLUDE

Song title: Living for the City
Artist: Stevie Wonder

V.

PETRIFIED: A TREE

GROWS IN BROOKLYN

Most evenings on ABC's Eyewitness News there was a shooting in Brooklyn. More often than not black people were pictured. When the reporters interviewed the black people, every sentence had a "Whaaa" or an "Aaaahh" taking the place of an idea the interviewee could never enunciate. I didn't want to move to that uncertainty.

Brooklyn also meant noise. How was I to rest in a city that never slept? I imagined taxicabs honking their honks at all hours of the night keeping me awake. What about college? What about leading Scotch Plains high school to another state championship? What other community in America supported soccer the way they had? I was meant to be there. It was all part of God's plan. And that was all gone because my mother couldn't get along with my aunt… Life sucked.

For the five months my mother, my sister and I lived on the corner of East 34th Street and Church Avenue with her boyfriend Mudd, I did not venture outside unless I was going to school, sent to buy groceries or lottery tickets. I'd meet my sister Annie after school and we'd walk straight home. Our school, PS 181, was only three blocks away so we never had to cross any busy streets. I was disappointed when I realized the school didn't have a PE class. There was no room in the five-story building housing close to eleven hundred students. I mean, how was I going to get A's on my report card?

I was even more surprised to notice how easily I adjusted to the new academic environment. Where there were C's and D's in Scotch Plains, my reports cards immediately began showing A's and B's in Brooklyn.

There could've been a variety of reasons for the dramatic improvement. For one, I again saw my mother everyday. There must have been an underlying comfort in that familiarity. After being around her all my life, there was total separation in Scotch Plains for days on end. I'm sure my mind never fully adjusted to that distance.

Around the corner in Brooklyn, there were bakeries and restaurants serving Caribbean food. I could taste the flavors and savor the scents of St. Vincent again. Being Vincentian mean a whole lot in America and for that I did not want any part of the culture. I still harbored animosity at my father and his Rastafarian friends, was still blocking most of my memories of life on the island. But living in Brooklyn, on Church Avenue, the [actual] center of the Caribbean world, I couldn't deny my island heritage. Except for the ocean, the warm weather and coconut trees, the Caribbean was, for the most part, outside my door.

At P.S. 181, my classmates were first or second generation Caribbean-Americans. I looked across the room and saw my skin, my nose, my hair, my lips, my eyes reflected back at me. My fifth grade teacher, Mrs. Cohen knew how to relate to us. She always encouraged me to do better and praised me when I did. I mattered to Mrs. Cohen so what she said mattered to me. With her positive feedback, school became important again.

There were prizes for doing right in Mrs. Cohen's class. She promised to give a portable radio to the student who read the most books by the end of the school year. I knew Mrs. Cohen thought I could do it and I didn't want to disappoint her. From mid-November 1986, I read every book I could get my hands on. For weeks, I would average one book each night. I read all the Judy Bloom books like *Superfudge*, *Tales of a Fourth Grade Nothing, Hello God: It's Me Margaret*. I even read about Ramona, her sister and all the girly books I had shied away from in Scotch Plains. I didn't care.

Each morning, I would walk into room 505 and check the chart at the back for another smiley face next to my name. Every morning, the gap between me and the other kids was growing. Even Jason Cummings, the real smartest kid in class even though the other kids said I was; even he was choking on my literary dust.

Jason was the kid I wanted to be. I was just lucky smart. Jason, he was brilliant smart. For a fifth grader, Jason was an encyclopedia of knowledge. He always had an answer for Mrs. Cohen and still found the humor to crack jokes that made all the kids laugh. Most important to me, Jason could articulate his knowledge to his peers. I envied his willingness to share himself.

Even though Jason was smarter than most of the other kids, he was a part of the class community. He sat with all the cool kids at the end of our lunch table playing Uno cards games and laughing. I never joined in, figuring they hated me for being a teacher's pet. They were one type of people and I knew I was another. The chasm between our two worlds was a grand canyon. Not once in fifth grade did I move closer to the cool end of the lunch table. I was to scared to.

Things were going well academically in Mrs. Cohen's class so my self-esteem was high. School became what soccer was in Scotch Plains. I found an identity and meaning in performing to the highest standards. I still looked forward to going to New Jersey and playing with the Spirit on the weekends, but the rest of the week, in Mrs. Cohen's class was all right too. When we started having PE, school got even better.

On Thursday afternoons from 2:10-2:50 PM, there was the choice of computers, art, dance, double-dutch or sports. The next Thursday, students chose do something else. I was part of the computer/sports program. When the fellas found I wasn't just a smart guy but could also run, jump and throw a football farther than most of them, I got a few friends I didn't think I could.

As positive as life was at school, home life was a drain. My mother and her boyfriend Mudd fought all the time about any and every little thing. In fifth grade, I couldn't understand what their adjustment to America was like. Like my own rude awakening, all the things they had been told in St. Vincent were lies too. There were no streets of gold or money to be found around the corner. Living and working in America was tough. They were two educated people having to labor twice as hard, often for less than minimum wage.

My mother spent the week cleaning up after rich families in Manhattan. (She worked for the violinist Itsak Perlman once). After being on her knees scrubbing their floors or making their food, she had to take the train to Brooklyn and listen to Mudd lament about being ripped off for the plumbing, electrical and masonry work he was doing. From what I overheard, Mudd's partner Charles was screwing him over. Charles got away with it because Mudd didn't have *papers* -- social security number, tax ID, green card or worker's permit-- to back him up. Charles was established.

If she got home early, my mother cooked dinner in and around the roaches, rats and other creepy-crawlers that squatted on the kitchen floor, on counters, shelves, in corners and appliances all over the apartment. The apartment was all the two could afford. Mudd worked out a deal with the landlord by fixing his other tenement buildings.

On one hand, my days were filled with the smile and encouragement from Mrs. Cohen. I took pride in knowing I could do the work many of my classmates struggled with. I was smart again, special again.

On the other hand, once I left the schoolyard, I talked to no one, shared with no one, meant nothing to anyone. Annie and I never talked because... well, we just didn't. I didn't ignore my sister. We shared the same room, so we must have interacted. I have no recollection of the specific things Annie and I did together. (Years later, she told me that I left her standing at a bus stop one day when I was mad, got on, but got off at the next stop to wait for her. If Annie had not told me, I would have never known I cared for her back then. It's unfortunate that good memories just vanish when you think the life you led was full of bad ones.)

I don't want it to seem as if what I called childhood was singular. Many kids have had it much worse than me and all kids go through some form of pain through their eyes. If anything, I was confused and spent a lot of time watching television attempting to escape the reality around me. Annie and I would use the TV volume to drown out the yelling and screaming coming from my mother and Mudd. I didn't want to hear my family, didn't want to be in my family. I wanted out and even had a master plan for escape.

All I had to do was get a soccer scholarship to a college in some remote part of the country. I'd take a bus from New York City, buy a one-way ticket and start fresh. No letters, no phone calls, no communication back home. If anyone asked where my family was, I would say they were all killed in an automobile accident.

Life was unfair. I was studying, praying, being nice to people and I got back nothing. God helps those who help themselves, but I wasn't being helped.

My mother was relying on food stamps and government cheese, butter and powdered milk to keep us fed. Those blocks of cheese were so thick, Annie and I had to use all four of our hands to cut a slice sometimes. And when the cheese was exposed in the refrigerator and got crusty along the edges, it was hell cutting up the cinder blocks.

Cheese was all Annie and I ever ate after school. I would dream about salami, bologna, ham or having other cold cuts in the refrigerator. Never was there any, only the blocks of cheese. Annie and I made grilled cheese sandwiches, or cheese, lettuce and tomato sandwiches. We pretended to be at McDonalds and made double-quarter cheese-cheesers with cheese. My sister and I ate so much cheese I thought we would turn into the rats we saw scurrying along the apartment floor.

I hated being poor. It wasn't fair. I knew what the other side of life was all about. I had tasted it. I was still living it with the Spirit of '76 on the weekends. Even in St. Vincent, I had money.

How could my mother settle for this life among roach droppings, where, in the winter, we had to get up early and boil water on the stove to take baths; where the noise from the storefront church services on the first floor kept us up Wednesday and Thursday nights. Annie told me she saw snakes at the church one Sunday. The women wore white robes and headdresses, danced uncontrollably and spoke in tongues. We were scared of the people who went to the church.

I was ten years old, didn't like my mother, didn't like where I lived and talked to nobody about any of this. The only place I communicated was in a journal Mrs. Cohen made us keep. When we came in from lunch, we would write for fifteen minutes. Mrs. Cohen was strict about stopping after fifteen minutes. Most of the kids dropped their pencils when she said, "Stop." It was a relief. Others had a lot to say and kept going. I sometimes wondered about their lives.

Did Corbin think he was all that because he wore the name brand clothes, the expensive basketball shoes and could draw real good? Did Julian get hurt when everybody reminded him he was Haitian? Being Haitian seemed to be the worst thing in the world in fifth grade. Maybe it didn't matter because he was the best-dressed kid in school. Did Cecile McKenzie, by far the cutest girl in class, really like me? I could swear she was eyeing me at lunch. Did Ahmed the Afghan kid even think about taking a bath every morning? And why didn't his family make him? I guess you can be as smelly as you want when your family owns its own grocery store.

Why did Nathaniel misbehave? Why didn't he put his pencil down when Mrs. Cohen said, "Stop"? Why was he so difficult? All his acting up was only going to hurt him. If Mrs. Cohen didn't like him, she wouldn't give him a good grade. Why did the other kids seem to like Nathaniel anyway?

I don't remember what I wrote in my fifth grade journal. I do remember one afternoon when I didn't feel like stopping. I remember hearing Mrs. Cohen say, "Stop." I remember even Nathaniel raising his pencil that day. I remember most of the kids stopping at once, which was a rarity. I remember Mrs. Cohen telling me to put my pencil down. I remember disobeying her for the first time but feeling like a kid when I did so; finally feeling like part of the class. All the other kids continued writing some days. Why shouldn't I?

I wanted to be seen as no different from anybody else. I could be bad. My classmates got up, fell down, said bad things, did worse things, fought, made up, fought again. They were together, the same. I was tired of being separate and unequal.

Mrs. Cohen walked to my desk and confiscated my journal pad. The rest of the class was stunned. By itself, the event was nothing. But summed together with the non-interaction that was my everyday life, it shone bright and got brighter when Mrs. Cohen looked over the last words of my entry, words I had rushed onto the page specifically for her eyes. When she looked at me, in shock, I felt remorse for writing, "**MRS. COHEN IS A BIG FAT PIG AND A WHORE**" in bold letters.

That night, on my bed, I listened for the phone to ring in the other room. Around nine o'clock it did. I knew who it was because my mother was trying to speak proper English. If it was someone she knew she'd have pulled out the island accent. The person on the phone was an American. It had to be Mrs. Cohen.

I stopped watching TV and crawled under my sheet, hoping my mother would think I was asleep. After the phone clicked down and she mumbled a few words to Mudd, no doubt telling him what she just heard, my mother walked into the room.

"Do you know who I just talked to?"

"No," I replied, my back to her.

"What did you do in school today?"

"Nothing." I could hear every thumping beat of my heart. Even my spit sounded loud as it went down my throat.

"So you didn't insult your teacher and call her a big, fat pig." By the squeaking of the floor, I knew my mother was getting closer to the bed.

"I didn't call her that," I protested. By now, my mother was standing over me, all five feet two inches of her. Her shadow, cast from the single light bulb hanging from the ceiling, seemed like Mount Everest. I had to look up now. Maybe I could talk her out of the beating if I explained things? But when I saw the belt, I knew it was coming. I could only stall and psychologically prepare my butt for the lashes.

"I swear I didn't call her that, Ma."

My mother edged closer. She was huge now.

"Are you calling your teacher a liar? Mrs. Cohen just now called me." My mother's right hand was raised, squeezing the belt like a viper ready to strike

"No!" I said, trying to wriggle free of the trap I was in. I put up my hands, almost praying for mercy.

"I didn't say it," I shrieked, "I wrote it down in my journal. She invaded my privacy." The inanity of my response sealed my fate.

"I don't care what she did. You should have never disrespected your teacher like that. You gonna pay, 'pickney neh-ga'."

The last words were said in her most Vincentian accent so I knew it was real. My mother always tried to speak proper around me. She probably thought I hated her, hated St. Vincent and everybody associated with it so much she tried to relate to what I was becoming -- an American-- instead of who I was. I didn't care what she sounded like. I wished my mother had never singled me out as the one to speak different to, wish I could've told her to speak to me the way she did to everybody else, including Annie. I wish I could've told her how much more isolated it made me feel. But there was no point in talking now. We were to be joined by her black, leather belt.

"You--whack--are--smack!--never--bap!--going--wablap!--to--splack!--do--wabup! (pause, looking for a new place to hit)--that--

blap!--again--smack!--in—wop--your   (pause)--kablap!--life.   You--
smack!--have got to--kapub!--learn--smack!--some--whack!--respect."

The beating seemed to go on forever. Before she left the room, my mother turned and said, "You're lucky we live in this country and they have all these people coming after you if you touch your children. As God, if we was home... You're lucky we're not in St. Vincent. You better never, ever, ever do that shit again or they might have to put me in jail. You hear me?" I didn't answer. My words were drowned in tears. The one time I remember talking to my mother in fifth grade was done through a belt.

That night, I wished the social workers came and took her away. She wasn't a mother. I prepared my own breakfast, ironed my own clothes, made my own snack after school. She never did one thing for me and I never asked for things because we couldn't afford anything.

I brought home a Student-of-the-Month award at the end of just about each month and never got squat. The other winners came to school the next day with something new. That didn't bother me anymore though. I'd gotten used to expecting nothing from people, gotten used to my mother not explaining the reasons behind all the fighting with Mudd, gotten used to figuring out the life I lived held no answers.

What was I doing wrong? Why didn't my mother make time for me like all other mothers seemed to make time for their kids? Those mothers had to work too.

"Did you hear me?" my mother repeated.

"Yes," I mumbled and rolled over to stare at the black shadow she left. I wished she was dead.

I cannot think of that possibility now. I am glad I saw my mother fight all my life because it taught me to battle for what I wanted. My mother's inability to create a relationship between us allowed maximum room for me to figure out life on my own. She was young when she had me and still had a life to live. In St. Vincent, there was a built-in safety net of extended family and neighbors who were like mothers and fathers to me. My mother could leave me and not worry about my safety or even if I would be fed or provided shelter. Somebody in our town would look after me, feed me and return me home. Anyway, Caribbean mothers were not touchy-feely. It was tough love, especially for the boys.

Good or bad, I became my own person because whatever my mother did or did not know about American-style motherhood at the time allowed me to develop along my own path. I don't blame her for anything. I can't. Our life then was what it was.

But that night, ten years old, flesh aching, tears falling onto my pillow, I wished she was dead.

I wished I was dead too.

VI.

<u>MARY McLEOD</u>

<u>BETHUNE ACADEMY</u>

Mary McLeod Bethune Academy (MMBA) was not the type of school the name may suggest. It was more like a military academy where the cadets were in charge and they didn't believe in rules. They couldn't because the school lay in the middle of a war zone and all the basic training became bull once the bell rang at three.

Across the street, up the block, down the road were abandoned buildings and what looked like drug addicts inhabiting them. It was 1986, the height of the crack epidemic in New York City. Crack vials littered the schoolyard we played in before morning line-up and at lunchtime. There were gangs outside waiting for their members before and after school each day. Once, my sixth grade classmates made the Spanish teacher, Senorita Clarissa, cry. The woman just stopped writing on the blackboard, walked to her desk, slumped down and began weeping.

"You kids are just bad," she tried to get out between heaves. "Why can't you just behave? You don't know what you're doing to yourselves." I felt so sorry for Senorita Clarissa. She was just trying to do her job and the idiots in my class had no sense whatsoever.

The idea behind Mary McLeod Bethune was promising. A pamphlet had come in the mail some time in fifth grade boasting of a gifted program for minority students who had excelled in math and reading. I looked forward to the challenge. After finishing as PS 181's salutatorian, the fifth grader with the second best grades, I wanted to deliver a valedictory speech in eighth grade and prove I was second to no one.

More than anything, I looked forward to walking from room to room instead of being locked up like a child the entire day. But, in the sixth grade at Bethune, movement was deemed too dangerous. (Actually, in the sixth grade, the school was still called John Marshall Intermediate School 210. The name change came a year later, a symbol of promise for the mostly black and Latino student body).

There were five or six of us in my sixth grade class who genuinely cared about learning. Aisha was Jamaican. Michael was a Black Muslim whose mother was from one of the islands. Keisha was Guyanese. The Caribbean kids wanted it more than the Americans. Our teacher, Mr. Ames, was from Barbados. Even though his accent, bow tie and tight, high water pants made him an easy target, the Caribbean kids never ridiculed him. Mr. Ames would say, "You kids don't know me. I have a master's degree in math-matics." He always emphasized "masters" as if we understood what that meant. American troublemakers didn't care about his academic resume.

Perhaps the kids acted up because we weren't labeled right. Our class was S-605. Technically, we fell short of being labeled *gifted*. The gifted classes at Bethune were E-601 through E-604. Maybe the American kids were letting off steam for being misplaced? I resented them for making it difficult for those with the drive to get to an E-class. I didn't want to look as bad as the rest so I redoubled my efforts to stand out as a top student.

"You are such a good student, Oronde," I was being told all the time by visiting teachers. I guess they thought they had to remind me or I'd end up like everybody else. At Bethune, I never accepted credit for my success. It wasn't me. I only looked good because the knuckleheads around me didn't apply themselves. I wasn't a shining star in a brilliant sky, more like a flickering candle in a dark tunnel.

I should have said something to my peers about their behavior but I didn't. I assumed they hated me for knowing the answers, doing the homework when they forgot or being ready for the surprise quizzes. Speaking out would only confirm I was into learning: a true nerd. Like anyone else, I didn't want that label. Devon, Corey or Jaleel, the thugin'est boys in S-605, would have probably beaten me up anyway. It was bad enough to walk to the bus stop with the fear of being jumped

46

always looming. To experience it in front of everybody would have been it for me.

I did get punked out once though. Two pip-squeaks grabbed my loose-leaf notebook as I exited the building one afternoon and threw it on the ground. Half the papers flew out in front of everybody. I was mortified. I thought about retaliating but what could I have done? Even though the two weighed a hundred pounds between them both and were a foot smaller than me, they had gang members nearby ready to tear into me. I walked off knowing that if the sharks smelled blood, they would pounce on me with more force than I was ready to take back then.

Despite the food fights in the cafeteria --at least once each week for the entire sixth grade year-- or the time I was held up for my bus pass by two kids with box cutters, there were good people at Bethune.

Mr. Hope was my sixth grade computer teacher. He must have been close to sixty years old and looked wise with his salt and pepper beard. I respected the old man. I respected any authority figure because they gave me meaning. Teachers, coaches, guidance counselors and deans were the few people in the world who made me feel special. Mr. Hope and I didn't have a particularly close relationship. He was there to teach and I to learn. It went no further than that. But that stability was enough for me. The misfits of S-605, especially Jaleel, were constantly compromising both of our jobs.

Jaleel was a troublemaker par excellence. At five feet three inches and close to two hundred pounds, with dark, coal-black skin, a wide nose and permanent scowl on his face, Leel was the boy I would steer clear of if I ever saw him on the street. He was antagonistic to everybody, even Mr. Hope. Leel stepped right up to the old man's face one day, pointed his fingers and began talking smack. He and Mr. Hope had gotten into one of their weekly verbal skirmishes. That day, Leel was intent on taken the situation to another level but Mr. Hope would not have it. The old man's energy was waning, but his [black] pride was still in him.

"Get your hand out of my face," Mr. Hope ordered. He looked ready to smack the fat punk. I was praying he'd do it for all of us who wanted to learn and were tired of Jaleel's antics.

"You black kids, you just don't know. You have no appreciation for what people like me had to go through for you to be here." Mr. Hope was pacing back and forth.

"Why don't you shut up," Leel yelled. Of course, that got the attention of anyone in the computer room who wasn't already tuned in to the fracas. There was the shuffling and howling that accompany these situations.

"Get out," Mr. Hope returned with equal anger. He walked over to the door, opened it and repeated himself. "Get out now, young man!"

"I don't feel like it," was Leel's comeback. He turned to his computer partner, trying to pretend nothing happened.

"Young man, if you're not going to do the work… if you persist in disrupting my class, you might as well leave."

Leel didn't move. For a second or two he was quiet. The whole room inhaled, waiting for the next move.

"I oughta put a cap in your ass," Jaleel finally said. Here we go again… Exhale.

That was it. Mr. Hope marched over to Leel's chair, grabbed him by his black and red, hundred-dollar Troop jacket and tried pulling him to the door. But Leel was too heavy. The boy's center of gravity was locked to the floor. Mr. Hope struggled but couldn't budge him. The rest of the kids were yelling and screaming and jumping on top of their chairs. Meanwhile, Leel began swinging at Mr. Hope's face, grazing it once or twice. In his wild state, Leel lost his balance and fell to the floor. Mr. Hope dragged as best he could.

"My brother's gonna kill you," Leel yelled.

"I pray he does," Mr. Hope said as he tried to drag Jaleel out the room. All the while the class was screaming and jumping around. I looked on in absolute disbelief. This was my gifted school? This was Mary McLeod Bethune's dream for her black children?

A part of me wanted Mr. Hope to beat the fat out of Leel. Another part feared that gangs of boys were going to kill the old man. Leel had an older brother outside everyday with his posse. Another brother was said to be in jail on Riker's island. That didn't look good for Mr. Hope.

With all the noise coming from the computer room, security officers ran in and took Jaleel to the principal's office. That was it. Within a few days the incident was forgotten and school went on as normal. At Bethune, fighting in the classroom was normal. Mr. Hope transferred a few weeks later when he found the two front tires on his car slashed.

When Leel came back from suspension, most people avoided him. I had never gone out of my way to talk to Leel but when there were chances to get on his good side, I took advantage as best I could.

If the weather was pleasant the sixth grade went outside after lunch. The boys played football or softball against the other classes while the girls skipped double-dutch or clung together and did whatever it is girls do in middle school. Leel always wanted to be on a team but nobody ever picked him. Outside, playing sports was the only place I saw him lose his bravado. No one was afraid of him on the football field because he couldn't catch a ball and wasn't going to outrun any of us. There was so much self-doubt on his face out there. I seized my opportunity to step in.

Since I usually ended up playing quarterback for S-605, I was the one who made players look like graceful swans or butter-handed ducks. Other quarterbacks stayed away from Jaleel because he would drop passes or wouldn't get far after a catch. I, however, went out of my way to find the right times to get him the ball. I came up with a list of scenarios where he might be an option and would throw to him only if those occasions presented themselves.

First off, I never passed Jaleel the ball on our half of the field unless it was first down, and even then, he had to be open by more than five yards. If it was second down and we were closer than twenty yards to the end zone, I might... I might throw him the ball. If we were inside the five and all that was needed was a simple shovel pass, there was a good chance Jaleel wouldn't screw that up so I threw to him.

If these simple rules were followed and Leel caught a few touchdowns each week, he was usually the first to run over and bear hug me if we won, especially if we beat one of the snooty E-classes. Leel was also less disruptive in class those afternoons. After a while, I realized that Leel just wanted to feel like being part of something. I could relate to him in that way. Moreover, my Good Samaritan work paid healthy dividends. When I'd see Leel after school hanging with his thug friends, I'd give him a nod. If he acknowledged me, I felt I could walk through the sea of gang members outside the building without fear. After all, he was my go-to receiver at lunchtime. Lionel Manuel to my Phil Simms, Al Toon to my Ken O'Brien, Jerry Rice to my Montana.

Even after the old man left, I still saw hope in the building.

I found a comrade in Bekim Austin, a kid I met in sixth grade PE. When there was a half-day at school, he would invite me to his house to play video games on his Commodore 64 game system. And what games they were. We'd play football, baseball, basketball or golf all day. "If only I had a system to practice on?" I thought. That pissed me off. Everybody seemed to have more than the Ash family even though we all arrived in America at around the same time.

A lot of the kids at Bethune were first or second-generation Americans like me, yet they had video games, their own rooms, parents with jobs that could afford video games and rooms for their kids. Bekim had it made. No matter the scores of the football games (61-0 in one tear-inducing loss between the Atlanta Falcons and the San Francisco Forty-Niners) I kept going back. I had to beat him.

It seemed the games were Bekim's way of getting back at me. While he labored for B's in school, A's came easy to me. Playing his games, I was the one struggling. No matter. He could have his payback. I got something in the deal too. I escaped my apartment for a day, felt normal and active, like one of the kids with the rooms and the video games and the toys and the family who shared time and meaning with each other. For a day, I wasn't cooped up in my apartment, sulking and seated in my own private agony.

In between games, I would say things Bekim's religious sensibility prevented him from thinking. I could be the funny person I secretly wanted to be. I could literally drink and eat the life I wanted.

Oh, to make a sandwich with salami, bologna, turkey, lettuce and tomato like in those mayonnaise commercials. Bekim's fridge had all the cold cuts, the fresh bread straight from the bakery, the meal cooked that same morning by a Caribbean mother who got up before she went to work to make sure there was food ready for everyone who came home before her. I think Bekim's mother was getting suspicious of my motives for playing with her son. I can't deny that food was a factor in putting up with the humiliating video game losses.

As much as he was into rap, R&B and could afford the name brand clothes to visibly fit in with the kids at school, I wouldn't say Bekim identified with the culture at school. At the time, I didn't follow rap music, found R&B love songs stale, had no money for Bekim's Timberlands, but I felt like I understood the culture in the building.

I don't know if it was from watching those *Eyes of the Prize* documentaries that surfaced on PBS every February for Black History Month or the ten-page paper on The Black Power Movement I had to write for Social Studies class. Whatever it was, I could forgive the loitering black men Bekim and I saw on his corner hour after hour, day in, day out. I was beginning to put a few things together about black social history in America. The reality of Brooklyn in 1988-89 was starting to click in my head.

Equal education was denied to an entire lifetime of black folks. The men I saw on the corner drinking their forty ounce malt liquors and shooting dice were not given the chance to follow the paths learning could've carried them. They had no examples to fall back on. Like me in my interactions with folks my own age, those fools refused to break from their static life and discover movement. Instead of growing as people, they were content to keep making the same mistakes and doing nothing to help their own cause. It was as if the social history of the black man in America could be summed up in my adolescent personality.

Like any man ready to conquer life, I was gifted with potential beyond reason. I could dominate any game I chose because I had an agile body and more importantly, a disciplined mind I could bend to my will. However, like many in black America, I refused to interact with my past, in my case, my immediate family and my connection to my island roots. Wasn't that the same thing black people were doing by not learning their African history?

My past, my blood --my mother and my father-- my land, my people were all cut off from me. The sad thing is all those elements were in front of me everyday in Brooklyn. I was a slave to my own inability to make those elements work for me. Everyday I refused to learn as much from and act to change my circumstance. It was too much work to get reattached to my history, much less black history. Black history was the shackle, the whip, the vices. At twelve and thirteen years old, there was little victory in reading *his-story.*

What had my own history ever done for me? Why would I want to remember my mother fighting in St. Vincent or a father who gave me marijuana to smoke? Why would I want to hear that scared little voice inside my head? I didn't want to get hurt by getting involved with, tackling, battling, raking every ounce of usable life from my past. That's what was happening with black America and its history. The memories of physical and mental slavery hurt so much we refused to study it in-depth and grow from its riches.

Forgetting my past, I had embraced America, the land where everyone could start fresh. I found success because I was willing to work and achieve. But in the process, I had lost touch with everything that had made me, everything latent inside me --my island accent, my island spices, my island spirit. Even at the heights of my middle school achievements I was a shell of a man. My American life had emptied me. That was the black America I saw in Brooklyn in the late 1980s, a shell of a people lessened by their days in America, circumscribed by its latent brutality. That was our reality.

"Why don't those lazy idiots get a job," Bekim would utter in disgust. "My father and mother came to America with nothing. Now we live in this nice house, they make sure I stay on the straight and narrow and we have God in our life. There's nothing you cannot do in this country if you make the choice to work hard."

I wouldn't say Bekim was naïve. His family was good Christian folk. I would purposefully curse around him just to test his mettle. I had recently parted ways with organized religion opting, instead, for a more personal conversation with God. I had grown sick of wondering why the Lord had forsaken me by giving me the worst family in the world. And worst still, God gave me the conscience to understand that I would be hurting even more if I turned my back on them. My brain never forgot the Seventh Day Adventists and Anglican Sunday school teachings from my youth. I still believed in The Almighty. I had to, for He was the only one who kept fleeting glimpses of salvation in my soul.

I think, like too much of black America at the time, I had seen life for the darkness it can be. Bekim's mother and father never fought fists and knives before his eyes; he never lived that dread. But I did. I had seen enough of family matters to make more pointed inferences about people. I'm not saying Bekim's perspective was groundless or that mine was something special. Hell, I didn't even voice my thoughts to anyone. A that time, I accepted that nothing I thought was important because it was coming from the mind of a naked, skinny, outwardly-normal-but-inwardly-stealthy, evil, no good, ugly, ugly, ugly, black son-of-a-bitch. And who wanted to listen to that kind of human trash?

Furthermore, voicing thought only led to verbal disagreements, which begot loud arguments that lead to conflict and strife, and those led to my mother and Mudd with fists and knives and me crying in my room cursing the Lord for bringing me into His world. Conflict on any level was something I avoided with the speed of the unholy running from truth on Judgment Day.

No matter how much I ran, conflict was omnipresent in middle school. Everyday, I fought inner demons to stay sane and keep the composure everyone had come to expect from me, the good black boy. I was an actor in life, playing the role of smart student and good citizen, but not the most important role of all: I was not a human being.

Deep down I knew I was not a human being. I was too withdrawn, too solitary, too detached, too insular. That was not what black boys seemed to be. Black boys were brash, loud, aggressive, out there. I was doing all the right things, saying all the right things to all the right people, hearing all the accolades, but I knew deep down it was all bologna and that made me battle harder to suppress my confused and hapless self.

If only the world knew the real me, they would see I wasn't the best at anything. I didn't learn for learning's sake. All I did was do my schoolwork, watch TV and play sports. There was more to life than that. I had never put my foot in the circle of life like my classmates were doing with ease. Even my sister Annie, who saw the same mess I did growing up, had friends who seemed to know her. I had no girlfriend, let alone a meaningful conversation with a girl. Didn't relationships count for something in the definition of the *good* person my teachers kept reminding me I was? I had never even been on a date.

Alexandra Aime. There was the person who deserved universal accolades. In seventh and eighth grade, Alexandra was a pain in our teacher's butt sometimes, but she was simply being herself. Alexandra went about the business of living and growing as a human being. Our teacher would single me out but I wanted to tell him, "No, no, look at Alex, she's the real brain in this class." She was articulate, inspiring, brilliant and unafraid to show it. What did I ever say to inspire folks? What did all the ideas in my head about blackness and the struggle for social change and power in America; what did that matter if I couldn't get those notions out? Wasn't action worth a whole lot more than words and thoughts?

Alexandra espoused her brilliance. She defended herself against male chauvinists and jealous girls who lacked her confidence. When was the last time I defended an idea? By defending an idea, I would be proving its real value to me. No one knew me, what I believed, what I really thought, and I refused to let anyone in. The last time I had a friend was in St. Vincent. We were six years old at the time, so that really wasn't true friendship, was it? I had no idea where that kid was. I couldn't call him up and reminisce about the times we did this or that. I had already blocked out what this and that were.

People at Bethune tried to help me though. Mr. Kearny was the sweetest man. In eighth grade, he stayed after school and gave us pointers on taking the New York City Specialized High School entrance exam. My eighth grade class was the first in Bethune's history with students who had a legitimate shot to get into the city's most competitive public high schools. Mr. Kearny reminded us how important in was to do well on the exam but he never let that pressure weight on our minds.

Mr. Parasram, a math teacher from Guyana, helped us after school as well. He introduced me to the coolest concept I ever figured out in middle school. It had something to do with a flying arrow and time.

Basically, an arrow is defined as being at rest when it is occupying a specific space and time. By that definition an arrow could, theoretically, be at rest even though it might appear to be moving. If the arc of a moving arrow were broken down into individual segments like frames in a movie reel, each frame would show the arrow occupying a specific space and time. In each frame, the arrow would, theoretically, be at rest. If it was at rest, then it never moved. Static movement? Made perfect sense to me back then. Like the arrow, I was getting somewhere but it was damn slow.

There was no applicable value to the flying arrow theory in middle school math and I have never seen it on any exam taken since. Mr. Parasram bothered to explain the theory because he thought we were smart enough to comprehend. The real value of the flying arrow theory was that Mr. Parasram thought we were smart. And since I was one of the first ones to go, "Oh, I get it now," I felt really smart.

Mr. Vernal Matthews was English teacher, disciplinarian, friend, father, confidante to just about everyone he came in contact with. He was the most gifted teacher in the school and the best one I've ever seen. In class 7E1 and 8E1 Mr. Matthews would say, in high dramatic fashion, "I'm leaving all of you and not coming back to this place next year." We knew he didn't mean it. Every year, despite the knuckleheads, the thugs, the wanna-be bad boys, Mr. Matthews returned to Mary McLeod Bethune Academy to teach.

His classroom had the most pictures, placards, colors and warmth in the building. He wore a three-pieced suit everyday and wrote with a black, Parker fountain pen. Mr. Matthews was disciplined, committed and took no back talk from anyone. Even the thugs who got the other teachers riled up listened to Mr. Matthews. He had absolute faith in me.

"Why can't you be more like Ash," he would say to my classmates. "Ash is a perfect gentleman. He never says anything hurtful or acts the fool like the rest of you. He just does his work. James, why can't you do that?"

I knew why James couldn't be like me. He was being a kid. I wasn't. I was some sort of scholastic machine working for the good of the building, never for my self. After two years of hearing, "Be more like Ash," I didn't want to disappoint Mr. Matthews. School became my job. I didn't want to mess up. I couldn't mess up. I'd disappoint too many people if I did.

"Everybody messes up," I'd hear a voice inside me say.

"Not me. I'm Oronde Ash. I can't mess up."

"Who says?"

"I... I say so."

"If you did more, you'd see you have a lot more than school in you. You should let loose like everybody else."

"I don't want to do that. I want to show these kids there is something other than what they see."

"Where did you get that idea?"

"I don't know."

"All those teachers telling you, 'Oronde, you're gonna be a leader someday,' is blowing up your head, huh?"

"Maybe? I just don't wanna be like everybody else."

"Why?" the voice asked.

"Do you ever get tired of asking questions?"

"Why do you ask that?" the voice retorted.

"Okay... I want to be different."

"But why?"

I thought about it. "Black power," I said.

Mr. Husbands --Social Studies teacher, dean, all around strict man-- made our eighth grade class do a paper on the Black Power Movement of the 1960s. After spending hours at the Brooklyn Public

Library, I began to not only realize, but to also internalize what black people had to go through in America to gain equal education.

My black power paper was about Stokeley Carmichael and The Student Nonviolent Coordinating Committee (SNCC), the Congress on Racial Equality (CORE), the Nation of Islam, the Southern Christian Leadership Coalition (SCLC). It was about the Black Panthers, Malcolm X, Dr. Martin Luther King, Jr., Angela Davis and W.E.B. DuBois. For days, we discussed the Civil Rights movement, its significance in American history, its promise and its demise. Mr. Husbands made sure we got the story straight. Nobody acted up in his class those days. We just talked and learned.

I wanted to share my opinions on the readings but I didn't. My voice was changing and I was unsure what it would sound like. Other kids talked. James talked.

"He spends time talking to people and developing opinions on things," the voice inside me said.

"Some of his thoughts come out at the wrong time," I answered.

"You're afraid to challenge teachers aren't you?"

"I just don't think…" I began.

"True," the voice interrupted.

"I have opinions."

"If you valued them, you wouldn't be afraid to sound them out. Let me speak," he challenged. I didn't say anything. "You know more than James but he's the one people hear. Aren't the kids seeing and hearing from the wrong person then?"

"I talk to people."

"No you don't."

"How can I play football if I don't talk to people?"

"Football… Football… Do you stay out there and chat to the kids on your block?"

"I have homework to do."

"They have homework to do too."

"But I have a standard to keep."

"You're afraid." I felt my insides tear ever so slightly. "You're afraid to fail at something."

"I can't talk."

"No, you're afraid to talk," the voice offered.

"They say… They say I sound like a white boy."

"You were living in lily white New Jersey for a year. How are you supposed to sound?"

"I'm different. I don't have the clothes or the video games or the money they have. I hate my life. I want to do more but I can't seem to. I hate walking into that apartment and hearing them argue."

The voice knew I was getting somewhere. "It's not your fault, you know," he tried interjecting.

"I know that. I'm old enough to know that now, but… I can't stop worrying. Every time I hear a voice rise up higher than it should or if something drops on the floor, I cringe like a scared little boy."

"I know," he replied.

"Then why are you asking me?"

"Because I have to. Who else but this voice enters your world?"

The comedians and troublemakers at Bethune provided me some other insights: there was fun to be had in school, a lot more to learn between the lines and outside the pages of the textbooks.

No matter how much control the administration tried to clamp on the less disciplined, kids were going to be kids. Even after the principal painted a yellow line down the middle of the hallway and tried to enforce a policy where students had to exit their rooms and walk to the next class without crossing the line, kids were going to cross the line, to fight, to yell, to kick, to kiss, to carve out a sense-of-self. Human development refuses to be quelled, even in a poor black and Latino middle school. Bethune didn't live up to all its pamphlet promises but, in middle school, I was beginning to understand a bit about my life.

Despite the fights, the gangs, the blatant fear factor surrounding the building, Bekim, Alexandra, James and the rest of my classmates graduated. Even though I didn't find a girl, kiss one, didn't participate in all aspects of school social life, I paid attention and studied that life everyday. At fourteen, I became a perceptive observer.

Who would have thought the biggest fad in eighth grade would've been chess. It was the weirdest thing. The smart kids, the thugs, the gang members, the brains, the wanna-be-any-things all played. The most ardent players were the toughest, roughest boys in the building. If Leel... If Leel would've still been in school in the eighth grade, I know he would've been playing.

"My boy's got you now," a spectator would say. "You in check, punk. You his now." All the kids the Board of Education had left with tattered, outdated textbooks, crumbling classrooms walls and little funding for extra curricula activities were settling their disputes on the chessboard. Kids were buying boards at Woolworth and bringing them to school. The whole scene blew my mind.

Chess presented my first extended glimpse into the dying destiny of my young brothas and sistas. I began to re-envision the power Stokeley Carmichael rallied about when I saw kids who did not believe in themselves in math class studying one of the most complex mind games man had devised. They all had potential. We all had potential.

Every single one of us has the gift to understand something, enjoy anything, do whatever. I saw that with my disbelieving eyes. Initially, it was irritating because chess took a lot of the boys who would play football at lunch. But that was OK. I witnessed something bigger happening.

Go on black man. Play your chess.

Go on black man. Heave out your chest.

Go on black man. Open up your vest.

Go on you super, black man. Show me your best.

Bethune students who weren't in class with me wanted to know two things in particular about me. Why I wore the clothes I did and what kind of music I listened to.

"You listen to heavy metal," a girl wondered incredulously.

At Bethune, rap wasn't doing it for me. It was good to dance to, but my ears weren't ready yet to really listen to it. Even though I was making sense of black history, I wasn't living that history yet and didn't understand rap was chronicling what would become my history. I was still studying black culture from the outside.

"I like Motley Crue," I told the girl that day. "I like Poison, Judas Priest, Anthrax, Guns-n-Roses." I didn't particularly enjoy heavy metal music. I heard samples when I went to Scotch Plains on weekends. The guys on the Spirit of '76 had tapes of everybody. Most of the time, I didn't like what I heard. Sometimes I did. (To this day, I still say Guns-n-Roses' album *Appetite for Destruction* is on of the best albums ever made.)

The question about clothes was harder to answer and I usually avoided it, not wanting people to know I was poor. They were poor too, but along with everybody else I knew, they managed to wear Triple Fat Goose coats, Kongol hats and the latest Jordans. I still wore my cousin Gerry's hand-me-downs or anything my mother found on sale at the discount stores on Pitkin Avenue or Fulton Mall.

For two years, my shoes were a pair of white, plastic high tops. Instead of laces, there was a big Velcro flap that usually unhitched because of the accumulated fuzz from my socks and pants. I'd have to stop running, peel the Velcro strip off, tighten the fit, then reset the strap. The Velcro always made the most annoying sound. I was sure everybody stopped and looked at me. When my mother finally got me a pair of brown, leather moccasins, all seemed right with the world.

My dress code didn't get too much flack at Bethune. Like I said, I rarely looked at people so I never saw them looking at me. If I was being teased, I never heard it. After a while, it was like I wasn't a member of the school. I was a thing separate, with my own rules, own code and expected behavior.

"This... This is wrong buddy," the voice inside me kept urging. "I don't want to live next to this lie." I blocked him out.

It wasn't that my mother couldn't buy the name-brand stuff. Those times were just far and few in-between. It seemed when I really needed a shirt or jeans she didn't have the money. When the money came, she bought stuff for my younger brothers and sisters. (My brother Keri was born in 1987. Randi came in '89. My youngest sister Teri actually arrived in 1985 with me, Ma and Annie. She was two years old then. Teri's mentioned for the first time here because besides picking her up from day care, I rarely did anything with her. I'll talk about my younger siblings enough in later chapters).

"You're trying to spite your mother, aren't you?" the voice inside would ask.

"She can't buy my affection now. It's too late."

"Do you know what the woman has to go through to get the money? Would you like to wipe down old people or cook and feed them day and night?"

I would have nightmares about my mother getting mugged, raped or killed on her evening train ride home from Manhattan. "It's not my money," I told the voice. "I didn't work for it so I don't deserve it."

"Who are you fooling? You're a spiteful little boy in denial. You hate her. You think every time you take a step to her, there's a fight and you have to go back to that spot you're creating in your head." I tried to tune the voice out but he didn't feel like shutting up. "By the way, that spot is getting bigger, getting harder. I can't grow if that rock is in my way," he warned. "I don't want that lie near me. It's poison. I need my space to grow, Oronde. Are you listening to me? Hey… Hey… Are you? Hello… Hello."

Chess. I will never get over that. The kids in school weren't bad. Provide them with an atmosphere to grow, teach them the game and kids could play anything. The room where all the chess wars took place became my alternative future for black America. "That's what it can be like," the voice would promise. "That's Black Power. Remember this. Remember this."

Mary McLeod Bethune Academy showed me other truths as well. I had to laugh more, joke more, mess up more, question more, expect more, do more, be much more in life. I wanted to crack jokes like James or just say "Hello" to Colette Clark and her posse of cute, eighth grade girls. I thought Collette was sneaking glances at me when we lined up in the lunchroom every morning. Maybe she had a thing for shy, brainy guys? Didn't that happen in Woody Allen movies? I wasn't that much of an ugly duckling was I? Cecile McKenzie did ask me to ask her to the fifth grade prom at PS 181. She was the most beautiful girl in Mrs. Cohen's class. All the fellas loved her long, straight hair and fair skin. She was from Belize and looked very exotic. And she had asked me to ask her to the prom.

What was it Cecile fell for? What was the only thing I ever showed the world? My brain. So my brain had to be sexy. Colette, the most sought-after girl in the eighth grade was in love with my brain. In my convoluted head, this made perfect sense. I accepted it as fact even after Collette dated my buddy George the entire eighth grade.

Surely the idea that girls found my brain sexy fueled my academic drive on some subconscious level. Some boys had their money, wore name brand gear, could recite Big Daddy Kane lyrics and do his dance moves. Me? I had a brain. There were many social wonders to engage it in. Most of my thoughts lingered on and off what it meant to be a black boy in America.

It pissed me off to see the black kids trying to talk, walk, dress, think, act and be the same monolithic stereotype. If lowered academic expectation was the legacy of the old school, I was, therefore, a leader of the new school and consciously tried to change the scenario.

The few times I talked, it was as if I had so much will and was ready to tackle the world at the beginning of each thought. But as soon as someone else's eyes were on me, I realized I was naked and had to put on the right clothes --the ones I could never afford-- to make sense in their eyes. By the time that fear hit, my voice had grown faint and trailed off, as did the meaning in whatever I was trying to say.

There was more to life than what Bethune students were seeing. Living in Scotch Plains had showed me that hard work and sacrifice were the things that got you the house, the dog, the white, picket fence. I saw it, felt it, I had lived that dream. Thanks to my surrogate soccer families, I was aware of what it took to achieve it. If only I could say it. If only I could teach it. If only I could enlighten my peers like the best of black America's heroes, the ones on Mr. Matthew's classrooms walls, had done. Differences make the individual great, not the same-o-same-o, generic crap I was seeing in middle school.

I had nothing in common with my classmates yet I felt special among them. I had achieved, not because I became like everybody else, but because I refused to be like anybody else. At the time, my philosophical stance had more to do with teenage defense mechanism, insulating my self from the world so I couldn't be hurt in the least, but it was proof that I didn't have to lower my standards to fit in anywhere. And all I gave up in middle school were friends, family, relationships, connection and a chance to find out about my beautiful, black self. If I could do all that and succeed; if I could continue living a lie; if I could keep selling out my soul, then anyone could.

"Madness. Utter madness," the voice hollered one night. "I know you don't believe… because there's no way… absolutely no way I… you believe that for a second. Life is not in accolades; it isn't in grades. You're getting straight A's but you're still unhappy. You don't even know how much you hate your self." The voice was steady. "Friends, family, faith in me, that's where life really is."

I thought, and thought and thought. I accepted this. After all, I was the smart guy. I had to accept the answer from my smart brain.

On graduation day I wore my red cap and gown like everybody else. My mother was there and smiled politely when teachers told her what a joy I was.

That day, my mother and I weren't connected in any meaningful way. It was not as if my teacher's kind words made her glow with pride, which caused me to beam back because my *mother* was proud of me. Nurture had long severed whatever I was supposed to feel when making her proud. I assumed she was proud but there was no way for me to be one hundred percent sure. Graduation felt empty and disjointed. I was acting happy instead of being happy. My valedictory speech was lacking.

Technically, the speech was fine. Mr. Matthews helped me add the most explosive adjectives and apt imagery where necessary. He and I practiced my speech during lunch for two weeks. "They don't think you can do this, Oronde," he reminded me. I had doubts too. "We're gonna show them. You're gonna knock their socks off." Mr. Matthews said he was a preacher. He even recited Shakespearean soliloquies in class. If he thought I could do, I knew I had a chance.

When I looked out at the audience that June morning, there was no one I felt communion with. I had never built a foundation with anyone at Bethune. All the A's on my report cards were for naught. I had worked for a piece of paper that ultimately meant nothing because I didn't feel emotion surrounding it.

From the podium, I watched kids who had struggled mightily in their work, had earned detention, been in fights, gotten suspended. Their families seemed overjoyed some of them had made it that far. I hadn't struggled in school. On paper I had made it farther than any other student, but I knew I fell short. Besides school and sports, I hadn't tried anything else in middle school. But there I was, the pride of

Mary McLeod Bethune Academy's 1990 graduating class, voted Most Likely to Success. Inside, I already felt like a failure.

Although I made it through my speech and got a cheer, my voice didn't show up that day. Later, he told me he felt ashamed.

What I keyed in on that day were the hugs and the tears. Parents were crying, kids were crying, teachers were crying. Why? What had I missed while I was busy studying and acting like a disciplined adult? What joyous imperfections had I passed up while trying to be perfect? What child had I forgotten to be? What a perfectly sunny, jubilant, poignant, empty, lonely graduation day it was, a pro poi of nothing.

In all the awards I gathered --valedictorian, Chancellor's Award of Excellence, Mayor's Award, blah blah blah-- everything else was fleeting. One minute the apartment I lived in would be stable and I seemed to be making friends and coming out of my shell. The next minute, my mother and Mudd would scream and holler and push each other around again and I was like a turtle back in the hole, never taking a chance on revealing the person intermittently peeping out between the raucous.

I remember walking into apartment 3R on East 52nd St. and being washed in darkness. Sometimes it wouldn't happen right away. I might have been with some schoolmates, always hanging on the fringes of their conversations. The light of our attempts at bonding might still have been following me into the room Annie and I shared. I paid attention to those groups of boys in middle school trying to figure out what, at fourteen, I was supposed to think and who I was supposed to be.

I began to see that each boy wished to dominate any conversation, to bring all the other boys to his individual vision of whatever the group was talking about. Each boy heard his voice as the right one, in some cases, as the only one. The logic I was familiar with in scholastic learning, where evidence is brought from opposing sides and weighed against each other, was not the rule in these discussions. A man could bend others to his will by deflecting attention from the topic with a joke, a pun, an indirect attack on his foe's dress style or character. A man could win an argument even though he made no logical sense whatsoever. The man simply had to be in control of his voice. For example:

Boy A: "Patrick Ewing should be traded from the Knicks."

Boy B: "Damn right. We ain't winning no NBA championships with him"

Boy C: "What are you talking about? Ewing's the only player the Knicks have. Charles Oakley's not gonna bring us a ring."

Boy A: "That black pirate is scaring people outta Madison Square Garden with that widow's peak on his forehead."

Boy B: "You right. Ewing is ugly with that widow's peak on his head."

As boys A and B laugh, boy C has no choice but to laugh. In the interim, A has won the argument without making any logical justification for wanting to trade Patrick Ewing. His delivery and comic timing were just better.

I was picking up these subtleties of conversation and interaction and began to study human relationships with the keen eye of an anthropologist. If I wasn't involved with people, I should at least learn as much as I could about them to be fully prepared when the time came to share my voice.

In summer 1990, with high school a few months away, my family ceased to be the personal liability it once was. Rather, I saw them as my human behavior laboratory. My mother, Mudd, Annie, Teri, Keri and Randi would be subjects in the grand experiment I theorized would result in making me the human being I wanted to be. They were going to teach me all there was to know about my voice and how to use it. And I could do it too. I mean… wasn't I just crowned the smartest kid in school?

VII.

Ka-GOW

"I don't want them to see me smile. They'll think they had something to do with my happiness. They must never see my emotions. They must suffer as I do."

Sure, I was doing things with people and laughing once-in-a-while, but inside I was miserable. Somebody should have caught on to that. I was once a vibrant, living human being. My mother and Mudd had made me feel awful about the life awaiting me thanks to their example. From fifth through eighth grade, I asked nothing of them. As long as my base needs of food and shelter were met, they'd done their part. I stayed out of their messy life and did mine: survive.

With my mother, I remained cordial. There were, from me, mumbled "Hellos" and "Goodbyes" whenever appropriate. I couldn't be an all-out brat about the situation. After all, the woman had given me life, raised and fed me, brought me to America. There was no logic in dismissing her. A wrathful God would surely have punished me. Honor thy mother and father was His commandment. And by eighth grade, I knew neither my mother nor Mudd was at complete fault for my feelings of inadequacy and self-doubt.

"You can still come out of your shell. You can still grow." The voice inside never gave up on me.

I don't know if it was hormones or what but that voice sounded deeper, more full of sense at the end of middle school. He talked to me during the everyday grind, in my sleep, walked me through my desire for change. My voice guided me to places I rarely tread. Those days, I listened more and more because the speed at which my mind and body was changing necessitated a steady, internal compass.

I wanted to become fully human, have a myriad experiences to learn from, maintain stable relationships without arguments and conflict. TV sitcoms like *Growing Pains*, *Who's The Boss* and *Family Ties* still hooked me to a world where if any child got hurt, the pain was only at the beginning of the half hour. Around the twenty-minute mark an all-knowing relative or caring friend would console the troubled kid and all would be made right between commercial breaks. My family never measured up. Even if we did, I refused to participate in our plot.

My mother and Mudd finally had money to buy McDonalds every so often and time to take my younger siblings to ride the roller coasters at Coney Island. My sister Annie tagged along. I never went. Ma and Mudd had their chance to imprint themselves on me when I was younger. That time had long passed.

There were Ash family barbecues in New Jersey where uncles, cousins, nieces and nephews came all the way from Western Canada to get together. I never went to any of the functions and my mother never made me. She would ask if I wanted to go and I would say, "No," just about every time. "She's afraid to alienate herself from you even more," the voice intoned.

In eighth grade, my mother got a job as a nanny to a wealthy couple in uptown Manhattan so there was more money, more food in the refrigerators, more stuff around the house. Spending money on her kids became my mother's way of showing love. Sensing that, I refused to tell her what I liked to eat, to think, to do, to wear. If anybody was going to *love* me, I wanted to be the one to do it.

"Just give me the money," is all I ever said around Christmas or birthdays because I came to recognize the power of manipulation parents are supposed to have from day one.

Like the FBI or CIA, parents are supposed to know their children's likes, dislikes, wishes, dreams and aspirations. It makes it that much easier for them to figure out effective means of control. I was able to see the subtle manipulations of the parent-child relationship because the ties that would have otherwise controlled me were severed. In our bondless state, my family lacked that connective force: love. From that lacking I became acutely aware of my need for love.

Love is something that had to be developed. If my mother had talked to me more when I was growing up or done more with me, our bond would have been tighter. But none of that happened. Once I began placing variables like power, need, time, emotions, history and the elements of day-to-day life into my skewed family equation, a clearer picture was painted. My picture was not clouded by involvement so I could be as objective as I wanted. I wasn't hurting anyone's feelings. To be hurt, a person has to be tight with whom or whatever is on the other end of the broken bond. Since I had no bond to break, I never got hurt. I refused to get hurt.

"This isn't the way," my deepening voice would promise.

"I'm going to control my own happiness from now on," I decided.

To convince me of worthwhile change, my mother had to practice a new lifestyle, one that recognized the emotional needs of her children. It's not that she wasn't caring. Like any decent mother, Ma loved us. She was just too busy and too tired to show that love with hugs, kisses, conversation and tender moments. I couldn't forgive her for denying me that soft shield against my black boy journey in America.

My sister Annie tried forgiveness. At thirteen, boys were entering her frame so a new shirt, shoes or name brand pants were appealing to what she was becoming. While I had sputtered and built icy walls around my heart, Annie had been melting. In her world, the falling waters helped her flower as a person. Even though she wasn't as *gifted* as me, I was jealous of Annie because she had friends, had meaning with those friends, had issues with those meanings. She was living.

"But they've bought her love?" I reminded my voice. "She's selling out."

I began to see the parallels between my detached experience of life and the possibilities for black people in America. Watching my schoolmates, my sister Annie, or even Bekim fall prey to the wants of materialism irked me. I wanted to tell them how foolish they were to spend money on clothes, shoes or jewelry when they should be worrying about experience. Because I lacked life experience, saw it as the thing that defined the individual. Yes, I seemed rich with God's graces, knew many things, could do many things, but I was poor because I was afraid to use those gifts. My limited life experience made me poor beyond my family's finances.

"You don't have the money to do anything," my voice would offer reluctantly. I had taught him that tired line. He knew better but had to repeat it. My family's poverty got my pride off the hook many-a-times. For example,

> "I would ask Collette Clark out, but I don't have the money for both of us to go to the movies... And I'm not going to ask Ma for money because that would mean listening to her, which would mean looking at her for more than two seconds, which always makes me want to hug her because I can see her crying inside. That would make me vulnerable and open and possibly cry too. Then we would hug and all would be forgiven and we would start to feel good. I don't want that. What about the war? I couldn't concede. Not now. She would only get into a huge fight with Mudd over some nonsense and I'll be crying and feeling like the smallest, most insignificant bug in the world. Then I will be back to square one --lonely and afraid... So why should I even think about asking Collette out? She'd probably say no. Anyway, I don't have the money."

Black Americans believed wants created for us instead of following our own paths to our own needs and desires. In my adolescent sensibilities, I figured black people would be so much better off if we gave up wanting material things. I didn't want anything and I was fine.

"You're not fine... You are not fine," my voice would say. "What do you really want, Oronde? Be honest." I thought about it, maybe for days, maybe weeks.

What I wanted was to experience a connection to life in some wholesome way. Why didn't black America see connection was the key to understanding and happiness? Black folks should have been more like me in wanting peace and understanding in my family. Nothing else mattered.

My mother knew I didn't want to do some of the things she asked, but I did them anyway. I went to the laundry with her Saturday afternoons watching the clothes turn from dirty to clean, waiting for our life to turn from dirty to clean. Every time I engaged with her, I was fighting every learned instinct in me to avoid her. At the laundry mat, it was as if I left my body and was dwelling in the world of ideas and ideals. Ideally, a boy should help his mother do things. That was decent. I was trying to live a decent life under God.

I knew it was right to talk to my mother, to be nice to her, but the mechanics of those interactions was not in my blood. My heart would race whenever she was near me, my eyes would dart left, right, up, down, my body would tremble a bit. But I knew I had to fight the discomfort because it wasn't natural. I wasn't supposed to be like that. My mother and I were not supposed to be like strangers around each other. I forced my self to practice kindness and compassion towards her even though those emotions were never real to me.

"Can you get this for me please?" my mother would ask. I knew she didn't need me to fetch the plate at the back of the cupboard. What my mother really wanted was to be acknowledged as I handed her the plate. My mother wanted to feel something from me, wanted to see if I was alive, wanted me to be her baby boy. And deep down I wanted her to be my mother and feel whatever it was a boy is supposed to feel for his mother. It was frustrating to know I hungered for something I was too afraid to make happen.

Bridging that gap between what I knew I wanted and what life had ill-prepared me to do was the saddest part of my family's social experiment.

Somewhere in me there was gold, oil, diamonds and pearls all shiny and sparkling. No matter what happened in life, I knew this. Nobody played sports with the energy I did if there wasn't that fire within. And I never wanted to dominate. On my block most of the kids were heavier and less athletic than me. When we played basketball, I drove to the hoop and gave them the ball for an easy lay up. When we played handball, I could have easily sprayed the court and made the fat boys run but that would almost be cheating. When they played the dozens on the schoolyard steps, I listened instead of insulting other kids' mammas. A semblance of compassion had to exist in me.

I went to school everyday, did all my homework, attacked no one, stole from no one, got good grades. That had to say something about my character. But what? And why didn't I own that character? I must have been that character some time, somewhere. All the teachers couldn't be wrong.

It would be another few years until I remembered the boy who everybody in St. Vincent seemed to like; the boy who felt affection and joy everywhere he went. As a child I held life in my palms on the island and gave freely to anyone. When other Vincentians visited apartment 3R on East 52nd Street in Brooklyn, I felt ashamed. I could never remember them but they always remembered me. I sensed their disappointment, or maybe it was my own. It was as if they were each waiting for another Oronde to talk; like the boy I was back home was destined for something beyond whatever I had become.

Vincentians were all noisy, expressive people, bellies full of laughter. They spat out Brooklyn's harshness, recognized that life in America was a hard, dangerous, deadly disappointment. But Vincentians were going to live no matter what.

In St. Vincent, The Ashes had food, clothes and money, but it could not have been material wealth that gave us spirit. My childhood friends and I would have the best of times without money. We were in the boy scouts together, caught fish, boiled vegetables and made soup and rice together. One day, we got the hide from a skinned cow and made drums together. We even went on a camping trip once and hiked through the mountains with all the *jumbees* --ghosts-- whistling through the bamboo and banana trees. It was on that trip I saw a glowing apparition in the woods. The white light was three feet tall and walking up the side of a hill. In the crazy machinations of my confused middle school mind, I began to think it must have been a vision of God blessing me.

The world must have thought I was a weirdo walking around with my head in the clouds never stopping to relate to the lives they led. I wasn't doing it to be snooty. I took the high road because the low road dragged me down with baggage. Surprisingly, in most aspects of my life, people let me be. I thought anybody else would have been a complete outcast for not participating fully with friends but I was allowed in and out of the lives of my peers.

I talked like a white boy, wasn't into hip-hop culture or Jamaican dance hall music, wore nothing name brand, yet I was never ostracized, at least not to my face. "God must be looking out for me."

Kids would ask, "Oronde, why don't you curse."

"I have no reason to," I'd say.

Maybe the kids respected me for not taking the low road. Perhaps my master plan for changing the stereotypes placed on black boys was working.

From wherever I appeared to be, the other kids seemed to think I could see more than they could. That would explain why they elected me their official answer man. And what was I going to do, reject one of the few means of connecting to my peers? If there was a question nobody could resolve, I was the last resort.

"Isn't it true that if the ice caps melt New York City will be flooded?" someone might ask.

"Yes."

"Yo, 'Ronde, what's the name of that show with the guy and the bike and he used to ride real fast?"

"Street Hawk."

"Ash, tell that fool that the capital of Saudi Arabia is Oman?"

"Shut up, Kayeem, it's something else."

"Actually, it's Riyadh."

"Told you. Told you."

While the others got back to their discussions, I waited for my next chance to interact with my schoolmates and experience some human connection. It was all bull and I knew it.

"Hey, 'Ronde, how do you pronounce 'shit' in Portuguese?"

"It's pronounced ka-GOW."

MUSICAL INTERLUDE

Song title:	It Takes Two
Artist:	Rob Bass and DJ EZ Rock

VIII.

THE HOUSE OF ASH

I f ever a place had cracks and fissures running through and through, The House of Ash, 58 East 52nd Street, Brooklyn, NY was it. Anger anchored the ceiling, pain and misunderstanding chipped the walls away, fear and frustration kept returning even after the bathrooms had been scrubbed of their grime, the freezer defrosted of its ice, the carpets vacuumed of their dirt.

There were eight of us living in the two apartments on the third floor of the six-family building --my mother, Mudd, Annie, Teri, Keri, Randi and me. With more money in her hands, my mother had enough of Mudd and his ways. The family next door to apartment 3R moved out so Ma leased apartment 3F and moved me, Annie and since there was more room, my Grandma came to live with us as well.

My mother shuffled between apartments 3R and 3F making meals and cleaning on the weekends. She may have been doing a bit more running but at least she had reclaimed part of her independence and gotten her kids out of a horrible situation.

Legally, Teri, Keri and Randi carried Mudd's last name. Keri was his father's son. I glanced over and saw him being shaped in Mudd's dirty image. For that, I rarely played with Keri, saving all my energies for young Randi. I was Adam in the household; Keri was Cain, too far gone. Randi was the Abel I was saving from Lucifer's hand. (I regret feeling so much animosity towards Keri. At the time, deflection and denial were practiced lessons in The House of Ash.)

Keri didn't know what was going on but he had ended up on the wrong side of my own private war. In my mind, my three-year-old brother had it coming after what happened on Monday, August 13, 1990.

Annie and I shared a bedroom adjoining the living room in Mudd's apartment 3R. A door made of two columns of square, glass panels that had been painted white, separated the two rooms. One of the square panels was broken and my mother put a piece of foam to cover the open space. Keri and Annie were doing something and Keri's finger got stuck in the loose, glass panel. He started crying. Mudd got upset and yanked out the foam from the panel.

I was trying to sleep but the newly created hole in the door brought the glare of the living room TV set onto my face. To get some privacy I took the foam and tried to duct tape it over the hole. Mudd saw what I was doing.

"I will fix that," he said. I didn't pay him any mind. I didn't need his help.

"I'm trying to sleep," I said. This was the first time I had said anything to the man in months.

I guess his expert carpentry, masonry, interior decorating or whatever-the-heck-he-did-for-a-living skills were bothered by my amateurish work so he ordered Keri to knock the foam down. I got the duct tape and tried putting it back in place.

"Leave that thing alone. I said I'd fix it when I have the time."

"You haven't done it yet. Somebody has to," I challenged, and continued taping the foam back to the door until I was satisfied. Then I got into bed and tried falling asleep. Three minutes later, the foam fell out the panel and I had to deal with the glare from the TV again. I got up, re-taped the foam and returned to bed. Two minutes later, the foam fell again. I could hear Mudd laugh as he ordered Keri to bring the foam to him.

"Can I have that back so I can fix it?" I asked.

"Look, I'm going to fix it. I can't have people come here and see that mess in my house."

"How am I supposed to sleep with the light in my face?"

"Turn your head and go to sleep," was his reply.

"I would if you fixed the damn door," I fired back. I wasn't backing down now.

"You think just 'cause your mama ain't here you da man in the house?" Mudd waited for my reply. He was ready. With my mother away in the Hamptons for the rest of the week with the family she worked for, Mudd saw the moment as a fight he could win. Bully. I said nothing. Silence had always been my most formidable weapon. It was my own means of nonviolent protest via passive resistance.

"You and Annie think you can do anything in this house. Your mudda don't wanna train you two right. You both have no respect for nobody and she just let you go wild. You gonna pay one day, though. If you two was home…" he began. I wasn't going to let Mudd badmouth me, my sister or even my mother for that matter.

"If we were home, what? You'd hit us. You're a coward." Mudd took offense and started to raise his right hand, open palmed, as if ready to strike but he didn't do anything. Instead, he took the piece of foam off the sofa, tore it to shreds and threw the pieces on the floor. Mudd then lay down and continued watching TV with Keri on top of him.

I went back to my bed and put a pillow over my face. That was it. I could understand Mudd, but my own brother? As far as I was concerned, I had only one brother, Randi. But if Randi started getting caught in the mudslide, I was cutting him off too.

I knew Mudd wanted to teach me a lesson that night but I wouldn't give him the satisfaction. For years when we passed in the apartment I never met his gaze. Not because I feared the guy. I actually wanted him to imagine evil in me. I had never entertained the thought of killing Mudd but I could have. Even that night, murder didn't come up. The guy was a non-entity. He had ceased to register in my head.

By the end of middle school I had perfected the ability to block out anything or anyone and focus on what I wanted. I had to do that at Bethune just to make it through days full of classroom brawls, gangs outside the school, drugs and violence around the corner. I had to use those same coping skills in the apartment to try to love my mother, my brothers and sisters despite my best efforts not to.

Later that night, I tried to tape a football game with the VCR but Mudd pulled my tape out. I said something, I don't remember what. I remember keeping a journal that summer. The entry for that day was,

"... Asshole Sr. then ordered me to take off the television no later than 1:00 AM. It seems I stayed up until 2:00-2:30 watching the tube. That was logical [Bills were always a spark for arguments] and I complied. Not because I was listening to him or give a fuck to whatever Asshole Sr. said, but because I didn't want him and my mother fighting. I've seen too much of that already and one more will not help. The real problem is that Asshole Sr. is trying to be the authority he isn't. I'd give more respect to the shit coming out my butt. Asshole Sr. is just trying to intimidate me, but Asshole Sr. will not succeed. He will remain the nothing he has always been in my eyes, and my silent war shall continue. Anyway, I'll get back at Asshole Sr. one way or another. You can count on that."

Mudd did much of his talking when my mother wasn't around. And when we were spread out over two apartments, he had to work that much harder to establish dominion. The guy craved power. He was a spin-doctor who operated on my grandmother with Machiavellian precision. I studied his scheming and treachery from afar.

When my mother was away, Mudd would get together with Grandma and talk about his troubles in the house. The two were true believers in the Caribbean version of family values --pseudo-male dominance and unquestioned respect for elders. They formed an enemy faction against my mother and Annie. To them, Annie should've been cooking meals, cleaning up after people and basically getting used to that submissive, female role. But Annie grew up in America, enjoyed spending afternoons skipping double-dutch across the street with her friends. Annie couldn't be blamed. In my mother, Annie saw a strong-willed woman who did what she had to do to preserve her dignity. Annie was being what she saw around her. All three generations of women in the apartment were just being what they were.

Grandma was old school, my mother had always been a survivor, and Annie, she was a teenage girl testing boundaries. If only the women could see their situation from the outside like I did, a lot of turmoil could have been avoided.

Grandma questioned the way my mother was raising Annie. Of course my mother never went for that. Ma listened, but she knew the reality for a girl in New York City. Annie had to grow a backbone. Grandma and Mudd didn't have a clue what it was like to be young in America. The two would reinforce their positions by tearing Annie and my mother down. I stayed out of fracas. I said "Good morning" and

"Good evening" to Grandma. Whatever she wanted me to do, I did. I couldn't blame her. She was being worked over.

There was a force in the apartment. I didn't think it was evil, but I knew it wasn't good. The fall of the House of Ash was eminent. I would leave for school each morning wondering if there'd be blood on the walls when I returned. I made it through school and friends and playing and such with my fear in check. Some may say I was mature enough to compartmentalize and get over. Annie, on the other hand, was not mature. She lashed out. I was scared she would do something grievous.

In times of complete desperation, my mother would threaten to ship my sister back to St. Vincent where she could learn some manners.

"Gyell, if you only knew what I had to go through down there," Ma would lament. "You think you a woman. You think you big," she would yell while administering what became a ritual --Annie's Friday night lashing.

I always thought my mother did all that for show. Two hours after the brouhaha, she, Annie, and Grandma would be talking again. I could never understand the nuances between the three women. One minute they'd be at each other's throats and the next they were going on about St. Vincent, cooking, fabrics for the dresses Grandma spent all day sewing. At least with Mudd, my mother took two to six days before they were good again. I was sure all the female problems had a bit to do with biology. Maybe my mother and sister were PMS-ing at the same time. That was my best guess.

Menstrual or not, I saw that my mother was being kept out of the limited information cycle floating around the house. I stayed outside the cycle, but I was close enough to pick up the wheeling and dealing in the two apartments.

Mudd had solid control of 3R with Teri, Randi and Keri. Grandma tried to influence 3F but Annie and I still held a grudge from her favoritism shown to my cousins when we lived in Scotch Plains. My mother cared about keeping the peace so she listened to her mother's side, her children's side and Mudd's side of every little thing that happened. Ma had to be going nuts. I started seeing this because the same thing was happening to me in my adolescence.

The more information I was starting the process, the crazier life seemed. There were no simple answers anymore. Truth was still truth but even that was starting to look relative based on where you were and how you felt.

All my mother wanted to do was relax when she got home. Instead, she had to run between apartments mending fences that always broke again. I don't think she ever figured out all that happened while she was changing diapers, reading stories or otherwise being a surrogate mother to two girls who treated her more like a mother than her own kids.

I was becoming a firm believer in rational thinking. There were lines of reasoning that worked. I needed life to work. Book rationale was what I knew and that had worked for me. To learn by the book, a person needs all the information available. What was happening in the House of Ash was not rational. My mother was fighting battles with half-truths and manipulations. When she hit Annie for something Grandma complained about, my mother was trying to discipline while being an obedient daughter to her own mother. And when she and Annie were laughing two hours later, Ma was trying to understand while reaching out to her daughter. What confusion. How could I not begin to sympathize with her?

Ma looked so pleased the night I walked into the new apartment 3F for the first time. Mudd had just finished installing the carpet in my new room. That moment, knowing my mother wanted me to smile, knowing she knew how happy I was to have my own space, knowing my smile would mean the world to her, knowing I wanted to give her my thanks with my smile, I refused to. I bottled my happiness and stood in the middle of the room, stark and indifferent.

"The minute I let my emotions go, I'm a goner."

"How will you know unless you try?" my voice asked.

"The more I show I care about her, the more she can control me."

"You still believe that."

"I can't deny what I've never felt."

My new room was not cause for wholesale forgiveness. I was still waging a war of silent, passive resistance until both my mother and Mudd acknowledged the damage they had done. I kept my talking and interactions with them to the bare minimum.

Even with all going on in my head, life was getting better. I had a new room for a new phase in my life. Mumbling a "Thank you" to Mudd for the carpeting --a very unnerving, almost sickening thing to do-- I left and went to move the rest of my things from the old country way across the hall in 3R to my new world in 3F.

"Mudd must never do anything to benefit my life in any way," I kept thinking that first night. I had nothing to say to that guy. As always, I would keep my mouth shut, listen but say nothing.

Everybody wants to be acknowledged for who they are. They want to be talked to, interacted with, thought about. Their humanity is reaffirmed with every word. "You" are talking to "them". "They" are answering "you". The process reminds both parties each is alive. By remaining silent, I was killing Mudd, killing his version of what it meant to be a man. He couldn't fight me, couldn't put me in my place. It brought me joy to cause him some form of pain.

Mudd wasn't a man. How could a man push my mother in front of me and expect me to respect him? How weak was the bastard? I had a book load of insecurities about being a man but I didn't take them out on anyone, at least not physically. I admit to playing mind games on the folks in the house by withdrawing my true self. I'm sure my cold demeanor was hurting my mother more than any of Mudd's physical assaults, but at least I didn't hit her.

From what I saw, my mother did her fair share of instigating arguments and fights. She had her own issues too.

"But he has the strength to cool down. He should stand back and let her rant for a little bit. She would calm down. She always did. Ma's not gonna hurt him with her bare hands." She was giving up close to a foot in height. What damage could she have done? But No! The guy wanted to be a dominant man of the house. No wonder my mother moved us out.

I sat down in my new room that first night, thought about everything that was happening and tried to make sense of it all. I thought back to that night three months before in August with the foam panel and the glare. Since then, I had started my freshman year at Brooklyn Technical High School and was playing soccer again after quitting for two years. A new phase of my life was on its way. Again, I was a leader on the field, the best player on the team. That success brought me some grounding no matter what else was happening in the house.

At the beginning of a new decade I was on the 38th parallel. To the South was all the baggage I had been carrying. I hated. I masked my hate. I hated my mask.

To the North was logic. It was simple, rational, overpowering. "You have to forgive and move on." I heard those sentiments everywhere.

Logic overtook me with the force of the November Revolution. I could not deny it. Human instinct started to pop up. I had two little brothers. I had to nurture them. "You don't want them to feel like you, do you?" Randi and Keri were not going to be like me. They were going to be better.

I had two younger sisters. I had to protect and love them. Annie and Teri were going to live a better life than their mother. I had to be an example of the good man they would need. Things couldn't go on the way they were. I had to grow up, become a 1990s man: intelligent, forceful yet open and willing to change.

The Cold War was over. The Wall had come down. I had a job to do on the home front: unite my family. It would be irrational not to focus on that task. I would never grow if I didn't do it. I would never be the man I wanted to be if I didn't do it.

MUSICAL INTERLUDE

Song title:	Right Her, Right Now
Artist:	Jesus Jones
Year:	1990

IX.

GATEWAY

Gateway was the name of a program at Brooklyn Technical High School whose aim was to get more minorities into the medical field. Students with exemplary middle school records were nominated to take part. The plan was to keep the students together in all freshman and sophomore classes and most junior and senior core courses. At the Gateway orientation, I saw Filipinos, Koreans, Hondurans, Venezuelans, Puerto Ricans, Trinidadians, Iranians, Sri Lankans, American blacks, white kids. The world was in my new school. Pick a country and there was someone roaming Tech's hallways with a tie to it.

New school year, fall 1990, I was again the resident smart guy; only this time, I wasn't the only one. I don't think the Gateway kids knew what to make of me. I never said or did anything to anyone, wasn't a pest to the teachers like some other know-it-alls. I did my work, was cordial, made no waves and went home. Some of the fellas found out I played on the Tech soccer team because I got my name in New York Newsday's high school sports pages. When they heard me talk about the New York Giants football games or the Knicks as easily as I tutored them in biology after school, I gained some cool.

For the most part, other Gateway students let me be. I was a nice guy. That blanket felt comfortable on me. (Looking back, I see *nice* as the worst adjective to describe another human being. It's the word used when someone has done nothing to distinguish him or herself good, bad or indifferent.)

My freshman year was without distinction one way or the other --just nice. Academically, I did what I was accustomed to doing: straight A's. I also got to know a few Gateway people. To me, that attempt at bonding was more important than any grade.

Each semester, Gateway arranged an overnight excursion for the students. They took us to Salem, Massachusetts on Halloween and we spent two days at Comsett State Park in Long Island on another trip. The boys looked forward to the legendary football games we heard took place at Comsett. The older Gateway students told us that the program coordinator, Ms. Cohen --not the same Mrs. Cohen from fifth grade-- was crazy about football and insisted everybody, even the girls, play a little. That was perfect for me. None of my classmates saw me play soccer for Tech so the football games provided a chance to impress them all with my athletic skills. After tossing a forty-yard spiral, Mrs. Cohen was made quarterback. Perfect.

Besides the football games, Comsett provided a chance for Gateway students to practice team building. We had each been successful individuals but the program's advisors wanted us to learn how to function in groups. If we were going to be doctors, we had to get used to working together. Best to start learning sooner than later.

At Comsett, we were divided into groups of seven or eight and asked to complete tasks. One task had us scavenger hunt around the sprawling estate with a map and compass looking for hidden items. Another required us to scale a seven-foot, shear stonewall. As soon as our guide explained what we had to do, all the faces in my group dropped because Vincent Johnson was with us.

Vinnie was five feet six inches and over two hundred and fifty pounds. He did not want to take part but the guide reminded us that everybody had to make it up the wall or the team would fail. Gateway kids didn't like to fail so we came up with a plan.

First, the boys helped the two girls in the group up the wall. That was easy. Then two boys jumped up top. The three other boys on the bottom tried putting Vinnie's thighs onto our shoulders and lifting him up but that promptly failed. We thought we'd make a ladder with our hands and help Vinnie up but that failed too. Finally, we came up with a scheme that was sure to work. By this time Vinnie was embarrassed and we had to convince him to keep working with us.

The three remaining boys on the ground formed a human step. We were on all fours, our sides braced against the wall. The plan was for Vinnie to step on our backs and have everybody on top who could reach grab his hands and pull. As soon as the people on top had Vinnie's hands secured, we would grab any part of his body and push from the bottom with everything we had. When Vinnie was halfway up the wall, we pushed against his thighs, his stomach, his massive rear end. Ten minutes after starting the exercise, Vinnie was on top. The grass at the bottom was torn away, my pant legs were caked in mud, but Vinnie was where he needed to be. To me, that moment exemplified all that was good about the Gateway program.

There we were, a group of minority kids in the middle of a grand Long Island estate, far away from the hustling City. With teachers and guides who worked to support us in every way possible, we could bare any burden or surmount any wall. There was no doubt in my mind that all the Gateway students would be successes in life.

In the middle of the first semester, Gateway arranged for us to take the Stanford-Benet Test. No one knew what it was for, just another exam we were used to passing.

Around Christmas, I got a letter telling me that because of my test score, I qualified to enroll in an SAT prep program at City College in Manhattan that would meet three hours every Saturday morning for six weeks. The program would then pay for me to take the SAT in February 1991. If I got a high enough SAT score, I would compete for a scholarship to something called Johns Hopkins University's Center for Talented Youth (CTY). CTY offered gifted middle school and high school underclassmen the chance to take college-level courses in math, science, computers, English and the arts.

I didn't want to spend another July in the apartment looking at my neighbors smiling under the spray of the fire hydrant, wishing to join in their reverie. Wasn't I supposed to be changing in high school? CTY was the perfect chance to go somewhere new and experience something different. For three weeks no one would know how coward and insecure I was. I could shed that skin and put on another one of my choosing.

I wasn't just a promising doctor. I was also a writer. Mrs. Laudi's freshman English class at Tech was teaching me to explore my feelings and present them on paper.

The book *Inherit the Wind* had swept me up in the scopes monkey trial. *The Sword in the Stone* made me think I was a magician traveling backwards in time. Like Merlin, I knew material beyond my years. Or maybe I was King Arthur, destined for greatness.

82

When we did our vocabulary lessons, I found clever ways to celebrate words. Standing in the front of the room reading a contrived sentence, I held the class in my palms. I could make them laugh out loud, smirk, wonder why they didn't come up with my sentence themselves. I painted pictures of what I thought, what they thought but could not say. I felt lighter when writing about or reading aloud my adolescent confusion. For once, I could touch my classmates like they seemed to touch each other.

The results came back from the February SAT exam. I had done it. The CTY application soon came.

"Ma, they need some information for the scholarship form."

"What do they need to know?"

"My social security number?"

"You don't have one, you know that."

"Maybe I can just make one up?"

"No."

"What's my insurance policy number?"

"You don't have any."

"What should I do about the social security number?"

"Leave it blank."

"How much money does this household make per annum?"

"Let's see. I make twelve... and he makes... Twenty-two. I think we make twenty two thousand altogether." I was sure CTY would send my application back because half the financial aid section was blank.

The day the scholarship acceptance letter came I was alone jumping up and down in my room. CTY was my doing; it meant nothing to anybody else in the house. To them it was another award I'd won. To me CTY was a different reward altogether.

I had dreamt of doing something, worked to do it and life didn't spit disappointment back in my face like it always seemed to do. There it was, a full scholarship to take an introductory writing course at Skidmore College in Saratoga Springs, New York in July 1991. I showed the letter to my mother. She smiled and congratulated me. I think, for the first time in years, she saw a glimpse of my joy. "That's great," my mother said.

That's great. Didn't Ma know how much CTY meant to me? Didn't she know CTY was the first thing I was not afraid to admit I wanted? Didn't she know I hated getting up early on Saturday mornings, especially when the apartment had no hot water, and riding the train to 139th Street for nearly an hour each way; all the trudging through the January snow, the chilling Nor'easters, the hours listening to professors dissecting practice exams and test taking tricks. Didn't my mother know I was scared the first Saturday when I got lost and had to walk around Harlem for thirty minutes asking directions. No, she didn't. I had never told her. She had never asked. Her saying, "That's great," was meaningless to me... What a shame.

There was no hug, no congratulatory kiss. I didn't need those things. I had never had those things... God, I wanted a hug or kiss from my mother, but I could never admit it. My wonderful accomplishment seemed tainted because I couldn't share my excitement with anyone.

No matter. I had done it. That was enough. Three weeks away at camp. I was going someplace to write. Writing was what I was beginning to love. Inside, my voice was growing louder with every sentence, every page, every idea I tried to develop and make my own. That voice, that work, that wanting to be true to my self was pushing me on, moving me on-up, from downstate to upstate.

X.

CARPE DIEM: ALEX

Love is real. Every troubled soul out there should take heed in the truth of love for it is undeniable and it is everywhere. Once I felt love, nothing could stay the same. Every isolated moment, everything good or bad on the road to recognition was reconceived as a plan woven to help me accept this most powerful force in the universe. In the light of love, once dark memories were transformed into mere hurdles to overcome, lessons I had to learn.

My mother, my apartment, my family ceased to be foes. Instead, they became teachers sent my way to teach me a wider, fuller wisdom of life. I had to stop burning the Ashes and let the fire die out. Any future moment I breathed, I had to take peace within, for each and every moment following love's discovery became an opportunity to recreate the feeling of its entrance into my life. I was less afraid of the future because every moment to come was full of this new force and had the potential to take me back to the instant I was given life anew; the moment I finally… finally became human.

That particular moment was open to anyone. There we were, all the students from the writing classes at CTY crammed into a small auditorium on a summer afternoon reading aloud to each other. The best stories from the first week were being shared with the throng. My twelve classmates heard my story in a peer review session and liked it. "What were eighty more people?" I thought. Was it not my summer of growth? Was it not my moment? I was prostrate, vulnerable, open to possibility. "It's either they hate it or…" I shuddered at the thought, but I was open.

Openness creates heroes. Think about it.

All the would-be readers were as scared as I was. Our names would be broadcast to the world only seconds before the glare of unknowing eyes turned and consigned each of us to their tastes, their emotions, their humor, their intellect, their heartache, their memories, their jubilance, their will. Before my name was called, I was no one to the listening audience and they were not people to me. Before my name was called, each of their worlds and mine were galaxies removed.

Then the moment approached, my blood flowed, sweat poured, my knees knocked, a voice rose in me. Somehow, I made it through and in the end realized… it wasn't that bad.

With CTY, my moment had been building. I had practiced reading my story again and again the night before. I believed in my story.

In the telling, the room giggled like I dreamed it would, echoed laughter like I never thought it could. For a moment, I owned a piece of time, had command of that space, had flooded my mind's heaven with just enough water, just enough sunlight, with just enough of my self for that particular moment to grow just the way I wanted. I felt justified in my talent, alive with brilliance, for my peers had accepted the workings of my troubled mind. A mind

> where I had lived and breathed foul air
>
> where I had slept for years and awoke without caring
>
> where I got drunk on spoiled nectar
>
> where I had cowered from light like a hermit's backside
>
> where I had shunned the day and all the moments past
>
> where I had been slain in the dark of my own
> perpetual night

I got the same cursory applause as the readers before me. But where they had dwelled on esoteric lyric, putting the week's writing lessons to practice, I dared to be satirical and funny. I had observed life in my own way and with their applause, the auditorium of genii told me they understood my vision. Not only that, they liked my observational humor. I was funny. Not many people had figured Oronde Ash for a comedian. Only two had ever known and they were my blood. Now, because of that moment, forever my moment, all the room was my blood.

I suppose it was this flowing bounty of life that hooked me up to its source. I had tapped the well of human feeling; no doubt I was awash in devotion. My body burst in the momentum as hungry cells tasting the fruit of the universe for the first time screamed for more. My mind expanded. I was sensing more, I was sensing her. She was on stage, she was reading.

The auditorium may not have had a sunroof, but her white t-shirt rolled up to her shoulders, her rope necklace, her shorts and sandals, she was glowing. I will forever swear to this. When I saw her, I was already aglow in the universal light. I suppose my mind made the logical leap. All this room is now mine; therefore, she too is mine.

I wasn't after tight ownership though. This girl was no slave; I was no master. What in the world would I do if I ever got her? I had never dated. I was boringly nice. I would be a fool around her, the girl would tell everybody and they would all laugh at me. I would walk around the world and the world would laugh at me. I would be hurt. I would feel the pain I always felt knowing I had the ability to do more to change but not having the guts to try. I would create a shell to protect my self. I would become a fetus again.

No. I had to meet this girl. Never in my life had I felt so sure someone had the key to something I desperately needed. There was no way the girl, whoever she was, would hurt me. I had no idea how I knew this but I accepted it as fact. Every cell, every fiber, every sinew in my bones told me I had to move toward the girl. It was that basic.

One plus one equaled two, Albany was the capital of New York, it was July 1991, I was feeling life for the first time and life was telling me I had to meet this girl. All this was undeniable fact.

The seven or eight girls in my writing class suddenly became my best friends because they lived in the same dorm as the girl. I wasn't afraid to talk to my female classmates because I was empowered by something holy. I was on a crusade, the girl my Holy Grail, my classmates my first knights.

"What is she like?" I would ask.

"OK," they would say.

"Where is she from?" I would continue.

"Someplace in New York."

"The City? Upstate? Where? Where?" I would persist.

"I don't know, Oronde. Why don't you ask Alex yourself?"

Carrie was getting tired of my questions. She was my first knight, the appointed go-between. What great people these ferries are. They are everywhere in the young world; fearless warriors, running between fate and destiny. Are they aware of their power? Do they understand they do the one thing shyness and fear will prevent the scared from ever doing: talk to the girl or boy of their dreams.

"Why don't you ask Alex, Oronde? Look, she's right over there... Hey, Alex," Carrie shouted.

"Shut up, Carrie. Shut up."

"You better wave to her. She's looking over here."

"I'm gonna get you for this."

"She's still looking. You better wave."

I smiled and I waved. For a week and a half, I smiled and I waved. At least this Alex knew I existed.

Mere existence was once enough for me. I remembered Colette Clark and all her popular eighth-grade girlfriends or the blond-haired blue eyed nymph Kathy or the exotic Belizean Cecile McKenzie in fifth grade. In the Gateway program, beauties sat next to me class after class. I'm sure they knew I existed but they seemed far, far away.

This... This Alex was different. Yes, she was beautiful, but her face had nothing to do with the attracting force I was operating on. I had no idea what the force was, thought about all that could go wrong and became afraid of calling the force love. In my life, love was always aligned with pain. But in the preceding months sharing some form of joy with my brothers Randi and Keri, this force was beginning to steer me. I opened my bedroom door more, talked to my mother and sisters more. My heart was rewriting my sad history.

Even though happiness was seeping into me, it was like a venom I ran from. Yet, here I was running toward this Alex, stumbling, bumbling on my own emotional wanting. If I wasn't to have Alex in reality, I held her in my mind. In my mind we talked for hours, she laughed, we kissed, snuggled. In my mind I was a stud. Why spoil that fantasy with reality?

People Magazine had a picture of Julia Roberts on their cover that week in July 1991. "The most beautiful woman in the world," the caption read. In my moment, that was Alex, the most beautiful girl in the world. I couldn't have Julia, so maybe my mind saw her in Alex and Alex in her.

Carrie was right. I had to say something, but where? When? The cafeteria. Alex had to eat. We all ate at the same time. Alex wouldn't make a scene there. At lunch one day, a few of the guys who knew how I felt pushed me to say something. I did. Exactly what, I don't remember.

The weekend passed. A second week went by. I had made friends at CTY. For some reason, the kids thought I was cool. They remembered my funny story from the reading and would mention it when they saw me. I was also the guy who beat people at basketball, soccer or tennis, the guy walking around Skidmore College with mirrored, silver shades on. I never went anywhere without my silver shades. I could look out onto the world but no one could look into me. I felt safe behind them.

> Me, Oronde Ash, weaving in and out of the
> kicking legs on the soccer fields or outstretched
> hands on the basketball court;
>
> Me, with the cool, silver shades and false security;
>
> Me, with the high top fade and the euphoria of
> Alex within;
>
> Me, one of the few black faces on campus
>
> Me, with that withdrawn air of the big city;
>
> Me, at fifteen, one of the upperclassmen in the
> program

Whatever vision MTV had painted of the urban black boy, these suburban kids figured I was it. They even thought I could dance. Ha! I couldn't dance.

The second Friday night, the guys in my writing class all showed up at my door before heading to the weekly dance. We hung out during the week but I didn't think I was that tight with them. It was as if the guys had to get a buzz from what was in my room before they had the balls to dance. Their presence freaked me out. Didn't they know I was Oronde Ash, that I was a nobody?

Week three. Five more days to tell Alex how I felt. I still heard my voice urging me.

My roommate Jim and I were talking like we did most nights after lights out. For three weeks, I was in close quarters with someone my age and I didn't die. Sharing a room with a stranger was the one thing I didn't look forward to at CTY. What would I say? I didn't have conversations with people, especially those my own age. I was sure Jim would get bored and request a new roommate.

I knew what boredom was, knew that it lead to jealousy, watching people in their interactions, the smiles, giggles, inside jokes I was never privy to. That jealousy had always gnawed at me.

It's funny how we all are at thirteen, fourteen, or however old. So concerned with how we look, feel or appear to the world, we only see the things we are not. He's great, she's beautiful, other people are funny but not us. We have yet to realize that our insecurities are universal. We don't know that funny guy or beautiful girl is probably just as insecure as us. The difference between them and us is that they've figured out a way to cope with their flaws. At thirteen, fourteen or however old, we haven't yet.

I was nowhere near figuring out a coping mechanism but I was acknowledging and accepting the things I knew I could change for the better in me.

Jim had gone to sleep and I was up looking out the window at the stars. The sky at Skidmore was clear. The light of the universe was not being blocked by the city's glare. This was a new country, a much different light shined on me here. In a distance I heard owls hoot. They were talking to me. In the play of the rustling leaves, I heard nature applauding my new discovery. I saw a shooting star streak across the night, connecting the world and all points of light. Was this the way the world had always been?

As usual Alex was on my mind. She fused with the night and became part of the natural poetry I was sensing.

The night was calm

    I had made it through two weeks

The night was bright.

    I was a personality. Kids knew me

The night was it's own singular song.

    I was unique, special

The night had meaning. It was there all along

    I had meaning

    I was there all along

Somehow, some mystical, magical, fateful way, I was feeling something strong enough to keep me awake and staring out the window until dawn. By the time the sun rose, I was convinced of a few things.

1. I was alive. For the first time in my life I knew what that meant and didn't have to logically come to the conclusion that I was alive because I was breathing or my organs were functional. No. I was alive because every pore in me was feeling the sun through the window pane, my soft mattress, the cool carpet, the crisp air, the limitless possibilities. I was alive. It was indisputable.

2. I had a purpose. There was a reason for me coming to Skidmore. There was a reason for me staying up all night on this night of all nights.

3. Fate and destiny were real and they worked miracles. Everything we do in life is for the better. All the things I saw and felt in my house for fifteen years was not a punishment from God. Rather, it was a blessing. There was a reason for it and for everything else in life. I was being crafted and reshaped like a poem on paper. I had no clue what that reason was or where my story was going, but I had faith that a reason existed.

4. There was good in me. These CTY people had seen it. One moment I could be funny, brilliant, charming and another I could be clumsy, idiotic, tactless. I could be a kid. It didn't matter. Moments come and go. One minute you're funny, the next you're not. That's life. I had observed that all along, but this was the first time I felt something for those I was observing.

5. Alex was my destiny. How else to explain the overwhelming feeling of connection? I was born to meet her. It was written.

How had I gotten to CTY? Through Gateway.

How had I gotten to Gateway? Because of my grades at Bethune.

Why did I get good grades at Bethune? Because the only way my mind could break free was through disciplined focus on academics.

Why did my mind have to break free? Because it was locked up.

Why was it locked up? Because I wanted protection from a gloomy life.

Was life gloomy? Not anymore. That night, it suddenly seemed promising.

Why was it promising? Because I felt alive for the first time.

Why did I feel alive? Because I saw Alex.

Why did you see Alex? To feel alive.

And what about the shooting star? That had to be a message from the universe. I had to talk to Alex, had to tell her how I felt. Wasn't that the way it worked in the movies? Two star-crossed lovers meet, they look into each other's eyes for the first time, music plays, the magic takes over. It all seemed right.

The final realization was easier to accept than I thought. For fifteen years, I had been content to be an emotional black hole. Everything went into me but nothing ever came out. I was smart enough to recognize the mess inside, how it got there and that my job was to do more than collect it, but I had no clue how to release the mess and clean up my life. That cluttered emptiness was my curse; until that night... Because... Because...

6. I was in love. Felt sure to the core.

Nothing could stop love. If I really wanted to, I'd get Alex. But it had to be fast, had to be clean. I had to attack her senses. How? How could I be smooth, persuasive, and cool? How could I get across what I wanted to say in the clearest way possible? Words.

I had just finished a one-day engagement at the auditorium where I wowed all the critics, Alex included. With the right words I could muster that magic again.

I tried finding the right words to capture what I felt but I couldn't. I wasn't satisfied with anything ending up on the notebook page. Then it hit me. The song. *Dreamer's Love Song*. The hand of God had been guiding me all along. There was proof of His master plan. How else to explain why I had written a song in January that made perfect sense in July?

The song was about a girl I saw on the train every morning on my way to Brooklyn Tech. Whoever she was, she became a double put in front of my eyes when Alex was unavailable. God had foreseen my future, knew Alex was waiting and made me write about her before I met her.

<u>Dreamer's Love Song</u>

I saw you on the train this morning & I so wanted to tell you my name
But the courage I thought was there inside I kept searching for in vain

The words were never good enough Or the time was never right
So I kept dreaming about the two of us Together day and night

I dreamt of all the fun we'd have The many good times that we'd share
Two people brought together by destiny With feelings they hold so dear

On those cold & dreary New York morns As I watched you pass me by
You brought a smile to my face that I still can't replace
When you'd just turn your head and smile

I dreamt of the moonlit nights of spring When we'd sail the ocean blue
As I hold you close and whisper in your ear Just how much I love you

I thought about serenading Alex but concluded that would be too sappy. I remembered one of the counselors --Dan-- had a guitar. I told Dan what was going on and he agreed to record my song on tape.

My plan was to give the cassette tape to Alex along with a brief note thanking her for moving me to do something so out of my character. No time to be scared. Same as the reading. Just do it. It wont be that bad. Just give Alex the tape. At least that's what I asked Carrie to do.

"Give this cassette to her, please?" I pleaded.

Carrie said, "I'm not gonna be your go-between anymore."

"This is it. Last time. I promise."

"What is this anyway?"
"A song."

"What song?"

"One I wrote for her."

"Ooo! This is getting serious."

Carrie and her family visited New York City for the Christmas holidays later in 1991. We met at a midtown Manhattan cafe to catch up. I still had my shades, still had my wall.

"Why don't you take those things off?" she asked. They make me nervous." I took them off. "That's better. You look much better that way. Now I can see if you're eyeing me up or not."

"You're funny, you know that."

"You talk to Alex?" she asked. "I still can't believe you did that. Why'd you stay so quiet though?"

"What do you mean," I asked.

"You did this wonderful thing for her, wrote that great song, and then you ignored her."

"Ignored her?"

"Yeah, you didn't talk to her for days. She thought you didn't care."

I cared. I cared that the job was done. Yes, I wanted Alex to respond, wanted her to be pleased. I convinced my self she was pleased, convinced my self she was glancing at me in the cafeteria. If I walked by, her friends would always giggle. Something had to be up.

That final, fateful Friday, instead of afternoon activities, CTY organized a carnival on the playing fields. While everyone was eating cotton candy, winning stuffed animals or whatever, I felt most secure tossing a football with one of the counselors. We were throwing for fifteen minutes when Carrie rushed over and grabbed my hand. Before I could offer any protest, I was standing next to Alex at a mock marriage booth. Counselor Dan played minister.

"Do you take him?" Dan asked.

Without a sign of emotion on her face, Alex said, "Sure."

"Do you take her?" I was asked.

"Sure." The word fumbled out of my mouth. I wasn't nervous. I wasn't alive. I wasn't even there.

"Here's the certificate to sign," Dan said.

Alex grabbed the paper and scribbled her name. I put my name on the paper too. The only other thing I could think of doing was smile, so I did that.

"Why don't we go over there," Carrie told the two or three other girls who were giggling throughout the ceremony. As soon as they left us, Alex said, "So, you wanna talk."

Later in life, a girl would tell me, "I like talking to you, Oronde. It's like I'm talking to myself."

"Is that a good thing?" I would ask her.

"Yeah. Most guys don't like to listen. They just want to talk. But you, you understand me. It's like I'm talking through you."

Understanding or not, I listened to anyone who'd talk to me. My gaze was the blind stare of the couch potato I had always been. I didn't talk back because I had no idea if what I wanted to say was right and I didn't want to sound like a fool. I assume Alex must have been talking through me that Friday. That night, at the last dance, she walked to where I was standing in the hall we called a disco and asked me to dance the last dance at CTY with her.

Was this not fate? Was this not God moving me?

I walked Alex back to her dorm. We talked. I found out she had two brothers, played on a soccer team, and was half Cuban, half Italian. She liked writing, had just seen the movies *Dead Poet's Society* and *Robin Hood* and thought Julia Roberts was indeed a pretty woman. "You look like her," I offered up. Alex thanked me.

"Thanks for the song," she began, "but I don't deserve it."

"Yes you do," I promised.

If only Alex knew what she had done. I was feeling something undoubtedly human. No one had ever made me feel this way, not even my own family. I was open. The real world was coming in and I wasn't afraid to let it happen. For years I had been trying without success. No one had ever moved me. They had to go out of their way to be interesting, challenging, charming or whatever. Yet, here this girl was, simply being herself, not doing anything extraordinary and every portion of me was responding to her. If anything, Alex deserved a lot more than my inadequate song.

The next day as everyone was saying their goodbyes, Alex introduced me to her parents. Before we parted ways, she hugged me and handed me a letter. I waited until I got on the Greyhound bound for New York City to open it.

I couldn't believe what I was reading. Her letter made up for the St. Valentine's Day massacre of years past. Here was a good-looking girl who liked me for being me. Not only that, she loved me. She wrote it herself. *Love, Alex*. Love was clear as my wanting to believe in it.

In big, bold letters, the final words on the page were **CARPE DIEM**. What did that mean? I looked it up: Seize the day.

In love's rationale, I concluded the universe was sending me a sign. Seize the day.

Seize the day and find happiness.

Seize the day and get the girl.

Seize the day and become everything you want.

Seize the day and change your fate.

Seize the day and become great.

With carpe diem, I now had a belief system to steer me. Nothing had ever attached to me like the idea of seizing the day. My soles walked Brooklyn proud when guided by those words.

As a matter of fact, carpe diem was beyond mere idea. Ideas beg to be thought over, questioned, refined, outwitted. Carpe diem was too simple to even think about. It was the same experience I had one day when I thought about that US Army tag line "Be all you can be" or

Nike's "Just do it." No wonder the two companies recruited so well. Eureka advertising.

- Wake up, get connected to life and the people who matter to you… Just do it!
- Count the moments. Enjoy the good. Learn from the not so good… Be all you can be!
- Manifest everything dreamt from the moment because there is infinite goodness there… Just do it!
- Grab hold of life, lock horns with it, engage it, steer it, strive to figure it out for yourself… Be all you can be!
- Fight for love. Find strength in that struggle… Just do it!
- Believe in that strength. Serve it.
- Believe in whatever is inside you that can do all things… Be all you can be!
- Get attached… Just do it!
- Get going… Be all you can be!

To be attached, you have to possess an inkling of the Creator's magic. You have to find joy in something outside your being. All my years in America, I felt no love for another human being, not in my family, not in school, not for any of my many teammates. All the while I was growing but I was without that magic. It wasn't until I accepted it was possible to love another human being without fear that I realized how beautiful soccer was or how moving music could be.

The song, the ball, they had both been in my life all along but never had I experienced them in the way I began to.

In the fall of 1991, with CTY stinging me with the nicest buzz I'd ever felt, golden trophies became mere symbols. The feeling of overcoming, triumphing as a team was the true reward of sport. I could not have seen that alone. The boys on the Spirit of '76 started making sense to me. No matter the game's outcome, they all had what seemed like loving families to go home to. What else, outside of air, water and shelter, does any boy need? Love helped me see the life-affirming meaning in everything.

I used to have trouble remembering people's names or the words in a song. I had never learned to fully appreciate another human being so a name or someone's words held little meaning to me. I never talked to people anyway, so why bother remembering their names.

I knew nothing about the history of soccer or even cared to watch the Sunday morning Italian Serie-A games on RAI TV or the Mexican League games on Univision. I didn't know the names of the world's best players, teams or leagues, in the way American middle school boys reel off the names, teams, batting averages of their favorite baseball players.

I'm not saying it's necessary to know a players' stats to appreciate the sport, but the lovers of the game are engaged enough to know these things and accept their need to know in the same unquestioned manner I now accepted the dictum, carpe diem.

Amazing! A game I had played since I could walk, with what I thought was incredible passion, seemed so new in the light of love. I wanted to discover love in soccer and in everything else.

I used to think it foolish to base a life around an idea, theory or philosophical dimension. I saw bases as platforms from which to strike out and cause strife. The person charging from a one ideological background wouldn't be open to understanding an opposing view. I saw how my mother and Mudd fought, never moving towards a solution, just jabbing from where they each stood.

But instead of being confining, a base sprung from my growing self-love was not the first march to war with another human being. Rather it was the most embracing thing I'd ever done. And it was all due to Alex.

After nervous weeks in Brooklyn, I worked up the nerve and called her. We talked. Actually, Alex steered our initial conversations. When I finally began sharing my voice, our exchanges grew longer. The telephone lines were enough of a curtain to allow me to be something without having to actually do anything.

My mind had always been expressive and the phone played on that strength. I began creating different personalities, different realities, being serious, dramatic, masculine, feminine, young, old. It was eye opening. The acting seemed natural and easy --possibly from the vicarious mass consumption of life through TV. Alex liked it so I acted more and more. Each conversation left a door ajar, inviting a new self to emerge from inside me.

The phone was good, but letters was where I tried to woo Alex. I was a junkie, drunk with her, high on her. Even as hard as I thought I fell, my rational, emotionless history was bent on keeping me away from heartache.

"You are no lover," the scared little boy inside me would propose again and again. Every time I tried to move beyond my self, the little boy was there to remind me who I was. *"How can you love if you have never felt love?"*

"I'm feeling something in my heart," I would answer.

"Ha! Your heart? Where do you think his power comes from? I'm the brain of this operation. I'm the one that saved you everyday. I'm the one that's gotten you this far in life. Your heart kills you. It has before and it will again. If you felt love right now, you'd... you'd be..."

"I think this is it."

"You think? You think? I think you should take it easy, baby boy. I'm not trying to deny what your heart feels. The thing's got a mind of it's own sometimes."

"Maybe it's not love but it's something. Something very real. Even you can't deny that or you wouldn't sound so scared."

"I'm no scared. I just know you're too young to be in love, boy. Have you ever felt it?" He waited in silence. I hated when he was right. *"No you haven't. Even if you had, you asked me to keep love locked away, didn't you?"*

"Yes," I said.

"Are you ready to let loose and be tugged around like a fool on a string?" The boy waited.... *"I didn't think so."*

"I'm going to change," I told him.

"What?" he asked. *"People like us don't change. I'm here for the long haul."*

"I'm going to change," I repeated.

"We'll see about that."

"No, you'll feel it," I commanded.

"I can't feel. You and I can't feel. How many times do I have to tell you that?"

"Wait... You will. You will."

Three days before my sophomore year began at Brooklyn Tech, I asked my mother to braid my hair. Something dramatic in my immediate appearance would be the perfect showcase for a world expecting the nice, ho-hum Oronde Ash. I had spent the summer changing and I wanted the world to see the new me.

I think my mother felt like a *mom* when I asked her to braid my hair. She didn't mind parting my high top fade over and over, didn't mind sitting down for three hours looking at my dry scalp, wondering when I would open my mouth and talk to her. I didn't mind the wait. It gave me a chance to out-duel the little boy inside me who refused to forgive and grow up.

My mother and I talked every few minutes. She'd ask about CTY, I'd give her my usual one-word answers. But at least we were in the same room, for once, doing something with each other.

When my hair was done, I hurried to the bathroom mirror. The mirror finally showed the image I spent three weeks creating at Skidmore.

In the reflection I saw dread locks on my head. I saw them short, then envisioned them long. They were flowers. I saw dreads as flowers. I felt like a flower, waiting for more light, more water, waiting for the world to help me grow. Flowers changed and matured into strong, sturdy trees. I saw my reflection learning more and becoming a strong, sturdy human being full of light, water, energy and love. I saw dreads as a positive reminder of my wanting to grow.

Everyday, when I stared into a mirror, I would see the flowers growing. Everyday, I would be reminded how much I wanted to grow, that I had to grow, that I had no choice but to grow.

Hair, flowers, people... We all have to grow.

XI.

<u>SOPH NO MORE</u>

T he first day of school my sophomore year, Mrs. Sigelakis began her AP European History class by passing around a bag with the inscription, "Before there was history, there was black history." I watched as two or three hands went up and words came out of my classmate's mouths. The room had energy. I listened, waited and tried to gauge the right moment to begin my new life.

"It's true," a boy said. "A lot of black history is not taught in school."

"I read *Malcolm X* when I was in the sixth grade," a girl named Kameron replied. "It was one of the most powerful books I've ever read. It really should be in schools. A lot of stuff should be in schools, at least in a school like Brooklyn Tech."

"I agree," began a boy with a black skullcap on his baldhead. His name was Gerbril. "You know. There's a lot of hypocrisy in this country... Y'all need to know a whole lotta stuff about what me and my people had to go through."

"But everybody had to go through something here. I'm Irish," the first boy began. "The Irish couldn't live in certain neighborhoods when we came to America."

"You're saying the Irish had it worse off than blacks?" Gerbril accused.

"I don't think that's what he's saying," Kameron answered. "Everybody had a raw deal in America."

"Some worse than others," Mrs. Sigelakis offered up.

"Right," the girl answered. The room grew quiet for a second.

"Isn't this supposed to be AP European History?" someone asked. What a dumb question, I thought. How could this kid not see the connections between all human histories? The slave, the Irish, the Jew, Malcolm X, Anne Frank, Frank McCourt, they're all connected by the same story of personal movement and progress. With love's help, I was starting to make the connections between all peoples.

Carpe diem. Seize the day. I raised my hand.

"I don't think anybody's story can be denied," I began. "We're all human beings with needs and histories, no matter who writes the words."

I was taken aback. There it was. The story in my mind and the words coming out of my mouth shared the same pitch, the same volume and were on the same wavelength. Truth came out of me. I felt released.

I found my hands going up in more and more of my classes. Since that first year in Scotch Plains, I seldom raised my hands in school. At Bethune, the fear was of being a black nerd. Freshman year at Tech, I wasn't the same shy little turtle but the pattern continued. "Because you let it," my growing confidence began. The answers were easy. All any good student has to do is read the assignment and follow directions. Explaining the answers, that was where the really gifted shine.

When I participated in class, it seemed I ingested more of the lessons, saw more sense in the schemes or bigger numbers on the page. I was learning more. And not just in my head. It was like living and breathing the words coming from within. Every time an idea made sense, it was I, Oronde Ash, the voice underneath all the shyness, the voice I knew was there all along, saying and defending that idea. I was affirming my real voice to the fake shell the world had seen for years. I was finally being me.

Once, I felt like two, three or four different people inhabited my body. Each one wanted room to develop and a need to be heard. It bordered on schizophrenia. But now, with each mumbling growing louder and enunciated with a developing confidence, one voice was taking control of the many in my head. I was beginning to talk. My voice was out among the living. I was beginning [to be].

I even changed the way I printed my name. Oronde Ash was small, compact, letters warring for room to breathe. It's the way I had signed anything since coming to America. It was the way I had always been, warring for room to breathe.

But **Oronde Ash** was a dramatic, catch-this-if-you-can John Hancock at the top of every paper I proudly handed in my sophomore year.

"I'm just glad to see you opening up and coming out of your shell," Ms. Floyd, my math teacher said one day in late September.

"I'm thinking about a lot of things these days," I told her, "and feeling good."

"You look like you have a lot of ideas in your head. You should share them more."

Ms. Floyd was black and beautiful and carried her self with a dignity that enveloped every part of her slight frame. She was the only teacher I knew who stayed home on Black Solidarity Day --the Monday before November elections.. She wore dashikis and Kente cloth, had her hair in Afro puffs, cropped or bound with colorful headdresses. Ms. Floyd was my first real life example of the black vision I was too afraid to be. But she was too compelling not to question.

One day I asked, "So you were in the civil rights marches and stuff, huh? I bet you still fighting the man, aren't you?"

"No," she laughed.

"Don't try and kid me. You look like you're a revolutionary from the sixties."

"You mean this old thing," she smiled, pointing at the green and yellow kente cloth draping her shoulders.

"Yeah," I said.

"I did my share." Ms. Floyd was still smiling. "Why you wanna know about me? You CIA?" She laughed. After that, I would kid Ms. Floyd about being a revolutionary. It became a running gag. In her teacher's wisdom, she saw I was searching for something. That's probably why she let me borrow her copy of *The Spook Who Sat by the Door* by Sam Greenlee.

The book was a fictional account of a guy named Freeman who became the first Negro *spook* --CIA agent. Freeman quickly gained the trust of important figures in Washington DC and while stationed in Chicago on CIA business, he met up with a gang of conscious Negro outsiders called the Cobras. Freeman trained the young cobras in the same guerrilla warfare the government had taught him. Nobody thought anything of it.

Word soon got out that Stud Davis, Sugar Hips Scott, Do-Daddy Dean and the rest of the Cobras were organized and ready for something, so the police decided to crack down on them.

In the middle of the book, the police shot a Negro boy and riots broke out in the ghetto. The National Guard, in the guise of restoring their brand of order, was sent in with the covert objective of infiltrating and destroying the Cobras. In the crossfire, Freeman was shot. The book ends with the Cobras having to go on without their wounded leader. I had faith they did.

The Spook was an in-my-face punch of what it meant to be young and black in urban America. I liked seeing black boys stand up and express the language of revolution. My body and mind were changing so fast every second made me an adolescent revolutionary.

The Cobras had an indomitable spirit. Their politics and their art were one-in-the-same. The fellas grabbed life and fashioned from it what they thought was true. The book made me question my blackness. Did I love it? Freeman was willing to die for what he believed a black man could be in the world. Was I even willing to live that possibility?

I was black on the outside. There would be no denying that. Even though it was purely psychological reinforcement, the dreadlocks on my head told the world I was into blackness. And I wanted to be but I didn't feel *black* --whatever that was supposed to be.

W.E.B DuBois was a name I respected for doing something incredible, but what, I never bothered to read *The Souls of Black Folks* to find out. Ray Charles was the guy in Pepsi commercials and not the genius of *Greenbacks*, *I've Got a Woman* or *Crying Time*. I'd never heard John Coltrane, Curtis Mayfield or listened to Stevie Wonder's *Songs in the Key of Life* over and over again. I didn't know that author Leslie Alexander Lacy rose and fell as a proper Negro or that Paul

Robeson is too magnificent a model for any man or system to erase from history.

I remember so-called friends making offhand comments in my presence. Once in the hallway, a guy on the soccer team came up to me and said, jokingly, "Assume the position," by which he meant for me to turn around and spread my legs. I wanted to tell the guy he was ignorant and insensitive but I kept my frustration contained. Growing up, I was always contained. I regret being that controlled.

Sometime later that year, we were changing our clothes after a soccer game when someone said, "I'm missing my necklace." Me, I never wore jewelry. Living in Brooklyn it seemed a dangerous habit. The only ornament I wore was a red, yellow and green beaded rope I bought at an African store near Tech. But the same ignoramus from the hallway spoke up saying,

"C'mon Oronde. We know you have it." He would always follow these comments with a giddy laugh like a hyena. The rest of us found it and him annoying as hell. That probably made it easier for me to dismiss his comments as that of an idiot and not as representative of white people.

There were two Orondes at Brooklyn Tech. One walked the hallways in a trench coat, wearing silver shades, trying to mask his manic confusion. He was distant and into his own thing. Unfortunately, in the language of adolescence, that seemed to mean *cool*. I could, and did get away with that dude. I didn't have to say or do much with him.

Then there was the guy wavering on the cusp of something and nothing all at once. His thoughts raced with every look, every slight, every word uttered in his presence. He liked people. Deep down the guy really liked people. He just felt more at home dealing with ideas and possibilities, truth, clean and pure, not the version people chopped up and often sullied. That guy was unsure if his truth would make it through the awkward translation to a reality with too many variables to be fully understood. Anyway, I could only see glimpses of that guy's ideology.

There were student organizations at Brooklyn Tech to help me figure things out. The Hellenic Club had many members. The Filipino Society met each week and so did the Latino Club. The Black Awareness Club (BAC) put on a fashion show but I never went.

"You don't have the time," I heard my voice say. "Anyway, it's those kids with the Polo jeans and name-brand gear," he continued.

"They're not serious about the intellectual side of blackness. To them, it's a fashion statement. You don't want to know blackness without substance, do you?" he asked.

"*They'll laugh at you because you sound intelligent,*" the little boy inside me interjected. "*They'll say you're trying to be white by playing a white sport and only hangin' with your white teammates. Then what are you gonna feel, huh? Yeah. You're gonna be hurt. And who's gonna have to dream up some place for you to hide? Me, that's who.*"

"If I wanted to, I'd go to the BAC meetings," I told the boy. "I just don't have the time. If I'm not playing soccer I'm practicing or doing schoolwork."

"*You don't want to be aware,*" the boy said.

"Of course I do. Why did I read *The Spook*? Why am I trying to listen to more hip-hop? Why am I trying to understand?" He didn't answer.

"*You're a freak,*" the boy said after a while.

"Where did that come from?"

"You should be hanging around more people," my voice intoned, trying to steer me away from the little boy's immaturity.

The more I heard this voice, the more I respected his thoughts. He had been listening to me argue with the little boy inside me for years and wanted to say more, but my voice bided his time. All would be as it should be.

The little boy asked, "*How can you ever know anything? You're an illegal alien to the world, baby boy.*"

"Yeah, I'm an alien but I have my voice."

"*Look, I'm not in your life to get hurt any more,*" the boy said.

"You don't get hurt." I told him, "I do. If I'm too shy, too unaware, too alien to interact with the world, I'm gonna at least try to understand it… And you're gonna help me."

"*You must be kidding,*" the boy answered.

"You don't have a say in this. You go where I go, remember?"

At CTY, I read Joan Didion's essay *On Keeping a Notebook* and started one the day I got back to Brooklyn. At Tech, there were five thousand kids from every corner of the globe. We were a microcosm of New York City --which was a microcosm of America-- which was a microcosm of the world.

"*You actually think if you can figure out Brooklyn Tech, then, on some mathematical corollary, you'd know the world?*" the boy questioned.

"Hell, I'd know the universe," I answered.

"*You wish, alien boy.*"

"You're the ET," I told the little boy. "Go home."

Spineless worm, I thought. For that, the boy gave me a headache.

When the headaches came, I wrote. When they went, I noted when, how and why. I kept a five-subject notebook at home and carried a red pocket notebook in my bag wherever I went. When an idea or issue became clear, I documented the moment. A lot of my early entries in fall 1991 were mundane details of the day-to-day. Most centered on my feelings about Alex. As the months went on, the writing got more personal, more pointed. I captured my thoughts on the page, reviewed and edited them. The world was my new wonder and I became its *Wonder Child*. Life was being kind enough to reveal its secrets.

I began to see the relationship between historical events and the present day. I saw the web of life and the connectivity therein. The world flowed into itself. Nothing was separate. Nothing could ever be separate again. It was impossible not to be involved, intermingled, dependent on something else. The more I dwelled on my burgeoning world connections, the more I felt a personal connection. Connectivity defined the human experience. It was in my genes.

The quickest way for me to connect to the kids at Brooklyn Tech was through hip-hop. The culture was omnipresent at Tech, in New York City, throughout America. In my neighborhood, I saw the teenage violence, drug abuse, guns, poverty, absent fathers and other issues the music addressed but, back then, I struggled to follow the actual lyrics of most hip hop songs.

Someone would bring a Walkman to lunch and play Das EFX, KRS-One, Brand Nubians, Onyx or whoever was hot at the time. All the guys would be singing along in tune. Even Nelson, a Korean kid at our lunchroom table who always wanted to be down, and Anthony Amalfitano, the Italian from Bensonhurst who acted like he was down;

even they knew the lyrics. Since I didn't sing along like everyone else, something had to be seriously off with me.

I didn't have the ear for hip-hop but my legs stomped, my body swayed, my head nodded; I couldn't deny the pulse in me. I wanted to understand the lyrics the same way I made sense of my textbooks. More than the rhythm, I needed hip-hop to, in a cohesive manner, tell a complete story of the person I was becoming. I was young, urban, black. The music was supposed to be about me but somehow, most of it wasn't.

Nonetheless, my vision couldn't deny hip-hop. It was the opiate of the adolescent masses. What was so addictive, so appealing?

Other music was starting to make imprints on me. Julius, a kid on the soccer team, copied Bob Marley's *Legend* for me. Sophomore year, Bob Marley became my radio. I listened to *Legend* everyday, consciously trying to program the soundtrack of revolution in my head. If I knew something of Bob, I figured I'd know something about the ties that bound us all.

Bob Marley wasn't just a black prophet. Conscious people the world over embraced his lyrics, his vision of mankind. Marley joined man to man, man to God and everyday reminded me of it all. His lyrics spoke of change for the better.

"One love, one heart... Let's get together and feel all right... Is there a place for the hopeless sinner who has hurt all mankind to save his own? As it was in the beginning, so shall it be in the end...

"Buffalo soldier. Dreadlock Rasta. There was a buffalo soldier in the heart of America. Stolen from Africa. Brought to America. Fighting on arrival. Fighting for survival... If you know your history, you will know where you're coming from. Then you wouldn't have to ask me, who the hell do I think I am..."

"Get up, stand up. Stand up for your rights... It's not all that glitters is gold... Now you see the light... But if you know what life is worth, you will look for yours on earth... Life is your right, so we can't give up the fight... You can fool some people sometime, but you can't fool all the people all the time..."

"No chains around my feet but I'm not free. I know I'm bound here in captivity. Never know what happiness is. Never know what sweet caress is... Won't someone help me 'cause life, I've got to pick myself from off the ground in this concrete jungle, where the living is so hard."

"Don't worry about a thing 'cause every little thing is gonna be alright... This is my message to you..."

My life at the time was on a forward march towards what Marley called, "Zion," and he was showing me word by word, beat by beat, how to be a righteous man.

I was a Buffalo soldier brought to America. I was beginning to see the light, believing that life was my right to live. For years, I never knew what happiness was. I refused to touch, let alone caress people. But love was loosening the chains around my feet. I wasn't yet free but I knew everything would be all right. I wanted the whole world to change like me, like Bob Marley's music was commanding me to.

I remember when Arrested Development came out with the song *Tennessee*. I hadn't heard it on the radio yet. At lunch, Carlson --a Trinidadian I'd met in PE class-- and Anthony Amalfitano --who was also in my Mrs. Sigelakis' AP history class-- asked if I'd heard this new song on the radio.

"It sounds like something you'd listen to," Carlson said.

"What do you mean?" I asked.

"It's kinda weird," Anthony answered.

"Yeah, that's why you'd be into it," Carlson added with a smirk. I wasn't offended. Carlson had inferred what I might have liked. In that sentence, I realized I must have been opening up to people even though I didn't think I was. Carlson thought he knew something about what I might like. I had to have given him some clues. I remember that day because Carlson brought his Walkman and was listening to *Scenario* by Leaders of the New School. He and Nelson began singing along and Anthony soon jumped it. Carlson and I both looked at Anthony and then at each other as if to say, "White boy knows this?"

"Yeah Anthony," Carlson yelled, giving him a pound.

"I'm down," Anthony mocked. We all laughed.

"That's a damn shame," Carlson began, eyeing me with mock disgust. "He knows this song and you don't, Oronde."

I was trying to learn the song but could only memorize a few phrases here and there: "Lyrical from the mind... Powerful impact, boom... When coming into my library... Here we go yo, here we go yo..."

"Do you even like hip-hop?" Carlson asked.

"Of course," I answered, knowing my blackness was being questioned. "I think Scenario is one of the best songs out. That and the Grand Puba song...ah..." I sang the line, "What goes around comes back around again."

"Three Sixty," Anthony said.

"Yes, that's it. The style is jazzy and melodic. It's amazing how they edit those beats into it. Fascinating."

"Does that mean you like it?" Carlson asked again.

"Yes," I replied. "I like it a lot."

To this day, *Scenario* remains one of my hip-hop primers. Busta Rhymes brought that sound bombing energy off the wax. Even the video, with it stylized cuts and meta-video look offers something new to find whenever I see it.

Unfortunately, there wasn't much in the rest of black music that made it both intellectually and emotionally stimulating. At age sixteen, music had to do both to reach me. Dance songs and R&B was all black music was in the early 1990s. If a song didn't hit me hard with the double dose for my mind and soul, I turned the dial.

I was already hooked to Z-100, the major radio station in NYC. There was more sonic diversity there. They didn't play a lot of hip-hop, but Z100 played alternative, pop, rock and dance. I didn't like everything I heard, especially the sad, nasal grunge music coming from Seattle, but at least it was different.

There was nothing separating most of the R&B I heard on the radio back then. Half the time, I couldn't tell who was singing. Was it Pebo Bryson, Freddie Jackson, Luther Vandross? Was it Jodeci, Guy, Mint Condition? Was it SWV or En Vogue?

I'd watch award shows and hear Patti LaBelle scream and wail with her magnificent control, pitch and technique. Patti was good but she was loud. After a while, she and the rest of R&B hurt my ear.

Then, all I saw was a monolith called Black Music. There was a spot created by white record executives for everybody and their stepmother's sister's second cousin who wanted to get paid. That one spot at record company X, Y or Z was the same spot with the same sound. Black singers, especially R&B singers, were slaves. Their records never changed, just another sad love song racking my brain.

As good as Luther Vandross and Anita Baker sang, they weren't saying anything their previous hundred records hadn't already covered. They weren't changing my life. I was ready to change my life. I never experienced the emotional heights Luther and Anita wailed on about. Heck, I was a virgin. How was I supposed to relate to R&B's sexual underpinnings?

The younger groups were pathetically worse. Jodeci videos would have them on stage showing lead singer KC's pre-pubescent physique trying to grind on any hand that came near his crotch. Even Bekim, my religious-minded friend, couldn't get enough of KC and his gyrations. Yes, KC could sing. Yes, the group could harmonize. But what were they saying?

Peel off the layers... As a matter of fact, it was right there confronting any listener. KC was saying, "Let's do it" or asking, "Do me?" That's it. No hidden meaning. That was R&B to me. Let's make love? No. Let's fuck, you and me, right here or later tonight. I'll lay you down girl and ram it in and out of you 'til you say stop. Even then, I might go on, cause your body's so hot. And black women ate this up? No wonder the teen pregnancy rate was so high in our community.

I was angry until I realized there were few alternatives. I couldn't blame my contemporaries for succumbing to trash radio. It was all they had. So called, "love songs" was what black radio recycled every four hours. There had to be more for me.

The first tape I ever bought was *Vivid*, the debut album for the rock, funk group Living Colour. Colour was saying the same thing as other conscious hip-hop artists but in a different form. In so doing, Colour was expanding the scope of black music. I soon heard music from Fishbone, King's X, Body Count, Bad Brains and other black rockers. Why wasn't anybody listening to those black boys?

Besides Z-100, I moved up and down the radio dial to find a sound that related to who I thought I was. Late one night, I came across 92.1 K-Rock. They played rock music from the sixties and seventies. By listening to rock, I thought I was taking a step backwards in my search for blackness but I didn't care.

Rock had always been seen as white music. It didn't matter. I craved aural stimulation. The angst, confusion, anxiety, above all, rebellion in the 60s and 70s rock music spoke to me more than any black music on the radio. Credence Clearwater Revival, Cream, The Almond Brothers, Led Zeppelin, The Doobie Brothers, The Beatles, Peter Paul and Mary, Crosby, Stills and Nash, Jackson Browne, The

Who, John Fogarty, Jimi Hendrix, Bob Dylan, Pink Floyd and other classic rock staples sang of an America, with all the warring and change, chaos and uncertainty, experimentation and transcendence. Their time seemed like perpetual adolescence. How could I not listen to my biology's inner drumbeat?

When classic rock got too heavy, I turned to CD 101.9, a smooth jazz station. With smooth jazz I didn't have to get attached to anyone's subjective notions on love, relationships or whatever. If I wanted --and I did-- I made up my own lyrics to Pat Matheny, Spyro Gyro, Stanley Jordan, George Benson's guitar, or Grover Washington's sax. I didn't even know the races of most of these jazz musicians and it didn't matter. The meaning in the music was under my control.

The problem was, as much as I liked Grover Washington's version of *Take Five* or Candy Dilfer's *Lilly was Here*, I could not afford to buy their CDs or go to the live shows at the Blue Note or Beefsmith's Rooftop Café. Smooth jazz was too pricey. None of my friends could loan me the latest Dave Koz, the oldest Chet Baker or Dave Brubeck, so jazz was out. With its over-sexualized nothingness, R&B was surely out.

Hip hop was the one music which had always asserted itself as dynamic, provocative and above all, affordable. So for the sake of finding a place among other adolescents, I had to listen to the music and pay attention to the culture. Hip-hop was a calling from beyond.

I realized that when my generation became the decision makers of the future, they would be doing so with a shared background in hip-hop culture. It was too big not to have affected everyone in some way. Love it or hate it, KRS-One was selling out shows in Tokyo. Japanese kids were listening to KRS-One's sound and copying his vibe. I couldn't deny something with that much power.

Hip-hop is one of those things --like the Enlightenment, the Industrial Revolution or colonialism's demise-- that had to happen. Hip-hop was the glue uniting my future.

In the early 1990s, the political right wanted to believe my peers and I were as accepting as they were to the new images pop culture presented them in the 1950s and '60s. But most of the kids I knew were savvy enough to discern what was real from what was not. We had spent too much time watching TV not to have made sense of what it was. Moreover, we could figure out the angles easier than our parents.

To sell meat sauce, there was no need to say, "Mama mia, that's a spicy meatball." We knew it was a meatball, knew the company was selling it to us. In the mean time, entertain us for thirty seconds. Maybe have an alien shoot the meatball or play soccer with it. There had to be more for my generation.

For me, more meant an even deeper search into black music and culture. I promised to read *The Autobiography of Malcolm X* especially after Spike Lee's movie created such renewed interest in his life. At our lunchroom table, students were talking about who was better: Malcolm or Martin? Most of the hip-hop world and the twenty five hundred other black kids at Tech sided with Malcolm. My mind appreciated the attempted discourse --all minds do. (The mind's job is to get better, to heat up. It wants all kinds of work, especially anything new; anything it can absorb.)

The conscious students and strap-a longs tried to absorb the movie. The Malcolmites believed Martin was too passive.

"He wouldn't be able to pull that [nonviolent resistance] off today," my buddy Nigel would start. "We ain't taking those beatings no more. No sir. You mess with me, you getting' a beat down. We ain't afraid to throw down on white folks these days."

I wanted to interject that Malcolm had come to see the error in his staunch nationalism and grown to embrace a wider policy of inclusion. Malcolm was done segregating what was not simply a national disgrace when he saw what was happening to black people in America as a global human rights issue.

"Oppression is oppression the world over," I wanted to say. "Spilling blood only spills more blood." (I remembered my mother and Mudd warring. There was always peace after a few days. Their ad hoc partnership was always better than separation because there was a greater good to worry about --the children.)

I was poised to tackle issues, picket and demonstrate, if only someone would show me how. I recalled Mr. Husband's eighth grade lectures about black power and having so much respect for the history of black struggle for progress in America. I remember reading Mark Mathabane's *Kaffir Boy* in eighth grade and wanting to be on a road in Soweto, South Africa marching for some noblesse. I wanted the sit-ins, the voter registration drives, the speeches. I knew they were no longer necessary but the energy in the process seemed so profoundly adolescent, so freeing, so human.

Soft no more, it was my duty to act hard. But when in adolescence, it helps to have others willing to do the same. I felt cheated out of that societal push the civil rights generation had to be active and the moral exemplars there to show them how. My peers and I didn't grow up in the atmosphere Jesse Jackson, Louis Farrakhan or Cornel West breathed in. The black leaders back then --our forgotten heroes-- had been killed, imprisoned, altogether given up on my adolescent ideals or worst yet, had been absorbed by the system.

My generation of conscious black and white boys and girls had yet to define America for ourselves; not in that way James Baldwin did with his writing, speeches, words and deeds, the way every black generation before us had to continually march down the Avenues within and without in search of an America they never saw. And even if my generation was defining our America, few were talking to me about what the new paradigm said about us. No one was on some stage leading.

Like me during *Malcolm X*, we all seemed to be waiting, not realizing no one but us would ever lead us. We'd been taught history, saw progress but we'd never figured out how to create it.

I bet every black generation before me was ennobled by the energy of progress. Every year was a forward march, some history created. I figured they must have thought each step was huge. (To a kid, the smallest thing can be the world.)

My generation may have felt the world was ours and the world seemed to think they had us figured out. Both sides had stalled. Black folks didn't step on the Avenue anymore --not like in those *Eyes on the Prize* newsreels. Reverend Al Sharpton would lead a march every now and again in New York City but he seemed in it for the ego trip, the self-promotion and the love of his own voice. I got the feeling my peers didn't think there were any rights left to be won, didn't feel like the black trailblazers we'd read about. We didn't know we could have been making history.

It's hard to feel excited about progress that never seems as big or as meaningful as it once was. This disconnection divorces too many from history's power and the need to keep the black progression, nay, the human progression going.

My time seemed ready. Hip-hop had been delivering the issues with a soundtrack we could all dance to. Queen Latifah, Sista Souljah, X-Clan, Jungle Brothers, Boogie Down Productions, U-N-I-T-Y, Power to the People don't delay, Fight the Power. Even rock music preached the call for black power. Living Colour's song, Pride, had lines like,

> "History's a lie that they teach you in school
>
> A fraudulent view called the Golden Rule
>
> A peaceful land that was born civilized
>
> Was robbed of its riches, its freedom, its pride"

There were definite signs in the air. Time and space were conspiring to put black America back on our historical march to Zion. Someone was helping my apathetic brethren and me. The directions were heaven sent. I was more than willing to walk the line and obey, if only somebody would lead me.

All through the *Malcolm X* opening and closing, I waited and waited but nothing happened. When the movie left the theaters, black consciousness, which we had been jamming to all summer thanks to Public Enemy's song, Fight The Power, went back into its darkness. Spike Lee had done it but my peers and I had not heeded the universe's call to action.

Maybe the movie was a brilliant marketing ploy to sell 40 Acres and a Mule hats and t-shirts? Maybe the film was just a movie and not a movement? Whatever! I didn't blame Hollywood. I internalized my frustration and despised my inability to act yet again. The revolution was calling! The revolution was calling!

Utterly disgusted, I did the one thing life had taught me to do in a critical moment of anger or frustration: I hated. Just like I used to do in the apartment, I locked away my faith in my brothas and sistas ever changing.

How could the sons and daughters born on the bicentennial, the most heralded call to action in Western history, not feel the inherent spirit of '76 and seize the day? How could we have been so senseless and not gathered the collective psyche of the times blasting through the radio, TV and newspaper ads? It was the fire that time. We were supposed to have blazed again, if not without, then we should have all been blazing within, asking, as Malcolm had to: What should America mean to me?

My schoolmates weren't blind. We saw that fifty-foot X sign when we got off the train in downtown Brooklyn every morning.

X: the unknown. The unknown: our definition of America.

Our definition of America: a fifty-foot X on my generation's gap.

The universe was utilizing the mediums we would latch onto to sound the trumpets and let us blast down the walls and ceilings still up in the 1990s. Movie, magic, action was the universe's call; action by any means necessary.

MALCOLM

I wasn't there, great prophet, when you walked

I wasn't conceived yet to be motioned by your talk

I've heard a word or three, some speeches, letters from Egypt

I wanna sting them, great fighter, with logic coded in your undeniable appeal

'Cause I feel what you feel

Even though I don't know…

I wanna learn them children somethin' 'bout fire

Kindle summer blazes from the winter us under

I want to transform, great writer, this apathy wherein

And continue the final passage denied you in the end

At Brooklyn Tech, there was a policy of mandatory volunteering. Each student had to complete service hours in order to graduate. If anyone volunteered at the hospital down the block, the soup kitchen and Salvation Army around the corner, worked to clean up Fort Greene Park across the street, they received service credit on their report cards. Credit could also be earned raising money for the Gay Men's Health Crisis' Aids Walk NY in the spring. We got the sign-up sheets in homeroom and already had a built-in market of five thousand people. There was nothing to do but bother students in the hallways, in the lunchroom or after school.

Every year, Brooklyn Tech bothered enough people to claim that the school's contribution to Aids Walk NY was the largest non-business donation to the cause. The principal and administrators were proud.

"That would look good on your college application," my guidance counselor would say. "Shows that you care?"

Did I care? When the announcements asked me to pick up the Aids Walk sign-up sheets, why didn't they ask if I cared to do so? I'm sure there were earnest volunteers. The die-hards pestered me for a penny here, a nickel there. After two years, I didn't have to be asked by the administration to volunteer. I took my sign-up sheets each spring and collected my pennies. But did I truly want to walk or was I conditioned to walk? Was it a pattern or personal progress? Was I a man acting on my own free will or a dog on a leash?

It didn't matter whether I was a man, a dog, a machine, or some permutation of the three. With Aids Walk NY, I was doing something. I may not have grossed the most money or sported a red ribbon, but I was affecting change. Wasn't finding a cure for human suffering cause enough?

The question of who was influencing me to act was one I grappled with more and more my sophomore year. At night, I would picture my body in the middle of a circle. On the outside of its walls were all the world's mediums of information and its institutions of learning --directly, like school and church and indirectly, like family and friends. My circle would spin at the speed of light and I was bombarded with questions about the images before me. All was a whirling blur, each flash of insight and trauma diverging into each other to form a mass of indistinct shape, size, color or texture.

"How am I to tell what is?" I would wonder. No one ever said anything back. I was alone to discern --alone to learn.

"Who is this?" I would ask. "I'm confused. I'm just a kid. Help me." No reply from the circle; just a constant, whirling dervish.

The dizzying blitzes made me want to pass out but I knew I had to get out, make sense and deal with the mess in my own way. Since I was feeling more of a connection with the students at Tech, I figured I couldn't be the only one in the circle. Others must be in the circle too. Some had ways of coping with the noise.

I saw kids with spiked hair, nose rings, tattoos. Some traded ethnicity --at least in language and fashion. The white kids dressed and talked *black*, the black kids put on Goth make-up and listened to Morrissey and The Cure. Others tripped on acid, smoked blunts, snorted cocaine. The kids did all the things associated with adolescent rebellion.

I thought about the Aids Walk. Why did more white students than black students pester me for donations? The brothas and sistas seemed to have better things to do than collect money for gay people. Maybe it was economics. Maybe we were going home to neighbors who didn't have the money to sign up. Maybe if we carried around the money we collected we'd be jumped and robbed. Or maybe... maybe black kids didn't care.

If Malcolm X, all the commercials, the hats, the shirts, the stickers, the fifty-foot billboard in downtown Brooklyn confronting us each day, the soundtrack or the bootleg tapes; if all that didn't spur us to action on an issue that had everything to do with our lives in America, then how could AIDS and the stigma of it being a disease for gay, white men spur action?

Black folks were not into action anymore. We didn't even walk. We waited at the line for someone else to sound a starter pistol. If the man didn't show up or the bang wasn't loud enough, even though we knew what a gunshot sounded like, we did not move. We weren't even on the blocks.

My hope for black America wavered when I'd see the same boy in the same Nike sneakers, baggy jeans, and headphones every three steps. Hope wavered when I turned on the news and saw him in handcuffs, trying to duck from the cameras as white police officers held his head up to shame me.

My will tripped when I witnessed smart brothas and sistas denying their intellect to fit into a group of other smart brothas and sistas denying their genius. Where were my people going if we were trying to fit this one image of blackness that, for the most part, we had no business in creating?

We didn't produce much of what we saw in the media so who was producing us? We were still in confines. This time, we were the slave masters and overseers in our own ill will to power. How then to churn out and let fly the new ideas to define a direction for young black boys and girls in the twenty-first century? Somebody had to break the mold.

When nobody seemed willing, I decided that would be my job. I wanted to start my own movement like Martin's SCLC, Stokeley Carmichael's SNCC, The Black Panthers, CORE, NOW. I wanted my own acronym. I wanted big things done by little people. Like Martin, I wanted to shame the world into change by leading the young and powerless on a crusade. Like Malcolm, I wanted action from righteous indignation. I wanted my conscious brothas and sistas walking the streets with black armbands, black berets, showing the world they were part of something bigger than themselves. The world would see the black berets and know something was coming.

There would be criteria for admittance to the new black intelligentsia. Smarts, creativity, awareness, a healthy body, empathy, among others. The members had to possess an inkling of the greater virtues. They had to be versed in history, had to know themselves or seek to honestly engage in the struggle for personal liberation.

Struggling to make sense of my life had brought me from bitterness and hatred and I wanted the means codified to produce a greater end for me and anyone who wished to follow. I had nothing to lose. I had no ties to the black community at Brooklyn Tech so there were no friends for me to embarrass, no group for me to get alienated from.

But I never put together my big, black brigade. At Tech, I never became the intellectual activist I wanted to be. I wasn't Kafka, Solzhenitsyn, Lumumba, Mandela, Biko. As a wanna-be intellectual, I cried freedom but never practiced it. Anyway, it seemed the black intellectual was a joke on any TV channel I turned too. Steve Erkel from *Family Matters* was the smartest brotha on TV and he was a buffoon.

The images I saw never showcased the guy I wanted to see. The college comedy *A Diff'rent World* came close but I wasn't in college yet. *The Fresh Prince of Bel Air* was catering to the hip-hop set with Will Smith as a 1990s version of Eddie Murphy in the mid '80s. I'd seen that smart-alleck, street-wise black boy before. Any young, black male character I saw --except for those on *A Diff'rent World*-- was a hip-hop Eddie Murphy for prime time.

Even if the black intellectual did exist --and I was sure that in the whole wide world, he had to be somewhere-- that guy was in a café or music hall or perhaps a walled up classroom. The guy I wanted to engage with was somewhere I didn't have easy access to.

It also occurred to me that the black intellectual may have been in the books in the Brooklyn Tech library or the New York City public library but I was not ready to get off my inactive ass and make sense of my plight by reading Richard Wright, James Baldwin, Langston Hughes, Ralph Ellison, DuBois, Countee Cullen or whomever else had gone through the black boy predicament before me.

I knew a bit about these people. History books always had a paragraph and some citations but I didn't know enough to feel secure in what these literary giants talked about but I promised one day I would. In the mean time, I had to start leading.

If I was going to lead, I could not ignore half the human population. So one of the first things I had to do was get over my fear and nervousness around women. The only way to do that was to put my self squarely around women. Heroes always challenged their fears head on. I had to do the same.

I had observed that women liked men who were the best at something. No wonder the ballplayers, politicians and even the nerdy scientists and authors got the babes. It seemed to me that adolescent girls lacked a definite sense of self. The world constantly told them what to do, what to be, what to wear, who they were. Most had no choice but to accept the crap fed to them --about them. A few women didn't buy into the commercialized ideal and did their own thing. Those were the ones I liked. I didn't buy the crap around me, so why should my women.

A guy seen doing the thing he was good at was a powerful attracting force to adolescent girls. Of course it helps if the guy is decent, kind, physically fit, and is appealing enough where the girl's best friends would want him for themselves. That dynamic created competition among the girls and seemed to play on their individual insecurities.

If a guy was good with kids, the girl he liked had to see him working in an after school program or the children's wing at a hospital. If he had physical strength, the girl of his dreams had to see him playing football or lifting sheet rock for Habitat for Humanity. If he knew Calculus, he had to be his dream girl's tutor. I had to put my self in a commanding role doing the thing I was the absolute best at.

Following that logic, I asked Tech's boys soccer coach, Mr. Yanakis, if he needed help with the girl's soccer team. The team had not won a game in years. Spring 1992 would be his first year working with the girls.

Mr. Yanakis was a good guy but knew little about soccer. Our first meeting for the boys team my freshman year he had plays drawn on the board. Soccer? With plays? No. Soccer is organic, unpredictable, evolving. Soccer is art; the grass is a canvas, the ball is a brush. When any player has the ball, there are a million options. Nothing is ever set. Some passing, dribbling or shooting options are better than others depending on where the ball is on the field, who is around it, the time or the score of the game. Other than that, soccer was up to the player with the ball and his or her teammates' ability to read what the ball carrier might be thinking and then reacting to those possibilities.

I wanted to share that concept with Mr. Yanakis and the girls. More pointedly, I wanted to be around the girls. I needed to get around the girls. Thankfully, Mr. Yanakis let me be around the girls. I even prepared a speech for the first practice.

"My name is Oronde Ash. I'm with the boy's team here. I was asked to come and help you out this spring. I'm not claiming to know everything about soccer but I've been around the game enough to know how it can be taught. I feel I have a lot to offer each of you but it's up to you to be willing to accept, understand and execute what I say as best you can. I know it may be hard listening to someone younger that you but it's just a few months. You never have to play soccer again --but I'd hope you do. All I'm asking is that you play the best you can and incorporate some of the drills, ideas, tactics and moves you'll learn. There's only one thing I hate about soccer and that's seeing it played wrong. So please, in practice or in games, give me something to work with. That's all I ask. That's what I want. That's what I expect... Let's get to it."

I never gave the speech. I mentioned some of the ideas throughout our troubled season. After four or five straight defeats, I stopped hammering the girls and began hugging them after games.

Through simple touch, bonds developed. Whether true or not, I began thinking that a few girls liked me. I'd watch the way they looked at me in practice or overhear whispers when they dressed. I got in the habit of taking off my shirt when the weather warmed up. I'm sure the fact that I had a lean, tight physique didn't hurt my appeal.

When walking the girls to the train station, we'd talk about practice, the game, other things. Most didn't join the team for competition. They were there for the camaraderie. The team was a social event. Ultimately, that fact meshed perfectly with my main motive. I found that one girl kept up a running gag with me about us having sex. Her name was Katie, she was a senior, a virgin, and had promised herself to be deflowered before she left Tech. I knew nothing would come of the dialogue but it was fun to engage in it.

There was also Paola, Kelly, Theresa, Jalissa, Cynthia, Shawnee. Shawnee was a cute Jamaican forward, the most athletic girl on the team. She lacked the ability dribble and pass but she was fast. Shawnee was our main threat to score so, naturally, I had to take interest in her. Any chance of winning depended on her speed.

While the other girls would tell me about their lives, hug or kiss me, Shawnee held back. I think it was her Caribbean upbringing.

Maybe she thought the other girls were being too forward, giving it up a little. Shawnee was not like that. I wished she were more forward because I wasn't ready to step to her. I gave attention to those who stepped to me. I was insecure and didn't want to put my self out there without a hundred percent certainty that my feelings would be reciprocated. The other girls on the team made the process easier by meeting me half way.

I sensed Shawnee's frustration --or maybe it was my own [black boy] guilt. When the other girls gathered around after practice, Shawnee stayed to the side. I knew what she was thinking: "Sellout." I thought the same thing too.

What was wrong with Shawnee? I liked her. She was older, could teach me things. We were both from the Caribbean. Had I explored the possibility, I'm sure Shawnee and I had a lot more in common. But like the soccer season, the chance to find out was over before I knew it.

Spring had sprung, Shawnee graduated and was off to some college upstate, never to be seen again. My loss.

"...Be willing to understand and execute what I ask," I had written to the girls. Was I following my own words?

A school year had come and gone. Had I explored all my options out on the field?

What shots had I passed up?

What goals did I miss?

How many balls did I have

XII.

<u>ALEX: PART 2</u>

After my freshman year playing soccer at Tech, one of the players --Mario-- asked me to join his club soccer team called Real Napoli. I joined Real Napoli in the spring of 1991, a year before I began coaching the Tech girls team, a few months before CTY. Napoli did well.

In October my sophomore year, the team traveled upstate to play Wallkill United. We lost 1-2, ending a twenty-game win streak begun the previous June. It didn't matter. All that mattered was that Alex came to the game. Her home was only twenty minutes from the field.

After the game, Alex stunned me, "Would you like to stay with us for the night?"

"We'll put you on the bus tomorrow, if that's okay with your mom," her mother assured.

What did I do to deserve this? I was sure my mother would say yes. She had to say yes... My mother said yes.

Alex's place was a resort in the woods. "Business people use it for meetings," she told me. It took me until the next morning to finally open up and be the personality I was on the phone. When we woke up Sunday morning I made her breakfast and we played pool. There was soft music on the radio, the trees were whistling, no one was around, just the two of us in a giant conference space. The bucolic, country surroundings must've gotten to me. The moment seemed right so I asked Alex to dance. She was apprehensive but agreed. We began dancing. I was beside my self. To this day, I have no idea why I did what I did next.

"Look into my eyes," I asked, like some vampire entrancing his victim. Alex agreed. I stared into her face for at least thirty seconds waiting for her to be overcome by emotions I thought would somehow transmit from my eyes straight to her heart. With all the letters I wrote, I figured she had to know how I felt. I must have looked creepy staring at her.

Alex and I were alone dancing to a slow song. I had just prepared her a meal. What else did I have to do? Just like in the movies, we'd kiss; my first kiss. Why didn't I kiss her? Why didn't I take the chance and carpe diem?

When I got back to Brooklyn Tech and told the fellas at the lunch table about my weekend, they thought I was lying. "You didn't do anything?" Nigel wanted to know. "Her mama invited you to her house and you didn't do a damn thing?"

"I didn't think it was right," I protested.

"Again... Let me get this straight. Her mama begs you to stay at her house. The girl takes you to see a movie, buys you food, gives you clean clothes to wear, you wake up, make this girl breakfast, dance with her and that was it?"

"Yeah. I got on the bus and came home Sunday afternoon."

"Where did you sleep Saturday night?"

"Upstairs."

"Where did she sleep?"

"Downstairs."

"Where did her parents sleep?"

"I don't know."

"I can't believe you, son," Nigel screamed. "What is up? I woulda damn well known where moms was and walked downstairs to get mine."

"I'm not you."

"Hell no you ain't like me. I woulda done something."

"It's not like that," I repeated.

You did nothing? You did nothing? I repeated the phrase over and over for days. Did Alex think I was gay? Saturday night we were watching the news when a segment on the Gay Men's Health Crisis Dance-athon was aired. Why had we seen that particular news segment… together? Nah! I was straight. I was just a gentleman. Then I thought, maybe Alex was just trying to be nice all along. Maybe she had put up with my boring phone calls, faked hours of laughter, was just being nice. Maybe she had seen something in me and was trying to get it out? Women could be motherly like that, couldn't they?

Alex and I kept in touch for another year or so. With each letter and phone call I was gaining more confidence in dealing with a woman. But despite that comfort, I still had a hard time accepting that she liked me. I could not give the boy inside permission to be liked. I wasn't worthy.

In high school, time began playing its sad song. My letters got fewer, hers were even farther in between. Where I spent days picking out the right word, the just sentiment to express complete honesty with her, Alex's replies lacked the depth of thought I tried to convey in mine. I didn't want to admit it, but I was realizing something grievous: Alex didn't feel for me what I felt for her. The strength of our relationship had been contrived and maintained in my head. I had to accept that truth.

I had created sentiments in my head that were not necessarily there. I wanted to believe in the two of us so much, I had come to see what I wanted to see. What I should have seen was a girl who had been touched by a stranger's kind act at a summer camp and simply wanted to get to know her admirer. Carpe diem was not a battle hymn from the universe, nor was it Alex's unconscious yearning for me. In fact, carpe diem was something she heard in the movie *Dead Poet's Society* that summer.

Whereas I saw the words as a scorching hot beginning to my new self, Alex wrote them as a cool way of ending a letter. No matter. What I learned those two years was worth it.

For two years, I dreamt about, saw my self living with, felt unbridled emotion for another human being. That was all new to me. Yes, the force of our relationship was borne of my own wanting, but so what. At least I believed in that strength.

Even if Alex was not the fire that lit me, she was the spark at the beginning of my new life. I missed sharing my emerging personalities with her. She was the first and is still one of the few people who categorically altered the course of my life. I wonder if she ever knew how deep she made me dig, how profoundly I was changed in such a short period of time. I started living my voice through her.

I wrote Alex a letter once but never mailed it.

"Hey!

Over the past few days I've been trying to figure out why you like me. I couldn't. I still have trouble seeing how we work. Then there was today. We have to read *The Odyssey* for English class. I came across these lines today.

'... We know the gods do not grant the graces to any man, handsome looks and good sense and eloquence together. One man is not much to look at, but God crowns his words with beauty, so that all may listen to him with delight. He speaks in a steady voice with winning modesty, he is notable where men gather together, and as he walks through the streets, all gaze upon him as one inspired...'

Conceivably, the word *speak* could be replaced with *write* and you got us. I just realized no one is God. It never hit home until today. No one is perfect. No matter how hard we try, we will never be. Unfortunately, I have spent too much time trying to be perfect, trying to right my flaws.

I have failed to realize there are good qualities about me. Among them is the ability to convey ideas through the written word. Instead of realizing not many people can write, I keep... I kept thinking I couldn't do something most people do with ease: talk.

Killing myself mentally, brooding over that one fault had kept me down far too long. After all, if I didn't know how to write, I would have never met you. I think you were the wake-up call, Alex. Now I treasure my writing talent along with anything else I seem to be able to do.

CARPE DIEM.

12-10-91"

When in communion with my voice

- I believe beauty exists in simplicity
- I believe the moment exists for each of us to conquer and take from it what we most desire
- I believe there is love in every moment
- I believe love should be conquered from every moment
- I believe a moment devoid of love is a moment devoid of life
- I believe every moment is part of a process to a greater fulfillment of the self
- I believe every moment is open to anyone open to love
- I believe in love
- I believe in love.

On my best days, I cannot deny love, nor will I again deny love because love never denied me. Love simply waited for me to rediscover it, then it wrapped me up warm and secure in all the life I was missing.

And since that singular moment of discovery, with Alex, *carpe diem*, CTY, my summer of change, my life has definitely been momentous.

...

XIII.

BIOLOGY

My sophomore year 1991-92, life was good. I knew people in school, people knew me. I was easy to spot because my dreads were getting longer and I had red, yellow, green, blue and orange rubber bands around some of them. I walked the halls of Brooklyn Tech as a black freak with a rainbow on my head and silver shades for eyes. It didn't matter. I was going to be free.

A lot of kids at Tech got lost in the hallways. I didn't mind the odds because I was used to not noticing people. However, when my new self started to get looks, I noted my pride. The more people eyed, the more I exposed. After years of digging I was unearthing a treasure, my precious, newborn nursling. This time, I was the mother, the father and the baby. I held onto this... this *Wonder Child* wherever I went.

From people's reactions, I started to realize I was becoming my favorite stock character from every 1980s teen film I had seen since my first days in America: the male freak. Every Savage Steve Holland film I liked had a middle class [white] guy struggling to either (1) get the girl, (2) beat the jock, or (3) find himself.

Movies like *One Crazy Summer*, *Better Off Dead* or *How I Got Into College* were, to me, classics in adolescent coming-of-age. As ludicrous as it is for me to admit, I identified with Hoops McCann.

In the movie *One Crazy Summer*, John Cussack played the socially inept, almost nerdy high school cartoonist, Hoops McCann.

Hoops spends the summer after graduation working on Nantucket Island and falls for Demi Moore's character. He uses his artistic ability to help save her family's house from a demented real estate developer. As with all of Mr. Holland's opus, I was laughing throughout.

Cussack's McCann was good, but Robert Downey Jr. typically played the stock character I most wanted to be. He was always the school oddball, wearing a trench coat in the middle of summer or dying his hair purple and green. Like the guy in *Back to School* or *Johnny Be Good*, his characters were smart, even brilliant. I knew they were going to college, would eventually change their ways and become successful. What's more, the jocks always left Downey the freak alone because he was liable to do anything. It was always the freak who got revenge when the main character's moral compass held him back from retaliation.

For me, the freak espoused an American individualism I rarely saw in young, black men. Where I was balled up, the freak was unbounded and the world let him be. By sophomore year, I wanted that freedom. It seemed as if life was demanding it. I had been left alone my whole life to stew and stir and sit and wait. I wanted to sip, to drink up, to get my belly full of the stuff of life.

My movie heroes threw a blow to my black identity. As much as I relished their freedom, it bothered me that they were white, middle class and living in suburbia. I was black, poor and slumming in Brooklyn. I wanted to be that All-American boy, wholeheartedly, but on my own terms.

I wanted to be free of spirit but grounded to a black, political consciousness. Those two ideals didn't seem to mesh. I lacked the example from my generation to model my self after.

Throughout high school, my blackness would remain my deepest, darkest fear. Like my relationship with my mother, I didn't confront it with the energy I should have. Both my mother and my identity as a black man were blatantly obvious and begged to be engaged with but my will was weak. That, and I started noticing other things.

"The women are looking at you," my ego would whisper in the hallway.

Even though I talked to women, I feared them because they reminded me of the one person I blamed for all my shortcomings as a man: my mother. But at age fifteen or sixteen, biology and human development would not be denied.

There was a Chinese girl who sat across from me in Mrs. Sigelakis' history class. She was timid, demure, not a blemish on her pale face. Her name was Elizabeth. I fell for her. Everyday, I'd walk into class and flirt. "She's starting to like you," my ego would boast.

"They don't date black," Nelson, the Korean boy at my lunch table confessed one day.

"And why would you want a girl with a flat ass?" Nigel came back with. "Now, did you guys see what Nadine was wearing today?"

Nadine was *the* black woman at Tech. Head cheerleader, BAC member, fine as hell and brilliant to boot. She sat next to Elizabeth in our history class. I didn't know who to concentrate on. Some days Nadine made the decision for me. When she'd wear her short cheerleader skirt, I'd swear my eyes were seeing the glory and the coming of heaven.

"I don't like her butt," I told Nigel.

"You don't like what!" he yelled. Heads were turning. "Are you buggin'?"

"I mean… it sticks out like… like she's cocked up when she walks."

Nigel laughed. By now, the other guys at the table were tuned in. "Cocked up! Hell yeah, it's cocked up. Because she's ready."

"I don't think she's like that," I said, trying to defend the wholesome image of Nadine I carried around with me.

"I know that, but it's a sweet, black ass. That's a black woman right there. Ain't that right, Nelson?"

"What?" Nelson replied, chomping down on a burger.

"Nadine's ass," Nigel repeated.

"Who? Nadine the cheerleader?"

"Yes," I said.

"Oh yeah. Her ass is damn fine."

"See," Nigel said. "Everybody wants that. Even him." He pointed to Nelson. "And he's Chinese, so you know he don't know nothin' 'bout ass." After the rest of the table started laughing, Nelson had no choice but to join in.

Nigel opened his fingers, outstretched his hand and grabbed some air. "If this was Nadine's ass," he began, "I'd …" He started growling like a dog and taking chops at the space he was holding.

"You're a pig, you know that."

"I'm just being a man," replied Nigel, biting off bigger chomps of air and chewing with exaggerated motions. "Tastes good, boy. Want some?" The whole table was in an uproar.

By Nigel's definition I knew I wasn't a man. I didn't walk around staring at women like they were pieces of meat, although sometimes, I couldn't help it --hormones were doing their number on me. I used to think the attention was all adolescent girls wanted.

"That's why they wear some of the clothes they be wearin'," Nigel would say.

"To have guys like you gawk at them 24-7."

"They can't deny biology, so why should we?"

"So you're a biologist now?"

"Look it up, genius. We're all animals. Men do the same thing. Why do we go to the gym and pump iron, compete for big time jobs or shoot up steroids? It's the same reason women diet, wear make-up or fit into those tight dresses. They want to be noticed. The human animal wants attention. It's right there in your biology textbook."

I asked my voice, hoping to prove Nigel wrong. "He's right," was the answer I heard. "We just got the bigger brains in the deal. Peacocks have feathers to attract mates. Birds do it with their song. Deep down, there is still that animal inside us all."

"We try to control it," I started thinking, "but it has to come out. The species has to keep going." That was in the biology books too.

I had trouble accepting Nigel's definition of manhood, feared what it could mean and didn't like being afraid. At sixteen, I hadn't gained any more insight into manhood than I had in middle school. After reading a couple psychology books I blamed my father for not being around and my mother for being strong-willed. I figured she had emasculated me.

"She can't teach me how to be a man. And what kind of a male role model is Mudd?" That's one of the reasons I stayed away from him. "I don't want to be like that."

"You're afraid his chauvinism and domineering is in you?"

"I don't want to end up abusing some poor girl. I'm not going through all this nonsense again."

"The only way you're gonna know is to go out there and talk to women," my voice said. Another thought kept creeping into my consciousness.

"*Maybe you're gay,*" the little boy in the back of my head giggled.

"Are you crazy? I may not talk to women, but I look. I get a woody like anybody else."

"*Think about it though?*" the boy said.

"I'm not gonna do that," I told him.

"Look, there's nothing wrong with being gay," my voice began. "Everybody goes through this questioning stage. Look, it's right there in your psychology book."

"Don't patronize me."

"Who's patronizing. It's fact. If you're the man I think you are, you'll listen to facts."

"I'm listening." I didn't want to listen, but where was I gonna go?

"The facts are these. You're sixteen and you're a virgin."

"So."

"I'm not finished. Not a single date... I know, I know, Alex, but you haven't kissed a girl, for God's sake."

"There's a reason for that," I said. "Freud says the mother..."

"Freud... To hell with Freud." My voice was mocking me. He rarely did that.

"But Freud says the mother-child bond is key. I hate my mother, therefore..." I was irate.

"... Therefore, you hate all women. Whatever! I know you, man. This ain't a The Ricky Lake Show."

"*Ricky Lake's a good show,*" the little boy charged. I don't think he knew what was really going on.

"Look. I don't wear a scarf around my neck all year. I don't sing show tunes or watch Barbara Streisand retrospectives on PBS. I'm a heterosexual man," I asserted.

"You're a closet heterosexual?" my voice asked wryly. I thought it over.

"Yes, that's exactly what I am… And what's with your tone?"

"You're confused."

"But that's OK," I answered. "They say everybody goes through this stage."

Sexuality was a mess. One day I'd think I was straight, the next I'd swear I had to be gay. There was a Gay and Lesbian club at Tech and I was tempted to sign up and find out once and for all. But that's normal… Maybe? I didn't know.

Maybe. My life was all about maybe. Nothing was ever definite.

"At least you're not cowering away anymore," my voice told me one day. He paused for a second. "Women are so curious, aren't they?"

"Where did that come from?" I wanted to know.

"Way back," he replied.

"I know where you're going."

"You know what I'm thinking?"

"I can read you now," I told him.

"I write you," my voice answered.

"Hello, I'm right here," the little boy said. He wanted attention. He was stunted. His fears had been invaded, his insecurity system broken into, locked up memories were being released. He was lost.

"Remember those two girls who asked you if you were gay? On the same day, no less."

"So what."

I almost bit off the head of the first girl. The second girl was different. She came up to me and followed the question with, "Because my friend, there" she pointed to a girl at the back of the room, "she wants to know." Her friend looked decent too.

"No. I'm not gay," I answered calmly, and walked out the room. On my way to the next class --twenty yards down the hall-- I started thinking.

"Maybe she wanted me? Of course she wants me. She never saw me with another girl, just me in the hallway, with the trench coat and the rainbow head. She stalked me for months and was so excited to have finally found out what class I was in, she got nervous and sent her friend. She probably writes poems about me in her diary and fingers herself, dreaming of me. Oh, yeah. Only a man can make a woman do that… I'm a man, damn it. Hear me roar. I'm a man. Yeah."

"Control it," my voice hushed. "There are other people here."

"I'm a man. Only a man can make a woman do that," I whispered. Unfortunately, my voice had practiced it's own logic.

"You're a little bitch."

"Prove it," I asked, as the crowds passed.

"The girl at the back of the room, she took the initiative, right?"

"But her friend asked me?" I tried thinking.

"Doesn't matter. She had the balls to say something. She was the aggressor. She was the man."

"You're saying I'm a girl because I didn't do the approaching?"

Yep. You're a scared little bitch."

My machismo delusions quickly evaporated. By the time the late bell rang, I hadn't opened the door to my next class, yet I had managed to be even more confused about my biology.

…

XIV.

<u>ME, MYSELF AND I:</u>

<u>CHANGE GON' COME</u>

I wore a black band on my left wrist everyday after reading a Sports Illustrated article on John Carlos and John Smith's black power stance on the medal stand in the 1968 Mexico City summer Olympics. Some students began seeing me as a rebel artist, a little different. They would ask what the arm band was for, what was my cause. I never told because I don't know if I ever picked one. Being different was enough.

This time it was a good different, free to say and do things only an artist could get away with. Escape into art gave me the room to both confront and run away from a black identity I was struggling to define everyday.

At CTY, we read an essay from James Baldwin's *Notes of a Native Son*. I had to hold back the tears as Baldwin described the poverty, helplessness, sheer drudgery of Harlem. "We shouldn't be reading this," I remember saying after one intense passage.

I didn't like the way the rich, suburban kid was reading Baldwin's urban, black words. The kid's voice lacked something. I didn't realize what it was until I heard a Dominican girl read a story in Spanish class. Someone started reading the words then the girl picked up the story in the middle. When she read her part, the words jump off the page. I felt the Spanish story because the girl could accent things none of the English-speaking readers knew.

I was moved to the core by James Baldwin's words and wanted to write like he made me feel. In him, I found a means to voice the disillusionment, the suppressed anger, the knowledge that couldn't come out, the family dynamic I never confronted. But every story I wrote in English class was a glossy, black tale. I remember sitting in my room and picturing white people in my head when I crafted my plays. I felt sick.

My sentiments were black, but the characters, like me, were shells. All I did was give the black shells names like Mahlik, Yusef or Kwame. In every other respect, my characters were white. As an artist, a James Baldwin wanna-be, the creative process was frustrating. I felt like a disappointment to my race.

I wanted to feel blackness all over my body and transmit it through the word. I wanted to go to the movies or turn on the TV and see a young, urban, confused black boy trying to find his soul in a world which had only taught him to hate his confused, lost, black self. When that day never came I finally turned off the TV set. If I did watch the boob tube, I tried to be more critical of the images that influenced me. If something didn't hit me as being an additive to the black man I was trying to create, it had to go.

Instead of network television, I watched PBS. A film on the history of Rock-n-Roll --or what is truly black Rhythm and Blues with a glossy, white cover-- changed my perception of black music.

"You should listen to more rap and R&B now that you know where those sounds came from," my voice told me.

"R&B is boring."

"You don't feel connected to it, huh?"

"You know the worst part of talking to you?"

"What?"

"You know everything... Of course I don't feel connected to R&B. It's about love and women, two things I don't have in my life."

"Just try listening again, will you?"

"I told you, we got no soul, man. We sell out our voices and say nothing with it."

"As much as you'd like to believe it's everybody else, you're the one with no soul. You're seeing what you're feeling, Oronde. Learn to embrace your rhythm, your blues."

"How do they expect anyone in the black community to feel love?"

"What are you saying?"

"I don't know what I'm saying."

"So think about it."

I paused... maybe for days.... maybe weeks. "I'm saying there's no love in the black community."

"You're saying there's no love in you," my voice answered.

"OK. OK. Hear me out. What if the only reason we're buying all the R&B love crap is because we are suffering for love. That's why those girls go nuts for Jodeci. That's why we went nuts for soul music in the sixties. That's what those writhing bodies in the painting *Sugar Shack* is all about. We want an aesthetic we seldom experience."

"OK," my voice begged. "Now hear me out. What if the only reason you think R&B is crap is because you have no love in you. You want love; you're dying for love. What if you're just jealous of Jodeci because they can create an aesthetic you will never know. That's why you can't go nuts for soul music, that's what your uninspired writing is all about. Black people have been through hell in this country. We've had our music repackaged, re-named, re-done, rehearsed and re-sold to the rest of the world as Rock-n-Roll."

"And?" I asked.

"And... And still we rise to crank out the soundtrack of America. Black rhythms and black blues made this country, Oronde. Black love made black music, therefore..."

"Therefore..."

"Black love made this country." I was still too young to accept truth when I heard it.

From what the news projected, black love didn't exist in America, especially among the young, urban and poor. Black love had never been re-enforced in my apartment, so it was easy for me to buy into the media negativity. What I saw often made me ashamed. Brothas were killing brothas over sneakers and gold necklaces. Black life seemed to mean nothing. I couldn't respect any black man --any human being-- who lived like that.

When young Gavin Cato was killed on President Street in Crown Heights --five minutes from where I lived --and the so-called riots ensued, I was appalled. When a Jewish man was shot in retaliation, I was distraught. The boy who shot the Jewish man was an old acquaintance. We used to play baseball in middle school. He used to smile a lot back then. He loved baseball. But when he was in the papers and on the news, the boy was never smiling. Brothas didn't smile in Brooklyn.

"Why do they have to do this on TV?" I asked. "We're just showing the world what they think we are --animals."

"Are they supposed to do nothing? A black kid got run over. The driver of the car is hiding in Israel. Could a black man get away with that?" my voice asked. "You really got to start hangin' out with more brothas, Oronde. At least listen to some Public Enemy, some Boogie Down Productions or something. You don't even know the people on this block. You can at least pick your head up and smile at the sistas around here."

"*They don't like him,*" the little boy inside me countered. "*They've never liked me. When I first got here. They thought I sounded white.*"

"They thought... They thought." My voice had been trying to evict the little idiot still in my head. The boy was coming between my voice and me. Even I was afraid for the boy. Where would he go?

"Did anybody ever tell you, Oronde, I don't like you because your voice sounds white."

"No."

"Are you starting to see something here?" I didn't want to think it, but it was there.

"It's all in my head," I said.

"Shonuf!"

"You're saying every negative thought I've had about black people is only a..."

"Keep going. Keep going."

"...Only a... a projection of the way I feel about me."

"Don't stop. Don't stop there," my voice urged, like a teacher finding his purpose.

"And if I start thinking positive about me… then I'll… I'll start thinking positive about black people."

"Not just black people. Everybody."

"Why don't they teach this in school?" I asked.

"They do."

"Then how come I never got it?"

"You never liked me… liked your self enough to learn," my voice said. "I mean, learn deep down in my soul so you never forget it."

"This can't be right. Life can't be that simple?" I wondered.

"It's a lot simpler than you think. Truth always is. The world just makes every day more complex 'cause man has to do something between sun-up and sundown."

"What kind of truth?" I asked.

"Love," my voice said simply. "A love of self is the most important thing anybody --black, white, brown, yellow-- will ever learn. Honestly, how do you feel these days?"

I thought about it. "I feel light."

"Not only do you feel light, you also see light, don't you?" I was confused. "The people in the hallway," my voice went on, "are not looking at the dreads or the glasses. They're looking at light. It's like you're born again. Who doesn't want to be born again? You said it yourself. These days you're like the mother, the father and the son all rolled into one. You're becoming complete. You're growing up. You're becoming human, my brotha… Human."

I didn't understand all that my voice was saying, but I felt good finally hearing him.

It would eat me up inside when I passed brothas on the corner drinking their forties trying to look hard. My emerging happiness seemed to signify I was white because, in Brooklyn, a black boy smiling was the act of a sellout.

"They have no idea what hard is," my voice commanded one day.

"So what is hard, then?" I asked

"Hard is doing what you're doing," he said. "Hard is fighting through darkness and walking out with light. It's graduating and going on in life. Hard is looking at the world square in the face and saying, 'I ain't gonna be denied. I don't give a damn what the statistics are for black men in America; don't care what might've been. I want to understand how it all came about but I am not bound by that history. I am and will be who I am and will be'."

"You sound like Dr. King."

"I don't know who else you got in your head," my voice joked.

I rarely stopped to chat with the fellas on my block. On weekends, while they were bonding, I was playing soccer. I didn't have time to remember the days when we all played wall ball, handball, football, softball or basketball games against the kids who lived on the next block. The one conversation I remember having with the fellas centered on clothing.

"What's so important about the name brand clothes?" I asked. I didn't see the point of wasting money buying clothes from designers who didn't care about the black community. I didn't see why a two-year old should be wearing Polo and Air Jordans. "Why can't people see you for who you are?"

"You'll get played out," I remember someone saying. The boy had been brainwashed into believing he needed a name-brand shirt or pants to represent him.

Yeah, black kids seemed to be the trendsetters at Brooklyn Tech, but what did that prove about us? What happens when fashion changes? All trendsetters are stuck. They have to adapt or lose their power.

Adapting was all I saw the young, urban poor doing. There was no stability. Television, radio, newspapers told us what to do and think. I didn't see black thinkers, black leaders, just a bunch of mindless boobs controlled by a system they didn't understand enough to fashion their own identity within. Identity was what the clothes were about. If those trendsetters were secure in themselves, they wouldn't need the expensive labels.

Everybody on my block wore the expensive labels, especially Xavier.

X was always looking fresh in Polo, Timberlands and a crisp baseball cap. He was the king on the block, had his own posse and everything. X's posse would fight against other posses while the rest of us went on with our games in the schoolyard. He played with us every now and again. When we were younger, X always wanted to play tackle football when we only wanted to play two-hand touch. He was aggressive even in his pre-teen days.

During high school, no matter if he was throwing dice, smoking a blunt or sipping a forty, X always said, "What's up" or gave me the brotha hug --right fist on my back, left fist on my chest. Hugs weren't my thing. Emotion wasn't my thing. Love still wasn't my thing, especially coming from a big, aggressive, black man --the scariest sight on the American psyche.

"At least X has the softness to admit and accept his aggression," I heard my voice say.

"You mean, his thug-life," I replied.

"X ain't no thug. He lets out his frustration onto the world because he can't control his unexplored [black boy] rage. Somewhere in him, there is an understanding of what this hypercritical, racist society has laid out for him. X is letting the world know what they are creating. You, Oronde, you know exactly what the history books have to say, what economics has placed value on in our community, what hard science and eugenics tried to claim about us. Yet you let it pass. You don't confront the world and tell them you hate them sometimes. You are in complete control of your rage. You're in so much control, suppressed that righteous anger so deep, you deny its very existence."

"You trying some more psycho babble on me, friend?"

"You tell me?" my voice returned.

My voice was right. I was the real black thug. I had the knowledge to understand black history and the events that had brought X and me to where we were in America, yet I denied how that knowledge made me feel. There should have been a holy tribunal like in that old Ice Cube video where he puts Easy E and MC Hammer on trial as sellouts.

"I should be made to confess years of denial and self-hate. I should be thrown out of the race." I reasoned.

"That's not gonna happen," my voice intoned. "As long as you understand what's going on, that's the important thing. The rest will come. You gotta keep on."

One night, I was alone in my room, and for no apparent reason, I just broke down. Tears began to flow.

"You look like a sissy," my voice reacted in the tone I had conditioned him to use at times when my emotions ran havoc on me.

"I don't know what's going on anymore," was all I could say.

"You know exactly what's happening," he commanded. "I didn't raise no idiot."

"What is it?" I asked over sobs and sniffles.

"It's hell out there."

"Why don't I hear other people talking about these realizations? I feel like the only one having to deal with all that's coming at me about school, women and men, politics, history, life in general. And not fully appreciating anything or anyone or knowing what I think and feel half the time." I couldn't hold it together anymore.

"You're not the only one," my voice offered. "You may be different 'cause you see things different. Most of your friends are doing what they should be doing at this age: living life without question. They're on the inside. You still like to stand on the outside thinking, Oronde. You can see more of the picture, but then what?"

"I can't do a fucking thing about it."

"Yes you can. You just choose not to. The only thing wrong with you is that you're treating the world like it's a classroom. The world ain't a classroom. There's no textbook for life, chapters to review then act on, no drafts to revise and edit. You don't learn to live life, Oronde; you live to learn life. When are you gonna see that?"

"How else am I supposed to look at it?"

"I don't know."

"How am I supposed to see a world that keeps changing every second?" I asked.

"I don't know."

"Tell me what's on the inside. I wanna know where you come from."

"But you wanna stay on the outside, Oronde. The truth is, you don't wanna know that it's a jumble where I come from. There, I said it. People make life rational when it ain't. Even then, people screw up. They know right yet they keep doing wrong. Some want more money or more power than they need. Some kill, some create. Some kill and create at the same time. The world ain't a classroom, son. Life is what it is and it's frightening."

"Why didn't you tell me before? You know everything."

"I can't learn you life," Oronde.

"Sometimes I feel like ending all this, cut my losses and say goodbye. The good die young, right? "

"There's a reason behind all of this," my voice assured me.

"What makes you so damn sure?"

"I'm here to help you. I challenge you sometimes, but I promise, it's all for the better. You gotta make it through this thing. Keep on. You got two brothers looking up to you and even though you don't show it, I know you love your mother. You can't hide that from me. I knew you loved her even back then. You used to push her to the back of my mind but I kept her for you. She didn't fall out... You're a decent kid. You haven't killed anybody behind my back, have you?"

"No," I said. My eyes welled up again. All the years spent in exile instead of helping my family grow together. Wasn't I the big brother?

"Then start acting like one," I heard my voice whisper.

Even if my emotions had failed me, my intelligence kept telling me there was a role to play in my family. I was the first son, the one to protect and counsel the rest, the one to go out and conquer the world. That's what I picked up from skimming psychologist Alfred Adler's theories on birth order and personality.

Psychology came at the perfect time in my life. We had taken the AP European History exam in May my sophomore year and had over a month until the school year ended. We needed to learn so Mrs. Sigelakis introduced us to psychology.

I read about Abraham Maslow's theory of self-actualization, read chapters on Pavlov, B.F. Skinner, Albert Bandura, Erik Eriksson and Alfred Adler.

Maslow showed me that my basic needs of food and shelter were being met, therefore, I should not complain, but instead, move toward the higher levels of human expression. Adler told me that as the first born, I had a duty to be successful and lay the groundwork for my younger siblings. Eriksson, Bandura and Pavlov explained that I had been conditioned to respond to people and social situations in only a negative manner, and could, by reconditioning, transform my life.

To be successful I had to master the dog in me, had to reorient my self, ring the bell again and again and get up like the champion I needed to be; like the champion my family needed me to be: like the fighter black America would always need. I figured I would cure my adolescent confusion by June and not have to pay a doctor thousands of dollars later on in life. Psychology was going well until we read the book *Clockwork Orange*.

When we watched the Stanley Kubrick film, I could swear it was me onscreen. I was the demented main character named Alex, running around causing mayhem. I didn't show it, but there was much aggression in me. The scene where Alex was forced to watch violent scenes from movies while his eyes were held open by mechanical clamps --that scene haunted me. I didn't want to end up like him.

"You've been saying change for a year now," my voice said. "And, by the way, I'd never let you get that crazy. What kind of monster do you take me for?"

I didn't want to find out the monster inside. To force some semblance of feeling into me I began playing with my brothers Randi and Keri even more than usual. It seemed like the right thing to do. I started calling Randi, "Buddy," because I wanted him to repeatedly hear the word. Randi was five, too young to understand what the word meant but I wanted the idea in his subconscious. As he got older and friendship began making sense to him, Randi would --deep down— have already internalized the meaning. He would connect me with "buddy". His subconscious would always have a friend. I didn't want Randi to feel the loneliness I felt growing up. Maybe it was all nonsense but I figured I was securing my baby brother's psychological future.

Whenever I got annoyed at Randi or Keri, I would wonder if it was my adolescent frustration, our age difference or my own psychological shortcomings.

"It's the age, you fool and all the that goes along with it." But when it came to my mother, I knew it was my shortcomings.

"Here I am, becoming conscious of my role in this family, learning about my future, my place in the scheme of things and she does this to me. Every time."

"You are one selfish bastard!" my voice interjected. He was being real again. "You have ears. You know what really goes on in this apartment."

"Every time I take a step forward…"

"Do you know how many leaps your mother has made towards you, you ungrateful little prick?"

"I hate her."

"You don't hate her, you moron. The little boy inside you hates her. I'm gonna kill that little piece 'a shit if I see him any time soon. Anyway, I thought you were reading your psychology books. Remember Freud? Remember your analytical hero."

"She's screwed up my life forever."

"Nothing is forever!" my voice yelled so loud my ears rattled. "Nothing!"

"Freud said the mother-child bond is the most influential relationship a person ever makes. I never made that crucial connection so my whole life has gone wrong. My mother never took the time to be with me --not in St. Vincent, not in Jersey and not here, not now, not ever. She screwed me up."

"You think you're the only one who realizes that? You think she doesn't know she's made mistakes. You think you're the only smart one in this house? And for your information, Freud was a base head."

"What?" I asked, a bit unnerved.

"OK. So you didn't have the TV-sitcom childhood. But who the hell does? I thought you gave up TV and its propaganda? You better get those celluloid dreams outta your head."

"I can't."

"Get up," my voice pitched. "Get up and go take a good look at yourself." He dragged me over to the bathroom mirror. "I made that," he said. "I've spent sixteen years shaping that. I ain't quitting on you and you're not quitting on me."

I looked in the mirror, past my reflection and saw the future for my two brothers. For the first time, I saw my sisters Annie and Teri too. Teri was nine, as old as I was when I came to America. Annie was fifteen, a year younger than me. They both needed me. For the first time in my life, I realized Annie had been next to me all along.

"If you had bothered to look across the room in 3R or on E34th St., you would have seen her crying right there with you," my voice said. My eyes fell to the floor.

It was me who had closed my doors all my life refusing to deal with the world. I had spent my American life locked away in my head. I could theorize and speculate, dream up fantastic delusions, perfect personalities for people I kept a calculated distance from. Intelligence made my delusions more complex, more real but no more.

Yes, life was chaotic, but even in its madness, it was okay and I was okay in it. I was seeing the world with new eyes. I wanted more of my vision. I needed the complete experience --mind, body and soul. It was time, high noon at midnight, time to set the clocks back and move forward. No rationalizing. No theorizing. I had to open up fully and let all my family in. All or none.

The Gateway program became confining. The classes, teachers, students were still a challenge but I was tired of relying solely on my mind to filter life. What about the heart? I foresaw graduating Brooklyn Tech with the empty feeling from middle school and I didn't want that. Who said I had to be a doctor? When did I want to be a doctor? I was more than that now. Unfortunately, I would never get to be more if I stayed with the same people all day for the next two years. I didn't know them and they certainly didn't know me. I was sick of report cards that never showed personal growth. I wasn't an "A" human being yet. I wanted to practice being an "A" human being. I wanted to get out of Gateway and open up my own program.

Was I getting good grades because I had been in a competitive environment since the seventh grade? Was it really learning if all I did was try to keep up with everybody? Wouldn't the smart guy show up no matter where he went? What if I didn't have the support system around me? What if I didn't hear teacher's kind words and encouragement? Teachers wouldn't be there to encourage me in life. What would I do then? I had to learn to crank-start my own life.

Gateway was about producing minority doctors. Me... I wanted to be a minority thinker. I wanted to explore more of the creative side the adolescent daze had been forcing me to escape into.

Whatever drug my peers were using seemed more liberating than the linear, functional geometry I was trapped within. I wanted to embrace a new logic --the one I was experiencing in my burgeoning consciousness. That logic was random, yet fixed, spontaneous yet determined, stultifying yet free. It was dark and light, riddled with love and hate, the angst and dread framed between heaven and hell. But I knew it was good. That logic in my dreams had reason and purpose. I wanted to find my purpose.

By the latter part of my sophomore year, my head was up most days instead of staring at Tech's hallway floor. The mirrored shades were gone. People were peering into my eyes.

In reality, I had been re-conditioning my self to look at people. Their smiles, their frowns, their whispers, for the first time, seemed positive. I was feeling comfortable being me so I thought people were feeling good about me. I felt wanted by women and admired by men. I was jumping into other lives more, starting to believe all the kind words teachers and coaches had been saying all along.

"You're going to be a leader some day Oronde."

"Why is he the only guy who wants to win this game?"

I was finding my self. He had been alive in me all along.

"I'm joining the football team," Nigel called to tell me one night.

"What?" I answered.

"I'm joining the football team," he repeated.

I wanted to laugh. "Are you serious?"

"Yes. I talked to the coach and he said spring practice starts in a couple of weeks."

"You're serious about this?"

"Yes, Negro. I've always wanted to play football. Sophomore year is the last year you can join."

"Nyge, you weigh ten pounds more than me. You're a twig. They'll break you."

"So what."

"So what? Where you gonna play?" I asked. "You're too small to be a wide receiver."

"I'm 6 feet 2," he stated.

"You're 6'1", if that much."

"I'm 6'2"."

"And weigh 155 pounds."

"You saying I'm not good enough to make it? You think you the only one in the world with athletic ability?"

"Nah, Nyge. I'm just saying…"

"You see," Nigel began, "This is why I'm leaving Gateway. Nobody there gives a shit. The teachers all hate my ass. I don't get along with any-a-dem fools. I gotta get out." He sucked his teeth in disgust.

"You're serious, aren't you?"

"Hell yeah," he said.

"What you gonna do next year?"

"I wanna major in Mechanical Engineering."

Brooklyn Tech was one of the few schools in the New York City that offered academic majors for juniors and seniors. All students applied at the end of sophomore year. Options included Electrical, Mechanical and Aerospace Engineering, Math and Science Institute, Chemistry, Biology, Graphic Communications, Technology and Liberal Arts and a new major, Social Science Research.

"I'm glad you said that, Nyge, 'cause I've been thinking about leaving Gateway too."

"Why? You're doing good in the program."

"Yeah, but I'm tired of the same faces all the time. I'm stuck in the same role for two years. I'm different from what they see. You know that?"

"Right."

"I gotta get out now. I feel this is the right time."

"What you gonna do?" he asked.

"I wish Tech had an English major. I'm probably gonna have to settle for Social Science Research. The brochure said that each student will have to write a Westinghouse Science Project his or her senior year. At least it's writing."

"That's good, man… Hold on… I gotta go. Moms wanna use the phone."

Nigel made me feel more optimistic about my decision. In our two years in Gateway, he had been a doer. Even if he didn't succeed, Nigel always tried. He would study for days before exams, get riled up and anxious. I always wanted to know what it felt like to want something as badly as he did. His anxiety seemed to be the stuff of life.

When Nigel saw a 75 or 80 on his exam there may have been sadness, frustration, surprise, disbelief, contentment, joy written on his face. I wanted to explore that range of emotions. School and life had been too easy for me. I needed to study, to worry, get rattled and anxious. I needed to fail. I needed the look of life on my face.

Mr. Ruzich, a Mechanical Engineering teacher, said something while we were carving plastic tic-tac-toe boards and iron pegs in machine shop one day. He said, "Anyone can do good in a subject they enjoy. The real genius is the guy who can get an 'A' in the subject he hates."

Mr. Ruzich was right. My junior year would be different. Once again, I promised not to be pigeon holed by anybody. I would miss Gateway but like Mr. Ruzich said, I had to get an "A" in a subject I was barely passing. In fact, I still felt the class of life was passing me by.

MUSICAL INTERLUDE

Song title: Redemption Song
Artist: Bob Marley

...

XV.

WOMEN

Junior year, sixteen years old, out of Gateway, feeling like a freshman again, but this time I know a few people to wave to in the hallway. Girls walking by, I'm eyeing them, they're eyeing me. More women at Tech... lots more women... all kinds of women. Where did they come from? I couldn't deny them any longer. Hormones, hips, breasts, ass; life was on parade.

I'd overhear conversations where the girl I wanted to get to know would say, "I can't believe John did that" or "Who does Duane think he is?" Some of the man-made mistakes were big. There was cheating, lying, not meeting the girl at the appointed time, forgetting an important date, physical violence. All that went on in high school too.

I listened, taking note of the errors, vowing never to repeat them when I got involved. I had no idea exactly what to do when I got involved with a woman but I knew what I wouldn't do. The memories of Mudd were always a scary presence. If anything, I would be the anti-Mudd. I would be clean. From all I had observed, I figured I knew exactly how to be the perfect man.

My road to perfect manhood had begun by coaching the girl's soccer team and continued with a Junior Achievement project in Economics class. The class designed and sold t-shirts patterned after Late Night with David Letterman's Top Ten List. We came up with the Top Ten Lies at Brooklyn Tech. The shirts were a success. Demand exceeded supply and the class had to reorder inventory. Each student made fifteen dollars profit from our ten-dollar investment.

But profit was not the hook for me. I was wrapped up in the marketing. I stalked the lunchroom tables and hallways looking for people to sell my shirts to.

At first I didn't have my rap down. Once I got comfortable, I grew bold, even began approaching women I would've never had the guts to talk to otherwise. The t-shirts became my conversation starter. There was no pressure. The women's guards were down, I was having fun with the process. My humor usually came out and the women could see that.

One day, I walked into the Tech yearbook office to take a photo. A tall, athletic, curly haired blond named Anna was behind the camera. She asked me to pose this way and that. For some reason, I started acting like a fashion model, pouting my lips and batting my eyes. It was like selling shirts, no pressure, just having fun.

"She's been asking about you," a buddy on the yearbook staff told me a couple days later.

"Really," I said, trying to maintain my cool.

"I think you guys would make a nice couple. She's the star volleyball player and you..."

"She plays volleyball," I interrupted.

"Yeah, she's getting a scholarship to play in college next year. She's one of the best players in the city?

That really got me interested. I was already more that pleased that a beautiful girl, a senior no less, was interested. My buddy kept egging me on to talk to the blond.

"Anna's still asking about you," he'd say if we passed in the hallway.

"Alright, I'll talk to her." It's not that I didn't want to talk to Anna. Although my confidence was as high as it had ever been, I wasn't sure I was ready for a relationship. What would we talk about?

Movies always showed the guy and his women at dinner then there would be a montage of images showing the couple running around laughing and having a good time. There would be no dialogue, just some happy pop song playing. At the end of the montage, the couple would be in bed or the camera would fade on them kissing. I always wondered about the time in between.

What did the guy say when he woke up after sex and they were mulling around the apartment? What was he saying to make the girl laugh so hard she had to hug him tightly? I didn't know the relationship protocol, the in-between talk.

I ended up calling to Anna in late November. For weeks, we'd talk on the phone just about every day. I rarely saw her after school because of volleyball practice so the phone line was our connection.

"You wanna go to a party with me this weekend?" Anna asked

"What?"

"A party. I'm driving out to Long Island to see a friend of mine."

"Sure," I said, trying to sound nonchalant.

"What time do you wanna leave?"

"Whatever's good for you," I mumbled.

"Where do you live?"

"East 52nd St..."

I suddenly realized I had no idea how to get to my apartment by car. I took the bus or subway wherever I went in New York City. "What if I meet you at Tech. That would be more convenient."

"Is six o'clock alright?"

"That's fine."

I couldn't believe what was going to happen. It was Thursday but I was hyped already.

Anna would meet me; I'd have a rose. She'd say, "That's so sweet," and give me a kiss on the cheek. We'd drive to Long Island and I'd make her laugh all night, just like the day we first met. We'd talk all through the party, oblivious to those around us.

On the drive back, a romantic song would come on the radio and we would both start feeling something. When she dropped me off, I'd do it, I'd kiss her. I'd get the first date and the first kiss over and done with in one night.

It had been close to a decade since I last kissed a girl. Her name was Monique. I was six. She stayed with the family across the road from us in St. Vincent. My best friend at the time, Jack, was her cousin. Jack knew I liked Monique and would tease me about it to the point of tears. He and his older sisters got together one night and spearheaded the fateful moment.

We were playing some variation of tag where you had to hold onto certain people at designated places to be safe. The night sky was pitch black, save for the half moon and the flickering lamp poles on the road. The moon was not bright enough for me to see it was Monique's hand I was clutching as Jack ran me down, growling like a mad dog. Before I realized what I had done, Monique turned her head and quickly planted her lips on mine. All the other kids started ooohing and aaahing. Jack initiated a round of, Ronnie and Monique sitting in a tree, k-i-s-s-i-n-g. The others joined in. Monique let go of my hand and ran to join her giggling cousins nearby. I was furious and bolted across the road to my house.

This time, however, I was determined to be ready for the moment. And it would work. There was something of destiny in it. My moment had been building. I'd been taking baby steps to gain more comfort around women. Anna would be my first real test.

Unfortunately, the universe did not cooperate with me that weekend. Snow pelted the New York area and made driving all but impossible. Anna didn't even have to call and cancel and I felt even worse when she did.

"Maybe some other time," she phoned.

"Yeah."

The next Monday, I walked into the yearbook office hoping to have a word with Anna. As usual, she wasn't around. I was about to leave when a petite, tight-bodied brunette walked in. The girl was stunning. She wore tight jeans and a light, form-fitting top accentuating every slight of her curves. I couldn't keep my eyes from following her body around the room.

"Hi," the girl smiled in passing. She stopped at the door, looked back and said, "You're on the soccer team, right."

"Yes."

"I used to play soccer..." (She had the biggest, greenest eyes. They seemed almost too big for her lithe frame, which made them pull me in that much more.) "Back in Ecuador when I was younger, I played futbol." I could hear the accent. "Your name's Oronde, right"

"How'd you know?"

"Anna told me."

"Really," I said, walking closer to the girl. We had something in common. Thank you, God.

"You should come and watch a game," I invited.

"Maybe." The girl looked at her watch. My friend from the soccer team walked in the door. "I'll see you tomorrow," she told him. "And nice meeting you, Oronde."

I couldn't keep my gaze off the girl's behind as she walked away. "Who is that chick?" I asked my friend.

"That's Roxanne."

"She's hot."

"Duh."

"Is she seeing anyone?"

"Aren't you seeing anyone?" my friend countered, grabbing some pictures and putting them in his bag.

"I guess... I haven't seen Anna in close to a week. She's always got practice or a game or something and when I do get to see her she's on edge. She's acting like she's not interested anymore."

My buddy turned around, put on his coat and backpack. "She's doing a lot of stuff," he began. "There's a lot of pressure on her right now dealing with these deadlines they keep changing on us. Believe me, working on the yearbook is a big pain."

"Why didn't she tell me this," I began, realizing Anna and I had not talked on the phone in days.

"Plus she's being recruited by college coaches. You know she's up for the Silver Horse Award."

"What's that?"

"Best volleyball player in the city. Her dad's been pushing her to win that thing every year now."

How did my buddy know so much about Anna and I didn't? Maybe they were seeing each other. Nah! He wouldn't do that. She wouldn't do that; at least not with him.

The next few weeks, I started bumping into Roxanne more and more. She'd come into my English class to talk to the teacher, Dr.

Weinberger and get stuff from her locker at the back of the room. Roxanne was in Doc's senior writing class and helped out with the school literary magazine named Horizons.

One day, I stopped by a Horizons meeting. Dr. Weinberger had been encouraging me to attend but I'd never gone because of conflicts with soccer. For some reason, I now wanted to go. Walking into the crowded classroom, I saw Brooklyn Tech's writers and artists.

Kameron Tell, who I thought was the most brilliant person I had ever met, was there. Sophomore year, she let me read two of her novellas, personal tales of a young girl coming into her own at home. They were well crafted but had little emotion. There was something else behind the words that never came out.

Kameron was a gifted speaker too, had an opinion about anything. I found that out in AP European History our sophomore year and in the first few months in Social Science Research. I looked to her as a young intellect I could pattern my self after. She was doing what I wanted to do, writing her life, speaking her mind. And I kind of liked her too.

"You like who?" one of the fellas said one day. "That fat, lesbian."

I refused to believe Kameron was a lesbian. Yes, she had a short haircut, hung out with a bunch of women all the time, wore pants everyday. But I loved her breasts. They were giant, fluffy, white sponges. She had alabaster skin that, when flushed, turned her cheeks a charming crimson. I wondered what it would be like watching us have sex, me, the night, she, the day --poetry in blissful symphony.

Skye Davis was in the room as well. Skye was the most interesting sista at Tech. She'd wear black lipstick, nose rings or fishnet stockings with holes in them. Skye was the only sista who wore Doc Martens regularly or dyed her hair. She was reserved, artsy, reminded me of Cree Summer's character, Freddie, from *A Diff'rent World*. There was something irresistibly cute about Skye, a far cry from the stereotypical neck popping black girl with sass and attitude.

Maybe it was the horn-rimmed glasses Skye wore. I had a thing for girls who looked like English teachers. I also liked the way Skye put her words together. She didn't challenge people like Kameron. Instead, Skye stated her opinions in a very motherly way, as if she knew you were wrong but wanted you to figure it out yourself. I figured her out.

We were in Dr. Weinberger's junior English class and would flirt. I talked to her on the phone a few times too. Found out her parents were hippies.

"Bet your mom's a social worker," I told her one night.

"How'd you know that?"

"Because I know you girl. 'Cause we're meant to be."

Skye laughed. I liked talking to Skye but I never asked her out. Didn't think I was ready yet.

I certainly wasn't ready for the tap on the shoulder, the wave and the smile from Roxanne as she passed me at the back of Dr. Weinberger's classroom. She strolled to the front where Doc was talking and sat at a desk facing the throng. Needless to say, I couldn't concentrate on whatever Doc was going on about. I kept sneaking peeks at Roxanne.

Roxanne's legs were hanging off the ground, too short to reach the floor. She was swinging them back and forth and in circles. Her mind seemed far away from the meeting. Maybe she was thinking about me like I was fantasizing about her? She'd twitch her nose every now and again and rub it. Looked like a rabbit with her tight, white cashmere sweater. Once, when Roxanne stretched her arms in the air, I saw her bellybutton and a mark near her hip. Got me a bit excited.

"And that's the end of this meeting," Doc said. "Remember, a writer always writes." She walked out, stopping to tell me, "Write me something, Oronde."

Everyone got up to leave. I had to stay seated at least a minute or face the embarrassment of watchful eyes staring at my crotch. Roxanne came over.

"What are you doing here?" I asked, placing my jacket across my waist.

"I help Doc. Isn't she great?"

"I guess." Teachers were teachers. They did their job and I did mine. Doc called Roxanne's name from the hallway.

"Are you leaving soon?" I asked.

"Yeah."

"Mind if I walk you to the subway?"

"No. That's fine. I'll just be a minute."

Roxanne and I walked two blocks to her subway station. I was nervous at first but her eyes eased my fears every time I made contact.

"How long have you been in America?" I asked.

"About six years."

"You like it here?"

"I'm used to it," she replied.

"Any brothers or sisters?"

"A little brother. What about you?" she asked.

"I have two younger brothers and two younger sisters."

"Wow. You're the man of the family, then?"

"I guess," I smiled. I couldn't think of anything else to say so I kept smiling. She smiled back. Ease. Calm. Finally Roxanne broke the silence.

"So… it's getting chilly, huh?"

"Yeah."

"I hate the cold."

"Why?" I asked, thankful that the conversation was going again and that I only had to ask questions.

"Because I keep getting sick every other week."

"I get those too," I lied. We had reached the subway stairs. What was protocol here? Where's the get-to-know-you textbook? Roxanne looked at me, smiled and squeezed my arm.

"Thanks for walking with me. See you tomorrow, okay."

"See you tomorrow," I returned. In my head, I was jumping up and down saying. "You da man. You da man, Oronde."

The next day, Roxanne caught me in the hallways outside Doc's class and gave me a hug. I'd never gotten a hug like that. The only other girl who'd ever hugged me was Kameron Tell.

I hugged her goodbye one day. "You call that a hug," she said before drawing me into her billowy bosoms and squeezing tight. Roxanne wasn't as big or as strong, but she was equally warm. So warm.

In the hallway or outside the building, boys and girls who hung out in the same group would snuggle, kiss, hold hands. I always wondered what that felt like. Roxanne had shown me. It was great. Felt like somebody in the world liked me. When Roxanne let go, I had to put my jacket in front of my waist so I wouldn't be embarrassed walking from the door to my desk at the front of the room.

I'd get a hug from Roxanne when I got to English class every morning. I'd wave to her in the hallway and whenever I saw her, she'd do the same. One day, right before Christmas break, I must have seen Roxanne ten times and she hugged me all ten. After school, she and I stood waiting for her friends in the main vestibule. We'd been talking, touching, edging closer. She said a few sweet things. I said a few sweeter things. The moment was open for us. Roxanne seemed to want it. I damn well wanted to but didn't want to mess up my first kiss, not with her.

Roxanne was so damn pretty. We talked for another five minutes before her friends showed up, but they left us alone. Roxanne moved closer. I moved in.

"Wait," she said, and sneezed.

"I'm sick. I have a cold. And aren't you seeing Anna?"

"Yeah," I said, "but we're not going out or anything."

"You're not."

"I haven't talked to her in a while, even."

"Ooh," Roxanne said. Had I known then what I know now, I would not have brought up the subject. It was probably a planned execution. I was a goner before I knew it.

It never occurred to me at the time that the reason I saw Roxanne in the yearbook office that day and the reason she knew Anna and my buddy was because they all worked together. I was too busy feeling full of my ego to put one and two in order.

I wasn't trying to be a playa or anything. It was just fun being me, especially after one woman showed interest in my goofball antics. When another woman --another senior woman --another hot assed senior woman liked me, I mean… that was just crazy.

When we got back from Christmas break Anna was still busy with her volleyball season. Not my fault. I didn't know the protocol there. What did the talking-to-one-women-when-the-other-is-busy textbook say? I thought about telling Anna the truth but reasoned that I wasn't doing anything wrong. I thought about how babyish the truth sounded. I'd be admitting I was a newborn in handling relationships. I couldn't do that, not with senior women. Presumably they talked to me because I looked or sounded or seemed mature. I couldn't spoil that.

In the middle of January 1993, when Roxanne and Anna finally confronted me, I was angrier about the situation than at both women. I expected them to throw food on me at lunch, tear up my coat or have one of their football friends beat me up like they do in the movies. Instead, the two women confronted me together and stayed together.

Dr. Weinberger had asked me to meet her after school to discuss the story I'd submitted to Horizons. After the meeting, I walked to the nearest exit, which happened to be around the corner from the yearbook office. Before I even cleared the threshold, I saw Anna and Roxanne holding hands, skipping like schoolgirls. They were moving as if on the yellow brick road, ready to unveil the wizard. I knew I was dead and stood in the middle of the empty hallway alone and afraid.

I didn't move. My brain thought it best I stay frozen, my pulse running into oblivion, body wanting to follow. Anna and Roxanne came to a jump stop three feet in front of me.

"Hi, Oronde," Anna said, bobbing her head to the left.

"Hi, Oronde," Roxanne said, bobbing her head to the right and smiling like a wicked angel welcoming the doomed onto a plane she knew was going down.

"Go ahead and make it quick," I thought. I almost stretched my hands out ready to be nailed. Surprisingly, the women did nothing. The two, still clutching hands and smiling the biggest smiles I'd ever seen, skipped right past me and headed for the stairs. I was more shocked than relieved.

"We're going to watch the divers. Wanna come?" Anna asked. Were they going to murder me in the stairwell? I didn't want to go but I figured it was the least I could do in light of the circumstances.

We walked down the stairs, the two still holding hands. I lagged behind. I got so far back one time that Anna yelled, "Where are you, Oronde." Roxanne followed with, "Are you alright?" I could hear them giggling. When I finally got to the pool in the basement, the two were sitting, watching the divers warm up. I sat behind them. Roxanne turned around and said, "There you are." I gave her a smile and quickly took it back. What were they up to?

I wanted to walk over to the pool, jump in with my bag, coat, my macho pride and sink straight to the bottom. I didn't want to be Oronde. He'd been a bad boy. I had never been this kind of bad boy. I had hurt two people I thought I liked a lot. I still wasn't sure if I had done anything wrong but I felt awful nonetheless.

I waited around for thirty minutes watching bad high school divers splash into the water. The room was muggy, I was sweating, it was boring. I thought it was a fitting punishment so I stayed.

"Look at the piece on that guy," Anna said, giggling again. She was getting on my nerves. The two had been making comments about the diver's packages and hooting and hollering like groupies.

"I wouldn't mind that," Roxanne answered.

The three of us hadn't spoken since we got to the pool. Every few minutes Roxanne looked around to see if I was still there. "Why are you so quiet, Oronde?" she would ask. "Is anything wrong?"

"No."

"Good dive! Good dive!" Anna would yell and whistle.

"Nice body too," Roxanne followed. Anna continued whistling while Roxanne clapped her hands and laughed.

Idiot! I knew what was going on. How could I be so foolish? The women were getting back at me by striking at a man's most vulnerable spot. They were making me listen to them talk about other dude's packages. Those witches. They were not going to affect me. I wasn't like other men. I was smarter.

"He is gorgeous," Anna said. She was biting her left index finger.

That was it. No more. I left the two without even a goodbye.

"Bye, Oronde," I thought I heard Roxanne say. The water splashed, Anna clapped and whistled. I didn't have to look back to know it was her because she and Roxanne were the only two in the stands.

The next morning, I caught Roxanne outside Doc's English class.

"I'm sorry," I began.

"That's okay," she promised.

"I didn't mean to hurt you." Deep down I didn't feel what I was saying. Sorry was the appropriate sentiment but I didn't feel sorry.

"It's alright, Oronde. I'm not upset with you. I just don't want to hurt Anna and ruin our friendship."

"I really am sorry," I pleaded.

"I'm not upset about it, really, I'm not. You're still my friend. We're still friends, right. I know you're a nice guy." She gave me a hug and walked away.

I hadn't talked to Anna yet. She'd smile at me when we passed, like the smiles I gave my mother when I really wanted to say so much more. I stayed out of Anna's way after that. Roxanne was a bit more cordial. That was more her nature.

It was a Friday in late winter 1993. The snow had piled up outside. The heat and hot water in the apartment alternated coming on and off during the coldest stretch of our mid-winter holiday. I took on their personality, changing constantly, on and off depressive spells over making such a stupid mistake.

It wasn't that I'd lost two women. I could deal with that. What I couldn't deal with was failure. I had stepped outside my wall of inactive comfort in an effort to be like everyone else and it had blown up in my face. Big time.

All the times I promised not to make the same mistakes I overheard or saw other boys making; all the observational analysis I'd done to be a more perfect man; none of it worked. I made the same stupid mistakes.

Even news that I'd been selected to the New York Newsday All-Brooklyn High School Soccer Team and voted Co-Player of the Year by coaches and writers --a heady accomplishment because Brooklyn Tech was a team that never advanced in the playoffs. Even that bit of news failed to cheer me up.

I brooded over Anna and Roxanne. It was the winter of my discontent. I had taken my first exam in Life 101 and scored a solid F.

Fucked... by women.

...

XVI.

MORE WOMEN

C"heer up," my buddy Julius would tell me. Julius was a kid I'd met freshman year on the soccer team. Besides getting me a copy of Bob Marley's *Legend,* Julius introduced me to Jimi Hendrix, The Beatles, Louis Armstrong, Bing Crosby, Led Zeppelin and his favorite metal band, Biohazard. He convinced me to go trick-or-treating with him one Halloween and then onto a parade in Greenwich Village to see drag queens and other oddities. When we came back to his house, we snuck into his older brother's room and borrowed a few men's magazines. I took two un-opened Playboys and slept well in the guestroom that night with my brown package. Julius was cool.

"I can't stand seeing them together," I told Julius one day. We were watching Anna and her new boyfriend Jeremy kissing outside economics class... again.

Jeremy was junior class president, knew all five thousand Tech students by name, had conversations with teachers, played in a band, maintained a B average, was chairman of our pseudo Social Science Research company that sold the Late Night at Brooklyn Tech T-shirts. I think the guy even came up with the idea. He showed confidence, was articulate, funny. Even though I was convinced Jeremy did all his extracurricular activities to bolster his college resume and not because he cared about anything in particular, the boy had to be credited for getting involved. He packaged himself well.

Smiling face, neat appearance, approachable, blue Speedo. Jeremy was the diver Anna was screaming for in the pool that day.

"Why is she persisting with these games? And with that phony do-gooder."

There were times all through the winter and spring when I wanted to hold Jeremy by his scrawny neck and strangle him. I didn't like the guy but I had to respect the package. He was doer, I wasn't. He was a talker, I wasn't. He had my girl. I was still dealing with my package.

"You should find a girlfriend, O. I know a lot of chicks who want to talk to you."

"Right?" I mocked.

"No, really. This girl Candy in math class talks about you all the time. She told me once she would cream her panties if she ever got to run her fingers through your dreads. And…"

"And what?"

"And do you."

"Really. You shouldn't say things like that if you don't mean it, J."

"I swear to you, man. Why don't you call her yourself? I have her number somewhere." Julius reached into his bag, pulled out a little black notebook and gave me Candy's number. "Call her up."

"She digs the dreads, huh?"

"Yeah, it's too bad you cut 'em off. That was you, man. Why'd you do that anyway? That was like your trademark."

"I got tired. I didn't take care of them like I should. Too many people asking me about 'em. It was like I was growing the hair for other people and not for me." I grabbed my bag and walked out the room.

"You gonna grow them back?" Julius asked.

"I don't know, maybe. If dreads can wet some panties, maybe I should. You serious about this Candy, right?"

"Yes." Julius saw his girlfriend at the end of the hallway talking to a group of her friends. "I hope she doesn't see me," he mumbled. "Let's turn around." Too late. The girl saw us and started running, arms outstretched, gleaming.

"Oh, no," Julius said, forcing a grin and opening his arms to receive her. He told me he wanted to break up with the girl but didn't know how. I affectionately caller her The Bird because she chirped all day, flew from here to there and dropped shit all over the place. "She's getting on my nerves," Julius would cry.

"Hi, hon," The Bird chirped. She was just too excited. She perched all over Julius, pecking his cheeks. J looked miserable, I had to laugh.

"What's so funny?" she asked, grabbing Julius' arm and flying him to where her friends stood. J looked back at me hard, asking, with his eyes, not to get him in trouble. She almost caught him looking but he smiled. She smiled right back and pecked him again. I laughed again.

"Everyone, this is… What's your name?" she asked.

"Oronde."

"This is Julius' friend Oronde." I gave a peace sign with two fingers.

I never enjoyed meeting large groups, especially people who already knew each other. They would be laughing at punch lines before I heard the end of the joke because they'd been together so long they knew each other's unspoken language. Anyway, the Bird's friends weren't people who I normally hung out with in school. My group was either me and the soccer team, me and Julius --when he had the time-- me and Nigel or me and a cadre of "What's up" acquaintances (because "What's up" is just about all I ever said to them.)

The Bird's group appeared to be middle class kids from Uptown Manhattan who were rebelling against God-knows-what. They had rings and chains hanging from every orifice. One guy had a chain linking his nose and ear, spiked his hair and wore black lipstick. They all wore black shirts, black socks, black jackets with holes ripped in them and black doc martens with the hard soles.

"You're ready, hon," The Bird asked, still clutching Julius' arm.

"Whenever you are." His smile seemed to pain him. I almost lost it.

"Where are you going?" I asked J.

"To…" he began but The Bird chirped…

"I'm taking Julius to this acting workshop my friends and I are in. He loves it. Don't you, dear? It's really neat. You would like it. You should come too."

"We gotta go," one of the other girls said, grabbing The Bird and pulling her from Julius. "We gotta be there by 4:30." The two started running down the hallway followed by their friends. "C'mon, hon," the Bird screamed back.

"Please come with me, man," Julius pleaded. "I'm gonna die if I have to be with that girl another day."

"Why don't you just dump her?"

"It's not that easy," he said. "I like her. She's not bad at all. I just can't stand all the hugging and kissing. Too much."

"Dump her then."

"It's not that simple. We've been together seven months now."

"You gotta do what's best for you though."

"I know but..." He was silent. "When you're together for seven months, you'll see what I mean."

"When I find a woman I'll be happy."

"I'm telling you," Julius insisted, "Candy... She likes you."

"What does she look like?" I questioned, realizing I hadn't asked that before.

"She looks good."

"Good personality," I questioned.

"Yeah."

"Black or white?"

"Black... Maybe mixed."

"Tall? Short? Skinny? Healthy?" Julius thought for a second.

"Tall and skinny."

"Now J, you wouldn't mess with me, right? She's not ugly or anything, right."

"I swear on my mother."

"Alright then."

The Bird came running at Julius.

"Wow," he huffed.

"I miss you, hon. Please come to the studio," The Bird begged, putting her head on his shoulder. Her back was to me."

"Please come," Julius mouthed to me. I waited.

"So where is this thing?" I asked The Bird.

"You're coming. Great. It's in Midtown. C'mon, we gotta go." She grabbed my hand and J's and we walked towards the stairs.

When I got back to Brooklyn that night, I called Candy. She was surprised to hear from me and wanted to know where I got her number. I told her Julius gave it to me and I hoped she didn't mind.

Candy and I talked about school, movies, music and other pop culture stuff for about an hour before I made some light sexual innuendo. Candy caught on and continued with the suggestive edge. She mentioned owning a black teddy and told me how sexy she looked in it. I had to get under my covers after hearing that. By then Candy was taking the conversation to another level. All I did was listen and add a "Yeah" or "Wow!" I tried to remember any sexy line I heard in a movie or on TV but drew a blank. Thank God it didn't matter because Candy was controlling the show. My ear was getting hot. From the labored breathing, she was too.

Candy suggested I come over and see her teddy with my own eyes. "I'll make you lunch and we could stay at my house all day."

"Sure," I said. But the more I thought about the situation and how easy it was, I had to ask, "Have you invited any other fellas to have lunch with you before?"

"Yeah," she said, and was real blasé about it. That was it. My ear turned ice cold; my hands retreated above my covers. This Candy wasn't so sweet.

I wanted to have sex, but not with her. I never called the number again. Even after Julius pointed her out to me --and she was hot-- I didn't want a taste.

Life was decent in the spring of my junior year. I helped coach the women's soccer team for the second straight season. The girls lost most of their games again but they tried to do the things I taught. The team had more players than in my sophomore year and I was convinced it was all due to me. There were a couple cuties too.

Cynthia was a tough as nails Korean defender. She was new to the sport. She lacked the proper technique but made up for it with guts. Cynthia backed away from no one.

Teresa Malcolm was a Jamaican who managed the boy's team for two years. She was a tomboy, had some skill with the ball but little athleticism. She and I grew close though. Once, we even started making out in the back of Mr. Yanakis' car on the way home from a game. He had to look back and say, "Hey, you two. Hey! Hey!" Teresa and I never went out though, not even after she wrote me a letter confessing she loved me.

I liked many of the girls on the team but going out with any one of them would have made my job complicated. I liked the attention from and the possibility in all the women and I didn't feel like choosing just one. Anyway, I was accomplishing my original goal: I was comfortable around them. My plan had worked.

In one year, I had talked to, hugged, caressed, flirted with, befriended, was teacher to, coached, helped, was an admirer of more women than at any point in my life. But I never asked any of them out. Fear of failure always kept me watching their lives from the sidelines… That, and my mother.

My mother became the focal point of all my female anxieties. Every relationship I tried to have ended up with me keeping the girl at a comfortable distance, the same way I stayed away for my mother. If I wanted to have a decent relationship at any point in my life either I had to find a way to live with the reality of my mother's history, kill myself or kill her. On a Sunday night that February, one week after my seventeenth birthday, I had my chance for murder.

I had just returned from an indoor soccer tournament in Long Island where my team had won --the first team from NYC to win the tournament. I was feeling great. I had my trophy in hand, ready to share the news with my brothers. As soon as I entered the building, I could hear the commotion coming from the third floor. When I got to the second floor, I saw my mother scamper across the hall from 3R to 3F. I knew I was walking into a fight and raced up the last flight of stairs and into my room. Once there, I closed the door and tried to block out the noise.

"Don't ever hit my kids again," I heard Mudd tell my mother. My room stood next to the front door to 3F. The two were right outside it.

"They're my kids," my mother responded. I heard what sounded like a body pushed against the wall. My mother locked the door to 3F.

There was an unwritten rule in the House of Ash. Annie and I lived in 3F and were my mother's kids while Teri, Keri and Randi lived in 3R and were Mudd's. He never said much to us and my mother was asked to leave the other kids alone. She could cook, clean, buy clothes, etc., but the younger ones were not really her kids.

It seemed the fight that Sunday began because a letter from Teri's school stated she might be left back in the fifth grade. Mudd claimed it happened because my mother didn't pay enough attention to the kids. (Sad to say, I had to agree.) My mother counter claimed that Mudd promised he would check all the homework himself. From what I discerned, Mudd trusted no one else's judgment with the homework and, therefore, he was responsible for Teri's faltering grades.

From my room, I heard my mother in the kitchen fidgeting with the silverware. Soon she slammed the apartment door and I heard footsteps rushing down the stairs. Minutes passed before I heard the door open and slam shut. There was calm. My mother walked to the kitchen breathing heavily. I heard the silverware clanging again. Just then, she opened my bedroom door and stormed in. She was still breathing hard, eyes tempered with frustration.

"I'm sorry, Ronnie," she began, "I know you won't like what I did but I had to do something."

"What did you do?"

"I slashed his tires and broke the antennae. I want him to come over here and hit me so I can call the police and get this thing over with… I know you hate me."

"I don't hate you," I replied, not believing what was coming out of my mouth. Then there was silence as my mother stood in the middle of my doorway. I was at the foot of my bed with my head in my hands looking at the floor. I could still hear her panting. I also heard Mudd walking across the hallway. He banged on the apartment door. When no one opened it, he kicked it open. I stood up, bracing for whatever would happen next.

During my high school years, my mother and Mudd's confrontations had subsided from physical combats to verbal pitches. Mudd wasn't stupid. He knew I wouldn't let him strike my mother in front of me. I didn't like her, but I was getting bigger. There's just so much a growing boy can take. Mudd was, however, still the Machiavellian schemer so when he stood directly behind my mother and said to her, "What do you think you're doing?," he said it calm and in total control.

"They're my kids," my mother replied. She was trying to insight something. "When's the last time you bought clothes for them, huh?"

Mudd looked at my mother. "Go discipline your kids in Manhattan. Go fuck their father too."

"He's probably better than you, you wretch," my mother scorned and pushed him out of the way. I expected Mudd to do something then but he didn't. Instead, he walked over to Grandma and started talking to her in a calm voice as if he was making peace. He kept repeating the phrase, "We're in this together." He was working her good, talking loud enough for me to hear.

"That woman ain't no mudda. She's never here. I'm the one who checks the kid's homework. I cook food for suppa. I shouldn't have to do that. That's her job. But I'm the only parent in this place."

"I bring my kids into the world and you not gonna take my kids from me, no goddamn way," my mother replied.

Mudd looked into my room. He knew how I felt about my mother and thought he could work me over.

"If you only know wha dis woman was like back home," he began talking directly to me. "She crazy. Why you tink your farda left? She drive him out. She do dis to all her men. Go ax your farda? Ax anybody from home." He sucked his teeth and left the apartment.

My mother got up and charged at Mudd but I held her back. It was our first hug in years. When Mudd closed his door, I stood next to mine fighting a losing battle with my emotions. A few moments passed.

"I'm sick of this, "I yelled." My mother waited.

"It's about time you said it," she answered as she walked over to the living room sofa she slept on at night.

I paced back and forth, grabbed my head, squeezed my skull and let out a roaring, "**AAAAAHHHHHH!**"

"I'm sick of all this shit," I yelled. "I'm sick of the fights. I'm sick of you two fucking with my life. I'm Sick! Sick! Sick! of all of you." I was pulling at my hair, swinging my arms, punching the air around me. I stopped pacing and gazed out the open door towards 3R, wishing Mudd would walk my way. I was ready to fight him but he didn't come back. There was silence in the building.

I went to the sofa and sat down next to my mother. She said, "Good... Good... You think I ain't sick either? You think I ain't sick of that asshole? You think I ain't sick of working all day to come home to this? You think I ain't sick of my children not talking to me. You hate me. Go on, say it." With that, my mother went over the kitchen sink, brought back a dirty steak knife and handed it to me. "Go ahead. Kill me. Send me to hell. I know you want to."

I clutched the knife handle in my right hand. This was it. I had dreamt of this moment when I was younger. I could be rid of her once and for all. I looked at the knife, looked around. It was just she and I. Annie had grabbed her jacket and stormed out the apartment as soon as I got in. Grandma was in her room quiet. There would be no witnesses. I saw the trial. I'd plea temporary insanity. The jury would go easy on me because I was young, smart and had been psychologically traumatized. I'd be sent to Bellevue psychiatric hospital for the remainder of my days. At least there I'd have doctors and drugs to help heal the scars.

I gripped the knife hard, looked up at my mother. For the first time, I saw tears in her eyes. I stared at the water falling off her face. My mother put her hands to her cheeks to wipe the tears away. She was human. I had never bothered to acknowledge that.

My mother always put up a tough exterior. I could not recall ever hugging, kissing or hearing an "I love you," from her. To me, she wasn't a woman. She was some thing I called *Ma*. If I ever needed spending money for a soccer tournament or hotel room; if I needed a shirt or a pair of pants; if I needed something for school, *Ma* got it for me. That was her way of being tender --female --human-- a mother.

Growing up, I should have used her guilt to my advantage and asked for more stuff but that would have meant manipulating her, actually having conversations with her, actually going back and forth with her. I wasn't ready for that.

In the tracks of my mother's tears, I finally felt something of her pain. She was dealing with the tension in the apartment too. So was Annie, so was Grandma. Everybody was probably as angry about his or her life as I was with mine. I was overcome with guilt for being so ignorant for so long.

"I don't hate you," I finally stammered, dropping the knife to the floor. "I'm just sick of watching you do this."

"It's not just me," she began.

"I know that," I interrupted, "but you can stop. You didn't have to slash tires to make a point. That just makes things worse. You don't believe this but I don't hate you. I'm just afraid you don't know what you're doing. You need help. Both of you need help or else your three other kids will end up hating you as much as you think I hate you. And the cycle will keep going."

I was done. In five minutes years of pent up emotion was released. The volcano inside me felt dormant, the roaring river calmed. I walked back to my room, closed the front door leading to Mudd's apartment and left my room door open to watch my mother sob.

The next day I began writing her a letter. In it I reiterated that I didn't hate her, that I forgave her for the instability in my life now that I thought about the roots of her problems. I told her that it must have been hard to watch her mother, older brothers and sisters leave St. Vincent when she was still a teenager; that it must have been a task to raise herself on an island with little security or opportunity for women. I told her that I understood Mudd was a bastard and that her father was probably a bastard too. I hoped she saw the connection.

I told my mother that I liked that she stood up for herself but not the way she did it; that I saw everything in the house even though it looked like I didn't give a damn; told her to build bridges with the younger kids through hugs, kisses, time and talk rather than through clothes, shoes and money. I told my mother that the only memory of her, Annie, my father and me together was a night in Barbados when Annie and I left the house we were staying in, climbed onto some rocks and cried because she and my father were fighting. I told her that wasn't good.

I told her the family dynamics I saw in the house, the three generations of women and their diverging beliefs, Mudd's Machiavellian maneuvers, the flawed information cycle filtering half-truths to her. Finally, I asked my mother to seek professional help for herself and for Annie, individually and together. I told her she wouldn't get therapy from me because I was still dealing with her. I asked that she give me time and space to figure out my next move.

Before I gave my mother the letter, I showed it to Dr. Weinberger. I wanted to find out if, as a woman, Doc thought the words were too harsh. Doc thought the letter was heart felt and recommended I read the novel *The Effects of Gamma Rays on Man-in-the-Moon Marigolds* by Paul Zindel. I never did. I gave the letter to my mother two days later. She wrote a note back to me soon after:

"Oronde,

I'm very sorry for all the embarrassment that I have caused you. These trials that I am going through are part of most women's lives. However, soon and very   soon it will be all over and I hope when this is done, you will forgive me and hate me a little less than you do now. I know at your age it is very trying and it's a lot of pressure for you to take. Just relax and remember who you are. Be yourself. I am very proud of your achievements and would like to say, "That's my son." Again, forgive me and just be cool... I hope your week will be a very productive one."

Sometime later that week, I cut off all my dreads and went completely bald.

I'm sure there was a lot more behind coming clean that particular week. The fight, the letter to my mother, the confrontation with Anna and Roxanne, Anna and Jeremy; something big was going on inside me. Something big had been going on for a while.

I remember challenging my sister Annie a few days later. I'd been waiting for over an hour for her to get off the phone. I was expecting a call from Myrna, a girl I'd met recently. We were going to have pizza some time soon. I was anxious and feared I'd miss my chance, just like Anna and the snowstorm. I walked up to the phone extension cord, grabbed the receiver from Annie's ear and hung up the phone.

"Are you crazy?" she screamed.

"I'm tired of waiting for you. That's the third call in the last hour."

"Just because you don't have friends..." she began, reaching out to grab the phone base and receiver from my hand. I put my body between her and the phone, extending it out with both hands.

"Give me the phone!" she exclaimed. Annie came at me again but I pushed my butt into her stomach and walked out her door. She jumped onto my back and began choking me.

"Give you the phone or what?" I asked.

"Or... Give me the phone you bitch. I swear I'll..."

"You'll what? Send one of your hoodlum friends after me?"

Although they never stayed around the apartment, I knew my sister was hanging with the neighborhood thugs. Sometimes, guys would knock on the door asking for her. Most would be wearing baggy clothes, braids and gold caps on their teeth. They looked like the worst young, black male stereotypes.

"I'll kick your ass myself, " Annie finished. With that, she got off my back and punched me in the thigh. It didn't hurt much. I clutched the phone tighter and continued walking to my room. I made one further step when Annie called, "Yeah, run you little faggot." I stopped. My sister had my attention.

I let Annie kick and punch me but calling me a "faggot" was stepping out of line. I turned around, put the phone on the ground and said, "You call me a faggot... You...you're a complete waste. What do you do with your life? Nothing. You don't go to school. You don't work. You just sit here and watch TV all day. Where's that gonna take you?"

"At least I have a life," Annie replied. "You just sit in your room and jerk off probably."

"Watch your mouth," I told her. I made a fist with my right hand and brought it close to her face.

"Go ahead," she said. "Go ahead and hit me. It's not like I haven't seen that before in this house." Annie started balling.

It took me a second but I knew exactly where the tears were coming from. It was the same place my tears flowed when I was alone in my room. I could only think of one thing to do so I opened both arms and threw them around my sister, pulling her body into mine. She put her head on my shoulders and wept.

"I'm not smart like you," she sobbed. My sister began heaving her words out. "I'm not... as... as strong as you. I don't... want... to do this anymore."

"I'm sorry, Annie," I offered in comfort. "I didn't mean all that stuff before. I was just mad." My sister continued crying softly on my shoulders.

What had happened to those days in St. Vincent? Annie and I used to be so close people would come around the house and ask my mother, "Where's Annie-n-Ronnie?" or say, "There goes Annie-n-Ronnie." No one said my name without mentioning hers. Back then we were one person. In Brooklyn we had grown up and grown apart under the same roof.

"I'm sorry Annie."

Two days later, I stayed home from school to clear my mind and wrote the following:

"2-25-93

"Went to the library and wrote for 3 hours today. The process brought out memories of my days on the island hanging out with my godfathers Scorpee, Funk, Red Eye, Trap, Ten Cents, my father and all the other rastas, going to Mustique, spending my days running errands and my   nights in the bunk house with all the other laborers; about watching westerns at the cinema that converted to a church on Sunday mornings; about going to Macaroni Beach, playing cricket, throwing up on the boat ride from Kingstown or running from those tiny lizards that scampered across the lawn in the villas.

As I am writing this now, more pictures are coming into my head. I never wanted to deal with my mother. I never answered when she talked about St. Vincent. I suppressed all the people I knew. It wasn't very healthy. I'm just glad to be making progress and recalling all my years. However the picture is just scenery. I see myself but I don't know if I'm saying anything. Was I always introverted and shy? Did I ask questions? Who was I? Who am I?

… Now, this week, my memories have been flowing. Intellectually, coming to terms with my mother has opened a pathway for a lot of stagnant and dying life… I want to go home and see my godfathers. I want to go to Mustique and see if any of the other guys are there.

At this very moment, my memories are calling me home."

…

XVII.

NATIONAL ANTHEM

"St. Vincent! Land so beautiful,

With joyful hearts we pledge to thee,

Our loyalty and love, and vow, to keep you ever free…"

A few nights after the big fight, Annie and I called our father in St. Vincent. We hadn't spoken to him in years. He wrote letters, especially around birthdays and Christmas, even sending a few dollars. It's not that my father forgot about us. I just never felt compelled to write back. I still could not forgive him for exposing me to marijuana at such a young age. I'm sure the little boy inside me also blamed him for not being around when I needed him the most in America. But that little boy had been dying for some time. The new Oronde was ready to forgive. As a high school student, there was even something cool about having a father who let me smoke weed with him. Times changed.

My three-minute talk with my father unleashed a lot of thoughts about the island. For days after, I'd visualize things I hadn't seen in my head since I left in 1985. I got a big part of my life back after that phone call. I remembered… I remembered…

Barrouallie was my home. It was not a valley or a village or a bay. Barrouallie was one of the six major towns in St. Vincent. I lived three blocks from the sea. Everybody lived next to the sea. Even if you lived under the hills, you lived next to the sea. The sea was a playground, a fish market, the office. The sea was life.

Most of the old men in town were fishermen. My dad's father was a whaler. Every morning these men would walk down to the sea and push their handcrafted, brightly painted boats off the sand and into the water. Some boats had nets in them to snare all kinds of fish. Some boats carried the whale and porpoise hunters. Those were the boats I wanted to be on at least once before I died. Even though the whalers reeked of blackfish oil and I often saw them stone drunk when they weren't harpooning, I secretly thought they were amazing. Everyday, the old men stared death in the face; no sonar or elaborate harpoon gun; just man vs. whale. And everyday, the old men came back victorious.

Some days, I saw the whalers hauling in two or three huge blackfish off the boats and watched women cut the bellies open right on the beach. Barrouallie was the blackfish capital of St. Vincent. Stories were told and songs written about our famous, fearless Barrouallie whalers. Even the island's most famous singer, Alston Cyrus Beckett, wrote a song about us.

"Barrouallie, I thank you,

For all the things you have done for me

You've given us, so much blackfish oil

To cure the sickness of every boy and girl

Barrouallie I thank you..."

My family lived on the main road in a two-story, cement house that was under construction. It used to be two full stories with four or five rooms, but that was before I was born. Back then, the house was teal green and made of wood like everybody else's. There was an aura about my house. Even as it was being torn apart and re-assembled during my childhood, after the upstairs was exposed with no windows or doors yet, even without the green paint I had seen only in pictures, my house was still a hub for town social activity. The main attractions --my aunts and uncles-- were gone, but the theater I called home was still open to the public when I was growing up.

Anybody who wanted to be known in Barrouallie hung out at my house. My uncles Rudy, Frankie and Kenneth were the town's soccer stars in the early 1970s. My father and his friends would amaze me with what seemed like tall-tales about my uncles' playing abilities.

"They would be on the national team, if there wasn't so much politics," someone would tell me. "Your uncle Kenneth was the toughest defender I ever seen."

I didn't know. I had never seen my uncle play but that didn't stop the stories.

If there wasn't a tale about my uncles, people talked about my aunts. Auntie Sonja and Auntie Elma went into teaching as soon as they left secondary school around age sixteen or seventeen, and, from what I'd heard, must've taught everyone in Barrouallie. But I had never seen them either.

What I did see were a lot of people. People came by the house to talk to my mother, swap gossip, ask for money or to simply get ice or drink a cup of cold water. If any Ash family was passing through, they stopped by the house. The only person who never came by the house was my father. He and my mother split when I was five and didn't speak at all. My father lived up the road at the back of his family's house. I would go and see him just about every afternoon. We did everything together. He was in his twenties and full of energy. I tried to use up as much of it as possible.

My father took me to the mountains to see the fields where he grew whatever he needed to eat or to the beach to play soccer. When I was seven, he enrolled me in a soccer clinic in Kingstown, the capital. If he couldn't take me on Saturday mornings, my father made sure I got on the taxi-van at 8 AM and had lunch money. He wanted me to be the best soccer player on the island.

People have since told me that my father would take me to the Barrouallie soccer field or to the beach and have me play with the older boys so I could get better, faster. In fact, at the soccer clinic, I was playing with eleven and twelve year olds when I was six or seven, and holding my own, according to him.

I do remember feeling safe around my father. The taxi-van rides to Kingstown were full of peril to my young eyes. At some points, the road was no wider than one and a half lanes of an American highway and the vans would careen around mountain bends that overlooked the sea or a coconut field two hundred or more feet below, unprotected by guard rails. If a van were to lose control and sit dangling off a cliff, I was sure my father would save us both.

My father was a mellow, spiritual man. He built a bench out of bamboo at the top of a hill outside his house and we would sit and watch the sun set on Barrouallie. He read the Bible everyday and knew more about it than the pastors I listened to on Sunday mornings. The only difference was that he called God, "Jah". I asked him why and he quickly pointed to a passage in Psalms. Anyway, he was a Rasta and all of his Rasta friends called God, "Jah" as well.

"Where did Jah come from?" I remember asking one day as we watched the sun go down.

"He's just dere. He made all and is all," my father replied.

"But who made him?" I persisted.

"Nobody! Jah live. He is everything and everywhere."

"But somebody had to make Him"

"He just is, son!" My father was getting frustrated. That's probably why he got me a black, leather-bound King James Bible as one of my first birthday gifts.

I was into religion then. All the kids in Barrouallie were. Our parents didn't go to church unless they were baptized or it was Easter Sunday. Everyone else under eighteen who wasn't a Rasta went to church. There were many churches to choose from. Barrouallie had a Pentecostal Church, Seventh-Day Adventists, Baptists, Jehovah's Witness, Methodists, Presbyterians, Anglicans and other small denominations that met in little rooms scattered all over town.

By far, the Anglican Church had the largest and most powerful congregation. A majority of the well-to-do people in town were Anglicans. Since it was the Church of England, and the island was under British rule until 1979, Anglicanism was island religion.

In Barrouallie, the Ash name was respected enough for me to feel proud to carry it. My mother's father owned a shop in town that was a staple of the community for years. It had all the latest toys from abroad, carried fabrics to make school uniforms, as well as food and baking needs. When I was born, we didn't have anything to do with the shop. By then it belonged to my grandfather's second or third wife --he and Grandma had parted ways. It did carry the Ash name though.

Back home, I had a lot of advantages other kids in town didn't. My mother was a schoolteacher and unless there was a strike, we had money. Mudd had his own taxi-van he drove to and from Kingstown all day so he almost always had money. My family wasn't wealthy by any means. Like everyone else, we still had to walk outside at night and go to the bathroom in a hole in the ground covered by galvanize steel, still had to worry about our house during hurricane season. I remember my mother having to ask neighbors for two or three fish to feed us some nights. We'd offer the same to them so it was no big deal.

All my neighbors were like family. The women had watched me grow up, changed my diapers or fed me at some point. I knew all their kids, played cricket, soccer or hide and seek with them. Some kids came from families like mine, others from families that couldn't afford food, shoes or clothes for them. My family had to feed my friends sometimes or give away any extra shirt or pants that no longer fit me, Annie or Teri. That's the way things were back home. There was a sense of a communal family. We looked out for each other's welfare.

If some lady heard me say something awful, she told my mother or told somebody and the news always got back home. There was not much a kid could get away with in town. Barrouallie was our playground but it was also our prison.

Any talk of escape always included America. I remember seeing a kid from up the road throw a laced-up, brown coconut one day.

"What's that?" I asked.

"It's a football," he answered.

"Why aren't you kicking it?" I followed.

"It's an American football." That's all I needed to hear to want to throw the brown coconut or kick it or do whatever you did with an American football.

My aunts and uncles had left St. Vincent for Canada and America before I was born. They were my connection to The Promised Land. After Annie and I came back from three months in Canada in March 1984 --Ma wanted us both to see snow-- I was the man for a while. I brought back ten gold-plated necklaces and wore them around me neck trying to look like Mr. T. Until the gold began to rust, I was the man.

One month after my return, the gold had washed off the chains and my friends and I were back to the trash heaps behind the local shops scouring for cigarette packs. We didn't smoke. We were after the silver --or please, God-- the gold foil lining the boxes. We would fold the shiny wrappers to make rings around our fingers, acting like we were Mr. T. (I pity the fool who didn't think we were cool, because we were.)

"We" were Jack, Jerry, Royston, Bravest, Roland, Deslan, me and a few other kids around the way. The guys all lived across the street from me and had parents who worked for the government as policemen, nurses or teachers --the only paying alternatives to fisherman, farmer, or taxi van driver. Jack's family also owned a shop in their front yard. We all had family in America. We were all special.

Besides scavenging for pretend gold and silver in dumpsites, my friends and I played soccer or cut down dried coconut branches and made bats to play cricket. At night, we sat in Jack's yard and talked, had races along the street, told *jumbee* stories or tales of Anansi the spider.

My neighbor Jerry was my best friend and big brother. He was four years older than me and lived next door. Actually, it wasn't even next door. There was no division between our yards. My yard ended and his began. When my mother and Mudd went to see calypso shows in Kingstown, Jerry stayed with Annie and me in the house. He protected me at the Barrouallie middle school. I cried easily then. If he could, Jerry made sure I didn't have to.

Jerry had a few goats he took to pasture in the hills each morning. Sometimes he would bring me along. After his family gave me a kid to look after --because I wanted to be like Jerry-- we were shepherd brothers.

When we found a good grazing spot and staked the ropes around the goat's neck to the ground, Jerry and I would walk down the hills to the Anglican Church. He was an alter boy there. I couldn't wait to be an alter boy. They were trusted members of the community, respected by us younger kids. Alter boys got to serve and drink the wine at communion and ate the waif. They also got women.

Jerry knew a lot of women. I figured they saw him in the spotlight every Sunday morning in his white robe and red sash. The girls loved that.

Jerry was also responsible for ringing the church bell. It was a big, iron bell like the Liberty Bell that hung about ten feet in the air, supported by a metal frame. Jerry rang the bell at six in the morning, at twelve o'clock on his way home to lunch and again at six at night. He rang the bell to call the holy to church on Sunday, rang it on special holidays and for weeknight prayer service.

The ringing of the bell was the number one reason I envied Jerry. Sometimes he'd let me do the duty.

Bong! Bong! Bong! Pause. Bong! Bong! Bong! He repeated the set of three bongs depending on the time of day. If it was 6 o'clock, the town heard six sets of three. The whole town heard the bell. That's how a lot of people got up in the morning. Before I had a goat, that's how I got up.

If the roosters crowing in the neighborhood didn't wake me, or Rupert's yelling (Rupert's family made sticks of chocolate from their home grown cocoa and sold them in the early mornings so people would have chocolate for tea. "Get you chocolate! It's chocolate time. It's chocolate time. Get your chocolate!" he would yell.) If Rupert's yelling didn't do it, Jerry's bell ringing did.

The church bell got my mother up and my day started. Ma made breakfast and got us ready for school. That meant ironing school uniforms if they hadn't been pressed the night before and forcing a comb through my hair, usually with me in tears. We ate together and listened to Radio Antilles for the morning stories --radio soap operas-- since no one had a TV.

I got to watch TV in the summer when my godfather Scorpee took me with him to Mustique. (Mustique is a private island off the coast of St. Vincent where world famous actors and singers have private villas.) Scorpee did the yard work, electrical work and regular maintenance in a villa called Cactus Hill. He would let me help him clean the pools, paint the house, send me to pick up supplies or relay messages to his friends at the other villas.

I looked forward to spending a week or two in Mustique each summer. The rich American who owned Cactus Hill built a little stream that flowed through his garden when Scorpee turned a switch. The American was never on the island when I visited but the place was always kept tidy and stocked with food.

Scorpee would buy groceries in Kingstown before we boarded the boat for Mustique. I'd see the cereals, cheese, fruits and biscuits and be tempted to eat the assorted goodies on the boat. Usually, the boat ride to Mustique, with the smell of diesel and the constant rocking made me forget about food. Instead, I concentrated on not upchucking all over the deck.

Even though Scorpee had a child of his own, I was treated like his son. Most of the older men I knew treated me like their son. That meant I had ten to fifteen fathers. It was great. Someone would pass by my house, scoop me up and take me to the mountains, the sea, the store, to watch the national soccer or cricket team play a match. My mother didn't mind and my father wasn't jealous because all the guys were his childhood friends. As long as I was enjoying myself, all was well. And I was usually having a ball.

Going to Mustique in the summer and playing in carnival were the two main distractions in my year. But even Barrouallie, with its postcard vista and communal feel, still had to deal with the island's poverty the rest of the year. The town was made up of poor people. The whole of St. Vincent was poor people. Unfortunately, poor people the world over seem to think the solution to poverty is to have more kids.

There were kids all over town, some with tattered, dirty rags on, their genitals out in full view, flies circling the living carcasses. Just about every boy I knew lived with his mother, siblings and extended family. Fathers didn't stick around to raise kids with their girlfriends. Fatherhood meant sending a few dollars every now and again to the mom or children.

If they didn't know someone in government, smart kids who just completed secondary school had a hard time earning a living wage. A lot of the young men like Scorpee went offshore to Mustique, Bequia or other islands in the Grenadines that catered to the tourist trade. They built houses, laid pipe, maintained the villas.

My first two summers on Mustique, Scorpee and I lived in a warehouse with bunks stacked three or four high. The place was smelly and loud. No one could be trusted. In truth, it was slave quarters. When he got a bed at Cactus Hill in a room that housed pool equipment, I was happy even if we shared that room with another male worker.

By American standards, the pay in Mustique was lousy and when you bought food, toothpaste and other necessities at the general store, you were giving the money back to the fat cats who owned the place. Needless to say, I saw a lot of rum and whiskey consumed in Mustique. I saw a lot of hard drinking in Barrouallie too.

When I went to watch the afternoon soccer games with my father, I saw men drinking. There was a rum shop five yards from every corner flag, one behind each goal and one at the midfield line on either side of the field. Rum made the men forget that they were men. Whiskey made them forget they had three or four kids by three or four different women and had to support all of them on what amounted to slave wages.

If young men didn't find labor in Mustique, they worked as mechanics, electricians, plumbers, welders, bricklayers and a host of other odd jobs. When the government was fixing a road or adding onto the primary school in town, people got *wuk*. Often though, there was scarcely wuk to be had.

So if you were young, you fished, drove a taxi van or found a plot of land in the mountains that your grandfather used to work before arthritis and old age got him. If your family didn't have land, maybe a friend had a plot you could help with. If not, you hung around or hunted. I saw young men disappear into the bush at night with a machete and a flashlight, unafraid of the devils that stalked the dark. The men reappeared the next morning selling iguana meat or meat from a *manicou* --a type of opossum.

Barrouallie nights scared me. There were but so many street lamps. Luckily, I lived on the main road, so there was a light every hundred yards. That was enough to keep me from falling into the gutters on the roadside or running into stones and tree stumps when we had relay races. The lights weren't enough to allay all my fears though. Dead spirits were everywhere. An *obeah* --black magic-- woman up the road was still practicing her arts. Somebody told me she was related to my father so she was my blood too. The woman supposedly put a curse on my friend Bravest's grandmother, Deeka.

As the story goes, dirt from a grave was sprinkled at the bottom of Deeka's steps. When Deeka went outside barefoot one morning, she stepped on the dirt and was cursed. Her right foot soon had boils and lesions all over it. Little marbles of puss bubbled up when Deeka walked. We all thought it disgusting and wondered why Deeka had never just chopped the foot off instead of walking around on her toes, with flies buzzing around her foot.

Deeka was a good woman though. She spent her mornings in the town's river washing her family's clothes, my family's clothes as well as clothes from the other families in the neighborhood. Deeka would stand in the water and grind the soiled garments against a washboard or beat them against the rocks. She was a good washer and got paid enough to keep doing it the whole time I was home.

When the white tourists stopped to take pictures of the women in the river taking care of their business, Deeka was the first to pose. Except for the times Bravest and his aunts did something wrong, Deeka looked happy. It was funny watching her hobbling on one leg trying to chase after the kids.

Deeka's longtime boyfriend Kaya was a tall, jet-black man with cheekbones that stuck out like tusks on a boar. The few times I saw him sober, he was on his way to the rum shop or hanging outside one. Kaya occasionally went *seining* --fishing-- with the older men or cultivated land in the mountains. But most of the time, he drank.

I'd see Kaya staggering up and down Main Street or Middle Street or Bay Street. I suppose he staggered in and out of Three Acres --the area behind my house-- in Paywood --where the Barrouallie Secondary School was-- up Glebe Hill, around to Kearton Hill and down into the next valley. For all his drinking and bumping into cars and almost falling into gutters, Kaya was an integral part of the Barrouallie community.

When sober or with a cigarette in one hand, Kaya was the best barber in town. He gave all my friends our haircuts when our mothers thought we needed to look respectable. There was the occasional nick and blood on the scissors --I never saw and electric shear until I came to America-- from jiggling hands, but we wore the scars with pride for having made it through the ordeal. Anyway, the haircut was usually good and that was the important thing.

Kaya was also the best *nointer* in town. Whenever a soccer player sprained his ankle, the guy came to Kaya. The injured boy would bring his own grease or Vaseline or whatever oil he had or Kaya would supply his own. With cigarette in the side of his mouth, Kaya would massage the blood-engorged muscle or joint. In those days, a nointing was entertainment for us kids.

I guess nobody knew it was best to ice a swollen ankle immediately after injury to reduce the swelling. Even if somebody knew, ice was scarce. Some people put pans of water in their freezer and made a small business selling ice. My mother did that at one time but mostly kept extra ice pans to give away in whole blocks or broken up with an ice pick.

Kaya would press and rub the blood-engorged ankle with the care and precision of the finest Swedish masseur. Anyone within earshot of the wailing and screaming would gather around and watch the nointed panting and shrieking. Others would climb a nearby tree or stand on boulders trying to get the best view. When it was all done and the young soccer player or whoever wiped his eyes and wrapped his foot in an ace bandage, everyone disappeared back to their life.

Don't get me wrong, Barrouallie was not a town of masochists. Nointing was how we knew to care for a sprained ankle or swollen toe. And it worked. I would see young men back playing soccer at the park two or three days after their ankle was the size and color of a ripened mango.

Kaya nointed my ankle once. I wanted to kill him while he was doing it, but I was walking without a limp the next day. The man was good. He seemed human then and almost made me forget how scary he was at carnival time.

Carnival was Kaya's excuse to drink himself silly. It was St. Vincent's excuse for those two weeks in July. The rum flowed, the calypso music and sexy dancing soared in the discos. Mothers and boyfriends sent their kids to their grandparents as they went to Kingstown to drink and grind on top of, to the side of, or behind anybody who was willing to have sex with their clothes on.

Carnival meant Kaya scaring the life out of us kids. He'd ground coal, mix it with water and smear the black residue over his already nightshade complexion. Kaya would put on a skirt made of straw that went down past his knees. He carried a stick cut from a thin branch of a tamarind tree. The stick was sharpened at the ends and had little branches coming off the main stem like the devil's trident. On his head, Kaya wore two goat's horns painted red.

Freddie Kruger and Michael Myers were cabbage patch dolls compared to what Kaya looked like to me.

Once the costume was on, Kaya would parade all around Barrouallie, stepping and jigging from one side of the road to the other. Crowds of young people would gather behind him building a massive throng in no time. They'd shout, dance, pick up cans, bottles, rocks or sticks by the side of the road and beat them in rhythm to Kaya's movements. This went on for two or three hours or until Kaya got tired and went to the sea to wash off the black paint. He was over fifty years old. He couldn't last too long.

For me, two hours was long enough. I usually hid under my bed when I heard the noise or saw the crowd approaching my house. Kaya did catch me once though.

I was playing marbles with Bravest. Kaya had just finished putting on his costume and paint. There was no crowd around him yet. He came over to where I was and stood in the circle with the marbles. I looked up and saw him staring down at me. He looked huge.

Kaya's white eyes were the only part of his body not blackened with coal, so those orbs gripped me. My knees began to tremble, my lips quivered, my head twitched from side to side. All the marbles fell from my hand. I wanted to scream and run but I couldn't move my feet and my voice wasn't working. Soon, tears rolled down my face. When he saw my tears, Kaya turned and walked away. He never said a word. He must have felt sorry for me. I ran across the street to my house and cried. I was five or six years old.

I didn't get over my fear of Kaya until I was eight. My cousin Wrenzo, who was always in the mob behind the devil, talked me into joining him.

"I hear he stuck somebody in the eyes with his stick," I told Wrenzo.

"Dat never happen. Not'n gonna happen," Wrenzo promised.

Wrenzo and I stood ten yards behind Kaya as he danced through town. Every time Kaya turned around, I sprinted to the side of the road, but the devil never came back more than five or six yards and no one was mauled in the eye. I wasn't scared after that.

Kaya and carnival was time to let off the tension in Barrouallie. If the fish weren't biting or the crops didn't grow, carnival made the people forget those worries. It spoke to the very nature of the spirit's need to let loose and trust in better days.

With the poverty and hunger and sickness and death on the island, Vincentians needed something to remind us of the inherent joy in living --even if it was just two weeks. No wonder it's the poorer parts of the globe where you see the bigger, wilder carnival celebrations. For those brief days, the poor get to feel a happiness their daily grind often forbids them to see.

Too bad carnival was just two weeks. After that, I returned to the major problem of my reality: my mother and her boyfriend Mudd.

Mudd was a decent enough guy back then. He took me to a soccer match vs. Grenada once. He never hit me, never yelled at or bothered me directly. I'm sure he knew my father would beat him up if he touched Annie or me. The guy wasn't bad; he was just an asshole.

My mother was who she was then, young and fiercely independent. She and my father split because his Rastafarian beliefs asked for a homemaker, child-bearer wife right out of the Old Testament. My father called his new girlfriends his *daughters*, so it was obvious he didn't see women as equals. Like most men on the island, he was a chauvinist.

After her mother and other siblings left St. Vincent, it was just my mother. She relied on relatives, family friends and her teacher's salary to raise her two kids. When my father left, her job was that much harder. Ma struggled and scrimped and went without so Annie and I could have. She had maintained the family house and earned respect in a place where women didn't get much --even though it was the women who really ruled Barrouallie.

Dealing with Mudd was a job all its own. My mother did the cooking and cleaning, but she never sat quiet and took crap beyond normal human levels. Mudd probably didn't know what he was getting himself into when he met her.

They liked each other once. It seemed that way sometimes. We would all get in Mudd's taxi-van and go to Mt. Wynn Beach for a picnic or to the rialto in Kingstown to watch a movie. I saw the break dance film *Beat Street* at that rialto. "Your Auntie Sonja works for that hospital in the Bronx," Ma said in the middle of the film. "We'll see that soon."

Mudd bought popcorn and made sure we got good seats in the balcony. The brakes on his van weren't working well that day, so sometimes, on our way back to Barrouallie, he had to stop the van, blare the horn and ease around a blind curve. The guy didn't want to kill us. That counted for something.

When Mudd and Ma did fight I rarely saw fists thrown. There were probably punches but I missed a lot of the action because I usually ran next door to Jerry or cried with Annie. Sometimes, Jerry's mom or grandmother or aunt or anybody would try to restrain the two. Ma would grab a knife and Mudd would do the same. Thank God there was never bloodshed, at least none that I saw.

Neighbors and sightseers young and old would gather on the road to watch the spectacle. Fights were entertainment in Barrouallie, just like the town drunk who gave away money.

The drunk didn't have any real money. He would stagger all over Main Street, stop traffic or stand in front of somebody's house and say, "Mrs. Daniels, I give you 8,764,256 dollars." Mrs. Daniels would thank the drunk; he would wave, smile and bow. Us kids would walk up to the guy and wait for our share of his millions.

"How much do I get?" someone would ask.

"I give you 5,836,920."

We'd say "Thank you," and return to our own games. No blood was shed, no disrespect felt or intended. Getting money from the drunk was an experience we each wanted to take part in.

When the neighbors came by the house to watch my mother and Mudd fight, the two became the town drunks providing a spectacle. I was embarrassed. The two squeezed out every bit of feeling I built up for them.

With each fight, my heart shrank tighter and tighter and the spaces for them got smaller and smaller. How could they not care? They were in their mid twenties, had both graduated from secondary school. Where was their sense? They pushed me away. That's probably why I spent so much time at my father's house. I'd take Annie and we'd sleep there and return home in the morning. My father was a calming third eye in the storm going on down the road.

I wished my father was at the airport in Barbados in August 1985 when Annie and I got on the 747 for America. He didn't have enough money for the flight. We said our goodbyes the night before.

I didn't cry walking up the airplane steps in Barbados. My mother didn't cry either. Annie and I had traveled alone before when we went to Canada two years earlier. We knew the drill.

The stewardess would take us both to our seats and buckle us in. When we got to Newark Airport in America, the stewardess would walk us out the jet way leading from the airplane and some relative would be there ready to take us someplace. The same thing happened when we arrived in Toronto in December 1983 to visit our uncles.

How far away that day seemed. Unlike Toronto is December, Newark airport in August was steaming hot. Barrouallie was hot, but at least there was a breeze always coming off the ocean. Newark had no breeze, no trees, just people hustling with briefcases, pulling bags, pushing their children.

"You gonna fly on the big plane two times an' I ain't even gone on the little one," someone told me before I left Barrouallie. Annie and I were veteran travelers.

"Hey, Oronde, I'm your uncle, Rudy," the bearded man outside the jet way said. He helped us unload our baggage and complete the airport paperwork, all the while smiling and talking to us. Annie and I didn't say much. I couldn't get over how hot it was. I could see heat rising from the asphalt outside. And Ma had made me wear dress pants, dress shoes and a button down shirt. She had them all tailor-made two weeks before we left St. Vincent.

Uncle Rudy drove forever. On the way I read the highway signs and looked at the billboards on the side of the road. I soon fell asleep and began dreaming about home. When I woke up, we were in Scotch Plains. Grandma came out and gave Annie and me big hugs.

After the hugs, kisses and welcomes were done, after the gifts had been exchanged --my mother had packed green mangos, tamarind, chi-chi cakes, golden apples, strong rum and other treats she knew her family missed.

When sleeping quarters had been established --me in cousin Jerry's room and Annie in cousin Carla's-- I ate and went to bed. It hadn't hit me yet that I was in America. That realization came three days later when my mother and youngest sister Teri arrived.

Finally, the Ash family was together. We were all in America. I waited for the day America would be in me.

"Whate'er our future brings,
Our faith will keep us through
May peace reign from shore to shore,
And God bless and keep us true."

...

XVIII.

<u>HOW I SPENT MY</u>

<u>SUMMER VACATION</u>

"**H**ello…who's this?"

"Nigel, it's me."

"Whadup, kid."

"I'm good. How was Jamaica?"

"Pops was cool. He's getting remarried next month… How your summer going?"

"Same old. No papers, no job."

"You still haven't gotten your green card yet?"

"Nope. I'm tired of walking 'round with no money in my pockets. I did go to the Empire State Games though. Brought back a bronze medal. First time a boy's soccer team from NYC got a medal... What did you do?"

"Yo, check this out. My dad hired this maid, right. Real cute girl; a little older than me."

"You didn't," I said.

"Hold on. Anyway, she'd come to the house and cook while pops was at work. When I got up she'd be in the kitchen making breakfast. I'd walk past her and pinch her butt."

"What?"

"Wait a minute. Let me finish. So she didn't seem to mind," he began.

"She probably thought she'd get fired," I said.

"Let me finish, man," Nigel protested. "So I'd goose her and she'd smile and hit my hand real playful. I start kissing her neck one morning. She turned around and I felt her tits."

"You're a dog," I said.

"Bow, wow, wow!" he laughed then continued. "So we ended up in my room grinding on my bed. It was nice."

"That's not cool, man."

"What? She didn't say no. She liked it too or she would've stopped me or told my pops."

"That's harassment... I'd really hate to be your wife."

"I'd hate for you to be my wife too. You'd make one ugly bitch."

The conversation soon got onto the usual topic: sports (more precisely, the Yankees vs. the Mets). Eventually I got around to telling Nigel what I had called about.

"You did what!" he screamed. I had to put the receiver away from my ear.

"I did it," I repeated.

"Negro! Who? When'd you pull that? Hold up. When did you get a girlfriend?" he asked excitedly.

"In April or May, I guess."

"And you didn't tell a Negro. You my boy. We boys."

"She's not really my girlfriend though. She's a friend and she's a girl."

"But you fucked her, right."

"Yeah... I guess."

"Whadaya mean, you guess. It's either your dick was inside her or not."

"Then, yes it was."

"I can't believe this," Nigel screamed even louder than before. I had to put the earpiece further away this time. "Hello. Hello... Are you there?" he repeated.

"Yes," I finally answered.

"You did it. I can't believe this shit. You beat me. You did it." I was confused.

"You mean, you still a virgin. Even after all those women you told me about. The cheerleader, the church chick that went down on you at the movies."

"Devina," he filled in.

"Yeah her," I said. "I thought she was a nympho."

"No. We got naked once but never did anything. Not like you, dog. I can't believe you. How was it? Did you make her scream? Did she have an orgasm? C'mon. You can't drop a bomb like that and not answer a couple questions for the brothas who ain't never had none."

"It wasn't a big deal."

"Are you buggin'! You're a man now, son. We gotta celebrate." He paused. Somehow I knew what was coming next, the question he had to ask: "Is she black or white?"

"Does it matter?"

"No... And yes... What was she? Please tell me she ain't white."

"White," I whispered into the mouthpiece.

"Noooo!" Nigel screamed, like Caesar to Brutus. "No. No. No. Why? Why? I thought we talked about this. Why is it that all you black athletes with a little fame turn around and marry white women? Nah, we gotta stop that. You shoulda told me. I woulda went out and found you a nice black woman."

"It's not like Sarah and I are getting married."

"Sarah… Sarah… Can't get any whiter than, 'Sarah'," he joked.

"You taking this too seriously, man. It's not like we even talking anymore." I hoped that would satisfy him.

"Why not?" he asked.

"I dunno."

"I know why. Told you negro: the blacker the berry, the sweeter the juice. White women ain't got nothin' on black pussy. They can't move like a sista. They can scream and carry on, but a black woman, boy… I can't wait 'til I get me mine."

I wanted to tell Nigel that Sarah was someone he would probably like. She was kind, forgiving, easy-to-talk to. If she had been Asian or Hispanic or Martian, I would have liked her still. Sarah made me feel a security in knowing, for the first time in my life, I was starting to open up and share my self with another person face to face, flesh to flesh, and that person appreciated me just as I was.

Sarah and I met at the Manhattan rehearsal studio Julius and The Bird invited me to that day. I went in, sat down and watched students doing weird movements while making animal noises.

"You have to know the beast within and let him out before we can communicate to an audience," some guy with an Australian accent was saying. His name was Ian. He was in his mid forties and according to Julius, had come to NYC to start an acting career that never materialized. Ian taught theater at City College and had won a grant to start a theater program for high school students.

"I want to help you tame the beast," Ian would say. "There's so much energy in youth. If we can harness it, then we can move the Empire State Building or at least drive other people nuts." He laughed.

"You," he said, pointing to me. "Who are you, son, and what are you doing on your bum? Everybody else is up. Get up." Ian walked to my chair and pulled me onto my feet.

"I don't know if I want to do this," I said.

"Don't knock it 'til you try it."

"C'mon Oronde," The Bird said.

"Try it." Julius repeated, "C'mon. Try it."

"Alright," I nodded.

"Good," said Ian. "Now we can get started."

That day, Ian had us doing deep breathing and spatial awareness exercises. We closed our eyes and walked around the room following specific commands. We also listened to a piece of what he called didgeridoo music and danced to the awkward rhythm. I had no idea what I was doing.

"Don't be afraid," Ian reassured. "We're all gonna look like fools sometimes. Better here behind these walls with these other crazies. If anyone here starts snickering at you, just wait for them to go up and snicker right back." He laughed a dramatic, diabolical, evil villain laugh and roared up like Frankenstein.

When the two-hour rehearsal ended, a lady poked her head in the studio door.

"Are you guys done, Ian? We've booked this room right now." The lady seemed annoyed, slammed the door and went back outside. Ian shut off the didgeridoo music and mimicked the angry lady. We all laughed. As I was leaving, he tapped me on the shoulder.

"Not bad for a weird talking white guy, huh? You better be back next week or else I'll be looking for you." He started imitating Marlon Brando in *The Godfather*: "I'll come and find your family, your wife, even your dog." I smiled. "Good," he said. "See you next Thursday."

I went back the next Thursday and the next and the next. Even after Julius and The Bird stopped going, I continued. I was having fun with the crazies. The other players didn't know me. We never hung out afterwards. Everybody took their separate trains back to their separate lives. What would they care how silly I was or what I was doing?

Acting in Ian's studio near 42nd Street and Broadway was make-believe but the experience wasn't. Ian was preparing us to do a show during the 1993 OFFestival, a series of off-off Broadway productions staged around New York City each spring. Acting was like being on a soccer team. The festival was the big game and I wanted to be in the best shape to perform well. I didn't have the most lines or wasn't the featured player on stage, but I kept moving into open spaces to receive passes and lines. I did what I could to make us all look as good as we needed to be.

It was in those minutes letting my self go in rehearsals when I first saw Sarah. She and I were chosen to be partners in a short dance routine towards the end of a production Ian titled, *Zen Puppies Unleashed*. All rehearsals would end with Sarah and me practicing that number. We kept messing up. It seemed like every other couple was in the groove except us. Sarah and I would laugh at our mistakes until Ian began extending rehearsals thirty, forty-five, sixty minutes because of us.

"C'mon you two," someone would whine. "I gotta go home."

"Yeah, I gotta take the R train all the way to Queens. It's crazy out there at night."

Ian would follow with something like, "I can't believe the two of you are wasting our time. We're bringing art to the people, Oronde. There's gonna to be some poor, black kid from the Bronx who has never been to a play before and he's gonna watch you, and he's gonna think that you are it; that you are Broadway. That's what I want, what you want, what we want, right? The only way that's going to happen... the only way that kid's gonna keep looking is if you and Sarah can't focus on each other and get this right. I'm not gonna be on stage with you. I can't help you then. I'll be just another stranger in the audience. And this is the OFFestival, man. This is my show. Get it together. Understand?"

We were only a few weeks from the OFFestival. Ian was nervous. He had helped organize the entire event. His work, his project, his professional life was being judged. If we did well, he would get more funding for his acting studio. Ian's tongue-lashing brought Sarah and I closer.

I was at the water fountain one day when Ian whispered, "I think she digs you, mate." I almost did a spit take and wanted to deny hearing him. If Ian was right, that meant I had to do something. But what?

"I see the way you two behave. It's my aboriginal sense. You two got the didgeridoo."

"I don't deny that I like her, but..."

"But nothing. Go. Do. Be." Ian began doing Shakespeare. "Fetch thee that wench and woo her with the did-geri you do... so well." He bowed. "Not bad, uh? Royal Queensland Company, 1983."

"I've seen better."

"Damn you," Ian proclaimed in high dramatic fashion. Then he got quiet and started looking around as if someone was following him.

Ian reached into his pants pocket, brought out a piece of torn notebook paper, shoved it at me and started talking with a Russian accent. "I 'ad to cross ze border and pass strew a field of vild sheep to retrieve theees secret number. Take it." He walked away, singing the mission impossible theme song. "Call."

When I got home that night, I called the number and wasn't surprised to hear Sarah on the other end.

"I know this may sound weird, I began, "but I got your number from Ian."

"That's OK," she replied. "He's my dad." Now I was sure Sarah liked me. Tired of waiting for me to make a move, she had made hers.

Sarah and I talked for about an hour that night and many nights after. I got used to our phone conversations and weekly dances. We went out on a date the first night of the OFFestival after she mentioned having extra tickets to the opening show.

"My father brought these two dancers from Germany."

"Is it Cats or something?" I asked.

"No," she replied. "This is off Broadway." I knew what off Broadway was because I'd see the ads in the Arts section of the Friday New York Times but I'd never seen an off Broadway play before.

That Saturday, I met Sarah at a theater in midtown Manhattan. It was my first date. How bad could a date be? Chances are, I would end up with a woman later in life and this was the time to begin learning how the dating thing worked. To top it off, Sarah was a knockout and she was brilliant. She attended Stuyvesant, the most prestigious of New York City's specialized high schools. Sarah had full, feminine curves, supple size C breasts that peeked through the white tees she always wore to rehearsals. She coursed with sexuality and was always more bubbly than not.

Sitting in the theater, I tried not to make it appear as if it was my first date. Even though I had no idea what was going on, I paid attention to the dancers. I'd say something every now and again to Sarah but I never felt I made any sense. I was bombing and wanted out as soon as possible. At intermission, Sarah brought me down to the stage.

"Hi daddy," she said to Ian.

"Take good care of her tonight, Oronde."

"Daddy!" Sarah said, embarrassed.

"So you like it or not?" Ian asked me.

"It's nice."

"You don't really mean that, do you," he smiled. "You can be honest. I expect nothing less from you. I've taken criticism before."

Was this a test? What's the protocol? Did I say I liked the dancers even though I had no idea what they were trying to say? What if Ian knew I was lying? Certainly, a man of honesty wouldn't trust his daughter with a liar. Thankfully, before I could answer, Ian started, "You know, it doesn't matter if you like it or not. What matters is that you understand that people are doing something they believe in. Even if you don't know what's going on, the dancers have to have some idea. You have to at least respect that."

"That's true," I nodded.

Someone motioned for Ian to come over. "Got to go dear. A producer's work, you know." He kissed Sarah on the cheek. "Have fun tonight," he said as he walked backstage.

"Bye daddy," Sarah replied.

The lights blinked twice and Sarah ran me back to our seats. Once the show began again, Sarah leaned her head onto my right shoulder. It was uncomfortable at first but I thought it best to hold on. That's what guys did in the movies. Anyway, I liked the smell of her lotion. (It was a kiwi and melon lotion from The Body Shop. For years after, I loved that smell.)

After a while, Sarah put her hand on my right thigh and started moving it up and down. I didn't know what to do. I figured I should do the same to her so I put my hand on her thigh and repeated what she was doing. Sarah then took her hand off my thigh and placed it at the nape of my neck, gently rubbing the skin. It felt good so I let her do that. She then moved her face off my shoulder, up the side of my right ear, began nibbling my earlobes before sliding her tongue inside. It sounded like the ocean through a big conch shell.

With her wet tongue and gentle touch, I was lifted from the theater and landed in a cup choc full of confidence. I sat up, sipped in, drank it up. That's the only way to explain me turning my head towards Sarah and kissing her. This was no pecking either.

On opening night, as I had done most of my life, I was bypassing the basic course and skipping straight to the advanced class. It was lip, spit, grit and damn if I was going for it.

Didn't matter that I almost bit Sarah's lips off and left a thick ring of saliva around her lips. Didn't matter that she had to stop and reposition my face three or four times or put her finger to my lips and tell me to stop breathing so hard. Didn't matter that she asked, "Are you shaking?" I was trembling but I told her my foot was asleep and I was trying to wake it up.

I was kissing a beautiful girl --not too well, mind you-- and she was actually kissing me back. I had gotten the kissing thing out of the way.

After the play, Sarah and I took a cab downtown to have dinner at The Russian Tea Room. She insisted on paying. I was broke so I had no problem with that. We walked along West Fourth Street in Greenwich Village, dancing into shops, eyeing the night scene. She bought us matching silver rings.

"I just love silver, don't you? So much prettier than gold."

"Sure," I answered, not really knowing how she wanted me to take her statement. Gold, silver, bronze, it was all the same.

We passed a gay couple snuggling. "Don't you just love the city? You see anything." Sarah waited for a response. I said something. She kept asking my opinions on the trinkets sold on the street, the music we heard, movies, plays, books. I never said much. That night, with the nerves and the hormones, there was some blockage from the opinion section in my head.

When I woke the next morning, I began freaking out because there was a dry taste in my mouth. I swore it was some female witchcraft from Sarah's kissing. That's why my male peers acted so stupid around women. One kiss or hug from the right woman and they were drugged. That was how women did it. In my mind, I imagined that in kissing me, Sarah had somehow inoculated me with some female drug that would make me want her more and more and go out of my way to please only her. And that kiwi melon scent I still smelled was part of the rouge. The girl was under my skin.

If that's what a woman's kiss did, well… it worked. Sarah got me. Things seemed right between us. My phone personality was back, our conversations always fun. I'd write her stories or read her my poetry. On hearing my work, Sarah knew I had deeper concerns. I always felt she wondered why she could never bring those ideas out of me face to face. She once told me I was different from the boys she had dated. For me, anything I did with her was groundbreaking. I think Sarah must have sensed that freshness.

One night, Sarah and I stepped outside a cafe in midtown. A breeze gave the air a slight chill. She shivered, I hugged her, we kissed. Not the tongue slapping I'd perfected by then. That night, the kiss was soft. We didn't have to communicate the change in style. It just worked. Holding Sarah, I felt my bones rattle. To me, that confirmed some chemistry. With the cabs honking, the city heaving, the whole world at a whisper, warmth enveloped me. I liked this girl; it was kismet. Like Alex at CTY, I was meant to meet Sarah.

Late June 1993. Had been four months since I first set foot in Ian's workshop and two weeks since the end of the OFFestival. All had gone well. A theater friend of Ian's even told him I had some acting chops. Actor? Me? Who knew.

Sarah and I had been seeing each other since late May. She phoned on a Friday night to tell me her neighbor was letting her watch his apartment while he was vacationing in Europe.

"I'm going to have it all to myself the next ten days," she said. "Wanna come over on Monday."

"Sure," I answered. Immediately, we started talking about sex.

"Are you a virgin," she asked. I told her I tried having sex in eighth grade but the girl complained that it hurt so we never went through with it. That was a lie. I heard one of the guys on the block tell that story in middle school.

Before she hung up Sarah asked, "What kind of condom do you like?" She mentioned the different condoms she had seen in Greenwich Village. We got onto talking about edible underwear and I suggested she buy some. "I know a place where they sell them," she said.

As soon as we hung up, I began anticipating Monday. Ready or not, I was going to do it. If only God had been lazy, I wouldn't have had to deal with Saturday and Sunday.

Sarah and I agreed to go to Central Park Monday morning for a picnic. I wondered if I would make it there without passing out.

That morning when I got on the crowded train to Manhattan, beads of moisture began forming on my forehead. My armpits started blotching my white shirt with a wet spot I knew would only widen by the time I saw Sarah. She would be repulsed. I had to remain calm.

We met near Columbus Circle and walked over to the Great Lawn. People were throwing Frisbees, footballs, hacky-sacking, tanning, running, reading, painting, dancing. I smelled everything from ketchup and mustard on hot dogs to dog shit and marijuana smoke. Sarah and I sat down under a tree and spread out a blanket. She brought spaghetti and apple pie she had made, two bottles of water and a fruit salad. We ate and talked.

I lay back on the grass and Sarah put her head on my chest. I rubbed my hand through her brown hair and caressed her as gently as I knew how. A breeze would blow every few minutes, wafting the melon and kiwi body lotion up my nose. It was like some scene from a Hollywood romance. All seemed as it should be.

The two of us soon fell asleep. When I woke up and looked at my watch it was close to noon and getting warmer. More people were coming to the park. Three nannies strolled into our area, sat down, took out books and began reading while their kids ran around.

One little boy wearing a pair of overalls and a red shirt kept chasing after a girl his own size. They must have been three or so. The boy would chase and tag the girl and she'd chase after him. The other baby, no more than eighteen months, was out surveying the strange, green carpet. From the many times the baby fell, she hadn't walked on grass much. A tiny bump in the earth sent her down on her bottom.

"That's so cute," Sarah would giggle after each fall. She'd point and smile that smile I loved --teeth clenched between her wide grin, eyes almost closed. "Aren't they adorable?"

"Yeah. Reminds me of my little brothers." Sarah kissed me.

We rolled around in the grass hugging and kissing. Everyone else was in his or her own pleasure so we weren't noticed, except by the nannies who stared at us as if we were two vile, perverted creatures. One of then shook her head and returned to her book as if asking, "How can you do that in front of these kids?"

The nannies soon grabbed the children and strolled away. By that time, the sun was directly overhead and blazing. Sarah was flushed. I was definitely hot.

"Let's go," she told me. We packed up, hailed a cab and went to her neighbor's apartment. Within ten minutes, we were laying on a bed kissing.

Do I just say, "You want to have sex now," or do I wait for her to initiate. The room was tense.

Sarah got up and offered me a glass of water but I refused, thinking that with the lump in my throat, I'd choke. Her fingernails tickled between my legs and I became bold. I figured I had ended up at Ian's studio for a reason, had stuck it out for a reason, had met Sarah for a reason. Right then, right there, me and her in bed was meant to happen.

"Turn over," I said, placing my body on top of hers. We began kissing, slow and soft, just like that night outside the midtown cafe. Sarah took off my shirt. I raised up her sundress and began licking her breasts and nipples. They perked up. I perked up as Sarah wriggled her body against mine.

"You don't have to do this if you don't want to," she began. "If you want, I can kiss you all day."

"I want to do this," I answered

As I began kissing Sarah's stomach, her navel, inching down to her panty line, she stopped me and nodded towards the nightstand on my left. There were condoms lying next to a blue, porcelain lamp. I grabbed one and tried to tear along the dotted line but my fingers were too wet. Sarah saw me struggling, took the pack and opened the Trojans herself. I tried one on but it kept slipping off.

"Can you put it on," I said. I'd never put a condom on my penis.

"If I was a guy, I'd be practicing this all the time," she chuckled. The girl definitely knew what she was doing. I was the one practicing.

"Hello! Hello! Oronde, are you there?" Nigel asked again. I had zoned out.

"What? What... Sorry, man."

"So," he persisted.

"So what?"

"You never said how it was."

"It was all right."

"I can never understand you. You just has S-E-X ... You know how many fellas I know have never had sex and you're not excited talking about that shit. I'd be calling everybody the day after."

I wanted to call somebody the day after. I wanted to call God and curse Him for making me the way I was. I went home that Monday afternoon and the other days that week having no idea if I enjoyed sex or not. I liked watching Sarah's face contort or hearing her holler and moan. She seemed to be enjoying my motion. Why wasn't I? All I kept thinking throughout the whole thing was (1) this is tiring and (2) I wonder if Sarah is really liking this? I had no idea and that terrified me.

I realized I didn't know Sarah well enough to trust her reactions. I was convinced she was pretending to enjoy the act. I thought she inferred that I was a tight, closed-off individual she could release with her feminine wiles. Maybe our whole relationship was a sham, her pet project? Maybe I was a fool in her company?

I imagined Sarah comparing me to other fellas she had. I had nightmares of her sitting in Times Square handing out flyers with my picture and the caption, "Stay clear ladies. This guy is the worst lay ever."

At my most vulnerable, I had reverted to the little boy in my youth, afraid and unable to open up and receive what I knew was all too real.

Fourth of July came. It was a Sunday. Everyone in my house had gone to the Ash family reunion in New Jersey. I said, "No," to my mother's invitation and lay in bed most of the day moping, thinking I must be gay. How could I be a man and not enjoy sex? S-E-X for God's sake. It was unfathomable. All the men in the movies looked satisfied. Why couldn't I be satisfied? I had a gorgeous leading lady with curves and full breasts just the way I liked 'em.

Sarah had made it clear from the beginning she had only one rule in a relationship: call her every couple of days. That night she wanted to take me to the Macy's fireworks display. I, however, wasn't in the mood for explosions, fireworks, oohs and aahs. The aural allusions would be too much to bear. Anyway, I hadn't called for two or three days and knew she'd be mad. Not saying anything after sex was a no-no. Even I knew that and didn't feel like dealing with Sarah's anger. I was pissed off enough for both of us. I stayed pissed off and sulked for a couple more days.

Soon, days became a whole week not talking to Sarah. By then, in my head, it was too late. I was ashamed to discuss something I couldn't make sense of in my own mind. I was embarrassed, felt guilty for letting the situation get to me when I knew the answer from day one was to simply tell Sarah the truth.

"You gonna talk or not," Nigel continued.

I wanted to tell him that the supposed greatest day in a young man's life was one of my worst moments in years. I wanted to tell him that sex was not as it seemed. It was hard labor. And not just in bed bumping and sweating.

What I began to note was that sex took place outside the bedroom. It happened the day you and your lady spent five hours talking on the phone about nothing in particular.

Sex happened when you told her your deepest, darkest secret and had no reservations about the revelations.

Sex happened when you called your woman afterwards and joked about the fart you made *in flagranti delicto* or her funny snorting when she peaked. It happened when the two of you were walking down the street and you reached for her hand first and held on, not to claim your prize, but just to feel her touch.

All those walks around New York City, the theaters, the parks, the shops, the studio spaces, the phone calls, the letters, the bedrooms, the bras, the latex, the summer heat, the practice, the play; I didn't have sex with Sarah. Yes, I felt relieved having checked off one of my adolescent goals. I was no longer a virgin. According to Nigel, I was a man. On the other hand, I longed for the emotional connection I knew deep down would have given the experience a bit more gravity.

Sarah and I cuddled after each act and caressed in the shower but I didn't feel clean. I didn't feel dirty, per se, but I didn't feel whole, complete, connected. By the fourth or sixth time that first week, sex became mechanical.

Get undressed, touch each other, get hot and heavy, insert penis into lubricated vagina, push against Sarah's body for sixty plus minutes, collapse, dry up the wet spot on the bed, cover my body, adjourn to the kitchen, re-hydrate, eat something, shower together, repeat process if feelings arose again.

One day I had a soccer game in Queens at 4:30 PM. Sarah and I finished showering at 3:00. I got dressed, kissed her good-bye and ran out the door to the subway. There was nothing tying me to her and that bedroom. Truth be told, at seventeen, I was not ready to have sex. Glad to have done it, but not ready for it.

I basically went from not playing the field all my life to starting the first game of the World Series... at Yankee Stadium... and I was literally, naked.

In the space of a few months, I had my first steady girl, first date, first kiss, first time. It was all too much too fast. Performance anxiety had tightened me up in knots. The same fears gripped me every time Sarah and I had sex. Not once in all our sex-capades did I ejaculate. Whatever was supposed to be released was still bottled up inside me. No doubt Sarah enjoyed that.

We'd lay down hour after hour, me slipping in and out, she moaning, me not releasing a damn thing. My sex was for Sarah and not with Sarah. The act became another performance. In bed I acted the part of lover. Out of bed, I didn't feel like playing a part anymore. I walked off the stage, turned down the lights and promised never to be a fool in Sarah's company. I never called her again.

"C'mon," Nigel egged. "You can level with me, Oronde. Sex was great wasn't it? Even if she was white an' all."

"Yeah," I said.

That was a lie.

MUSICAL INTERLUDE

Song title: Fragile
Artist: Sting

...

XIX.

SENIORITIS,

FULL RIDE, DEPORTATION:

THE WONDER YEAR

In the second half of my junior year and for much of my senior year, I suffered an almost crippling case of senioritis. I went to class but there was little in the books and lesson plans for me. Brooklyn Tech's hallway was more fun. Ditching Ms. Weiser's 8:05 Pre Calculus class and eating a full breakfast in the cafeteria offered up more interesting conversation and a better start to my day in spring 1993.

Why pre calculus? I had no need for slopes, asymptotes, functions, conjugates, linear theorems, vertices, scientific calculators. As an exercise in thought, the class was fine and Ms. Weiser was a good teacher, but the material was not for me and I knew that. I got high on people, on the energy in the building, the energy in Brooklyn. My learning was happening off the page, outside the classroom.

By the beginning of senior year, most Brooklyn Tech students had earned enough credits to graduate according to the standards set forth by the New York State Board of Regents. I was no exception. I had just about earned a Regents Equivalency Diploma, good enough for admissions to most colleges. For all intents and purposes, I had graduated high school. The class schedule my senior year was busy work prolonging the inevitable. I was leaving Tech and there was nothing the teachers or I could do to stop it.

In addition to the NY State regent's requirements, students had to do extra to earn a Brooklyn Tech diploma. We had to perform community service hours each semester and we each had to learn how to swim. If a Technite didn't learn to swim, he or she didn't graduate. I was born on an island two blocks from the sea, so swimming wasn't a problem.

My problem was my academic major, Social Science Research. The students spent the bulk of the senior year completing a Westinghouse Science Fair project. I had begun a study on the role of television and its effects on inner city youth. (I figured I had watched enough of the boob tube, might as well figure out what it was doing to me.) I went to the 42 Street Library in Manhattan, read books, articles, journals, watched documentaries. I handed out a survey to over one hundred Tech students, entered the results into my teacher's computer program, analyzed the statistical variance, the null theory, my margin of error. For a time, I was very much into my project.

Then one day I looked around and saw that other students were gung-ho about their projects. Those kids were coming in early, sat by their computers for hours analyzing data. I tried coming in early, sat at my computer but I was not putting in the extra effort the gung-ho kids were. (Two of my classmates became Westinghouse semi finalist. For students researching sociological issues in what is traditionally a contest about hard science, two was a significant accomplishment.)

I wasn't concerned about my project. I liked my idea, but I was not *into* my idea. I figured if I wasn't working as hard as the others were I was cheating my self, cheating the class, cheating the major, wasting time. I didn't deserve to be a part of the Westinghouse field. I could not win like that. There were young researchers eager to get noticed by college admissions officers. I wasn't. I was going to college with or without my project.

After leaving Gateway my junior year, most of my classes seemed easy. Teacher's expectations were half what they were in the Gateway program and still my new classmates were struggling. It was still Brooklyn Tech, still tougher than most high schools, but the work was easy. Teachers seemed to have given up on students turning in quality assignments, so my haphazard, lazy efforts usually got a B or higher.

When there was no assigned seating for a class, I sat in the back. With the last name Ash, I was always in the first or second seat all my life. In the back, I chose whether or not to pass notes, join conversations or play cards when the teacher wasn't looking. I chose whether to make the extra effort on a paper or even hand one in. I didn't have to study the long hours I had in Gateway so I had more time for phone calls, music, writing, hanging out. I'd cram the night before an exam and pull a B.

As a freshman and sophomore, I got straight A's but I was always worried. By the end of my junior year, a solid B was my new standard. B students had more time for friends, parties, music, the opposite sex. They seemed more well rounded. That complete human being was what college admissions officers looked for, what I had spent my high school career trying to be.

Inevitably, B's became C's and the occasional D showed up on exams. By the second report card senior year, I was getting the worst grades of my academic career. I cut class, sat in the cafeteria and people-watched or went to the 42 Street Library and learned what I wanted to all day. I read books on my Westinghouse topic but I also flipped through the works of my new academic heroes: philosophers, thinkers, makers of men.

Why did I need a high school teacher to interpret primary truth? Why not read the works and draw my own conclusions? All the books mentioned in my favorite classes became my new obsessions. Franz Fanon's *The Wretched of the Earth*, James Baldwin's *The Fire Next Time*, Frederick Nietche's *Beyond Good and Evil*, Paolo Freire's *Pedagogy of the Oppressed*, *The Communist Manifesto*, Mao's *Little Red Book*, Hobbe's *Leviathan*, *Candide*, *The Republic*, *The Holy Bible*.

I skimmed through the names in my history and English classes: Socrates, Plato, Aquinas, Shakespeare, Milton, Longfellow, Copernicus, Descartes, Jean-Jacques Rousseau, Martin Luther, Galileo, John Locke, Ralph Ellison, Langston Hughes, Henry David Thoreau, Ralph Waldo Emerson, Chinua Achebe, Mark Mathabane. These were my new teachers.

Why did I need Tech's curriculum? I was smart. And hadn't Tech's teachers done their primary function; show me where information was and how to access it. They didn't have to tell me to learn more. I'd been doing it on and off the past four years. More importantly, I knew what I wanted to know. At least I thought I was headed in the right direction.

I would lie down at night to face a recurring dream. In the dream, I was suspended in a clear bubble above the ground sometimes, above existence itself sometimes. It had to have been existence because all of history, all the present and the future were in plain view. I was in the center of the bubble but I could sense everything about me. There were no lines or ropes fastening me to the bubble but I was secure and never worried about falling or being hurt in any way.

The only odd thing was that my perspective on existence and on my self would alter dramatically in my dream. Any given second, I would see the world up close, as if the bubble was a microscope allowing me clarity. A second later, I would be in a corner, like a fly in a web, all the world looking big and imposing. On those occasions in the corner, I spent hours bouncing around the bubble trying to break free. I struggled mightily those nights.

On my brightest days, I woke up drenched in new knowledge. The levees holding the world back had broken in the night and I floated in the silt, the mud, the debris of life. Tree limbs were rafts, mud banks offered refuge. I was unafraid. I woke up and accepted, in the pit of me, things I had always known. On those days, all life fell into place.

The night before, I would forget to do a math assignment or study for a test and the next day the teacher would not be there. Or I would decide to take a sudden turn down a road and run into someone I had recently been thinking about. There were innumerable coincidences, countless déjà vu moments, things that seemed beyond mere happenstance. In fact, my days seemed more like divine design. I was the designer, the model and the object of my own creation. There was purpose in my life and I accepted that fact unquestionably. I started calling the feeling *knowing without knowing*.

It was as if all the world and everything in it was out there to teach me some lesson in the present that would make me a better man able to create a better tomorrow for the world. I was a good man, more secure in my self and would create a world as secure --a good world.

It may have been adolescent ego but I saw it as something else. At seventeen, I had reached the zenith of my youth. Everything I had learned about life up to that point was bubbling around in my head and I was ready to engage and share it. I could feel the hemispheres of my brain fusing, felt my heart bleeding as the activity and the need for more activity required more pumping from its center. I was transforming before my eyes and I was actively aware of it. I considered my self an aged soul trapped in a young body. I saw too much behind the words people said, the things people did and did not do. I was a senior in my youth, a wise senior; I was *The Wonder Child.*

As *The Wonder Child* I engaged life everyday with intent. Not only was I listening to someone for their words, I was also trying to decipher the hidden message in their language, their movement, their being. I assumed people talked to me because I had to learn something specific from them. I had been learning from books all my life and was good at that. There was no challenge there anymore. I would be dealing with people for the rest of my life, so learning from them became my new challenge.

Realizing people had as much to teach me as my schoolbooks, placed school on equal level with the people in my life. When I found out how much more stimulating learning from people was, school took a backseat. I did enough to get by but in the margins of my junior and senior year notebooks are scribbles about any and every idle notion that poured into my head. My heroes documented their thoughts for posterity so why shouldn't I.

According to my history books, philosophers were men of leisure who spent time thinking about life and how to make it better. They had time to think because some wealthy patron or their own family's excess allowed them a certain leisure. They didn't have to worry about the bottom of Maslow's hierarchy of needs and could move up the pyramid contemplating the eternal. What a life?

I welcomed my life as a man of leisure. My mother was feeding and clothing me. I didn't want for food, water, shelter, was reasonably happy, felt good about my place in the world. I realized that at no other point in my life would I have the energy to devote my thoughts solely to my place in the universe. College was a few months away and with it ten-paged papers to write and soccer games to win. After college, I'd have a job and probably a family and kids, no time for philosophy and the eternal then. I saw how tired my mother and Mudd were, no time for family even. I'd never think about all these wonderful possibilities for the world again.

I was scared I'd lose the child inside. It was as if a new person had been born from all the disparate voices in my head. He was the benevolent dictator bringing sanctity to the echoing chaos. I had to save the child, had to show the future Oronde that he had big plans and worldly notions at some point.

When life killed *The Wonder Child*, which I knew it would, I had to have a record of his dreams, his visions, his striving, his mess.

So, when I felt I had to look at something more closely, I did. When I was compelled to smell, to taste, to feel, to write, I did. Didn't matter what time of the day or night. I sensed, I scribbled, I noted, I wrote so I'd never forget my self. I wrote…

11-2-92

"My problem is that I'm going into unknown territory for a black man, coming upon problems never before faced; and I'm doing all this as a teenager --confusion upon confusion. I don't know why I'm writing this? Should I be writing this? Is this all leading somewhere? And if so, where?"

11-4-92

"Bill Clinton is prez. Don't know how I feel about that…Been reading a lot of first person articles on schizophrenia and it got me wondering if we each have a case of schizophrenia in us? Are we all crazy? The black issues I've been thinking about are all jumbled in my head, as is, seemingly, everything else. What is the young black man's place? Someone told me once that as a teenager, we find out that the world has an endless list of problems that lack answers. Maybe my job is to solve as many as I can... The problems we encounter as black men are spirals within a helix encircling a whirlpool of nonsense --of which we know nothing nor had a hand in creating…"

11-16-92

"Maybe the very purpose of our being is to dwell in the *collective unconscious*, to see only the fibers which bind us together; thread across the intertwined webs of our distinct realities without fear, love, hate --like babes before breathing life eternal-- knowing, feeling and judging nothing; just coexisting."

12-3-92

"… I am going through a transition, learning how to think for myself and how I learn. I will have to update my study habits and have learning be ongoing, day to day, intertwined, criss-crossed. That means finding the time to review my class notes at home and coming up with questions and comments on my own, make up my own pneumonic devises and study questions based on my own life. Everything in my day must tie together to make

sense... I realize that I don't belong to much or have much to associate with. I realize I don't have a country, a culture, have no idea what it means to be Vincentian or a Vincentian-American. I realize I have no idea what it is to be a Black-American -- racism is so subtle, so psychological these days that I think only the pre-civil rights blacks knew what being Black in America meant. I realize I don't have any religious, ideological, social or moral codes on which I base my judgments. I realize I don't know a lot about many things. But that may be a blessing...To make yesterday complete, Alex called. Unfortunately, I wasn't home. But she did call. I do wish to see her again. I think I've become more personable since our last meeting --a total disaster. We hardly spoke that night. All I remember saying were "Hello" and "See ya around." That really hurt whatever friendship we had. Fortunately, things are on the upswing. I see that we're good friends and have suppressed any romantic feelings that may exist. She probably still has the notion that I'm crazy for her but that feeling has waned. I hope we can patch things up and sail smooth again. Life is smooth. I AM VERY VERY VERY HAPPY!

12-23-92

"Today may not have been as impressive as the last entry, but there were memorable moments nonetheless. We got out of school at 1:30 PM. My last class was Spanish. While the students filed out, Mr. Cacheiro, Gerbril and I ended up talking about the legalization of drugs, the degeneration of American society, where America was headed and what's it going to take to reshape us. On that, Gerbril felt the answer lay in religion and the establishment of a uniform, religion or definite moral and ethical codes. Being a Muslim, I expected something like that from Gerbril. However, I don't see religion helping American society. And even if such a thing were possible, which religion? Gerbril would say Islam, but what about Mr. and Mrs. Smith in Small-town, USA?

...Mr. Cacheiro mentioned something, which I didn't quite pick up on. He said that the 1990s will bring about a change in structure, where there'll be no going back. By structure, I think he was referring to ideological beliefs. Maybe the 90s are to bring about a new belief? That would go along with my theory that this is the decade that will shape human --America --world-- history forever. I should talk to Mr. Cacheiro about it more when we get back from Christmas break. Maybe he can help me figure out what I'm thinking?

Something else happened today. I think I'm going out with someone. Her name is Roxanne. We had been saying "Hello" and hugging each other everyday. We were near the first floor staircase waiting for her friends when..."

2-4-93

"Cruel irony --Primitive man had the world at his fingers, dared to dream up the constructs we now frame life within; he is the shadow in our nights. But now that we have gained the capacity to alight the laws of the physical universe and move beyond our constructs, we are running scarce of materials to work with. In the end, life is just the construct..."

2-14-93

Definition of Her

in her, frankness and truth will be a blessing. open-mindedness and respect for my complexity a necessity. ability to bound through human action and human thought will be welcomed. must be nothing but who she is --an untapped goddess in wait. must be willing to roam the deserted plains of her forgotten selves. have the learning potential of a blank page. a seeker and a wanderer, imaginative, personable.

3-1-93

"The realization that the second half of my life has begun and must be mastered has dawned on me today. I was with Myrna and Ari at the pizza shop and then to Manhattan. I like that Myrna. She seems to like me or why have me around. For some reason, I think a lot of women at Tech see something in me. I don't dress like, act like, talk like, walk like the black guy they have in their mind. Yet there is something unmistakably black about me. Ms. Floyd sees this; Dr. Weinberger wants me to write from that voice, Nigel wants me to talk more about it.

... I am beginning to feel the brunt of my self-loathing. The fact that I have stood on the sidelines is killing me with Myrna. I like her, but have never tried to do whatever she is expecting me to do. I have the power to attract, but it means nothing if there's no action after that. Today with Myrna, I was mute. She's Filipino, a gorgeous mix of white, Spanish, black. Looks a bit like Natalie Merchant. And she writes for Horizons. I want this girl. I'm wasting the opportunity. And if I'm wasting her time and mine, I have to move on. In life, I see I'm not going to be as happy unless I put all that I have into whatever I decide to do. All my energies into soccer when I'm playing, all my energies into the pages when I'm studying, all my energies into Myrna when I'm with her. I want to go somewhere with this girl. Whatever my heart and mind want me to do with her, I'll obey. I have to test myself now.

I realize I've made significant progress in the last year but I have a ways to go. Six months ago, I wouldn't have had pizza with this girl. I did. Twice. I can't blow this without seeing where it leads. I screwed up today but tomorrow is another. Go with the flow and see what happens. Enjoy the day, wherever it leads."

5-9-93 [Mother's Day]

"… Life in the past few months of awareness has made me dig for truth in everything about me. There are no rules in the digging. We each must make the rules as we go and hope they are good decisions. But there are no bad or good decisions; no need to fear choice, for choice offers the opportunity to learn. And learning is the secret to life. When the individual stops learning, he dies and the world suffers. We must never stop learning.

I went to a Zendo --a Buddhist holy place-- with Sarah last Wednesday. I had to put on a black robe and sit in the lotus position for five hours. The idea was to clear the mind. I thought I thought I would   reach nirvana. Naiveté. The experience was soothing --I think. Odd enough, I had the most trouble breathing. And my groin was killing me.   After about an hour, I relaxed a bit. It wasn't until I left that I realized what I should have been doing. I was supposed to have focused on where I was --sitting in a dark room. But my mind was everywhere. I tried to concentrate on each event that flashed across my consciousness but it wasn't working.

The experience was healthy though. I left the Zendo relaxed. My knees hurt, but my mind was at ease. For once, my thoughts, my facial expressions and my actions seemed to fit. For one night, I was together. I want to be me together, to know me completely, to feel, experience and be with me completely… all the time."

October '93

6:00 AM Black CONSCIOUSness

Awakened by a passion long dead within. The waters which move about are more inviting. Memories jolt from springs forever alloyed to floating magnets clamped frozen in the wintertime of my hard ship.

I feel ready to dive in, to swim with the current, to be engulfed by the powers, to be drowned in the depths. I feel secure. I know I will resurface, I won't be held down for sure, I won't be drowned black no mo'. My mind is jigged into something cohesive. I understand it. I can call it... My life

Excerpt from a speech imagined:

"... And you notice when you mix the colors together, the red, the yellow, the purple, the green, the white, ; you mix them all and you get black. That's right. All the colors lead to black. Black is all encompassing, see. It's beyond the understanding of any one or two colors. It's not two or three or four colors. You need them all to begin... to even think of looking black. I tell you, they haven't found all the colors yet. There are colors beyond our spectrum. You can mix orange with... ah... ah mauve and you got yourself a new color. Go out. Play scientist in your backyard. Mix the paint in your garage. See for yourself. That new color you just made; the new color that never existed until you just made it; that new color will help make black. In fact, it was already in black to begin with. Black is beyond anything singular. It's not fully known yet... How does that make you feel? You ain't known yet. The world don't know you. You don't even know yourself. You can see white. You can see brown, yellow, red. You know them all but you don't know black. Black is too complex, too deep, too much work. It's hard mixing colors... You mix them colors I was talking about. What happens? They fade into black, get lost in the black. When you finally see the black, you can't see the other colors no more. The black is too strong... Oh, black doesn't run you into the ground with its power. It just is. And as it is, it's too powerful for anything else..."

10-3-93

"I stink. Can't remember if I've bathed all weekend. Ms. Desiano's American Studies homework is due tomorrow but I'm thinking about soccer eligibility and college scholarships. I will probably not play high school soccer this season because I cut so many of Mrs. Weiser's classes last spring. I know what I did. I have to plead with Mrs. Weiser to help me. No one thinks she will. I have to try.

I'm giving serious thought to leaving Real Napoli this fall and playing with the Brooklyn Italians --Napoli's bitter rivals. I will have a better chance to get noticed by college coaches because Joe Barone [Brooklyn Italians coach] has the connections. I've practiced with the team a few times. There's talent there, much more than at Napoli.

Joe's got all the kids who made the All-Brooklyn Team last year. Bomb squad. And I'll be the center midfielder orchestrating it all. NC State and UCONN have already called him about me but I haven't been able to get back with them. Not a good thing to do to people who can make a huge difference in my future. I'm afraid to tell the coaches I may be ineligible for the season. What would that say about me?

Deciding to leave Real Napoli was an easier decision than I thought. It's driving me mad, soccer is. Will I play? Will I change teams? College scholarships? There has to be more going on in my head. I need to start writing songs, playing the keyboard, reading poetry, drawing again or I'll go crazy.

I'm calling Ralph tomorrow to let him know I'm leaving then I'll tell the team on Tuesday. I love Ralph. He's been a father. I could do no wrong by him. He let me run practice, gave me confidence to do whatever I wanted on the field. He used his insurance to pay for my hip flexor injury, "found" a pair of Copa Mundials someone "left" at a tournament in Long Island. Ralph fed me, drove me all the way home on the other side of Brooklyn after practice. He trusted me. I could have never asked for a better coach the past two years... But I have to do what's best for <u>my</u> future."

When Mrs. Chang was carrying on about the Krebs cycle in AP Biology, I wrote in the margins.

Dear Beth,

I have yet to study for one of my senior classes. I am still passing them all with 80+ but with little reward. AP Biology continues to be a bore and I use it to read the NY Times and attempt to finish the crossword puzzle. I could console myself in the fact that a lot of my fiends are getting this "senioritis" but what is that saying? I am not my friends. I am *The Wonder Child* and I'm afraid I've forgotten what it means to be him. I know he wanted to experience something grand in life. I have forgotten what it is he wanted. I don't know what I want. (Imagine, this is just the start of adulthood and already I don't have grasp of things.) I thought I'd become more aware at this point in my life. I don't need to know about the infinitesimal parts of the human body. I'm just beginning to enjoy looking at the whole damn thing. It seems so pointless to come to this class. And yet I do it. I made the choice to take AP Bio so I have to live with my decision. It was the first semi-adult decision I've made this year. I am not happy with what I've decided but I guess this is to allow me to make better decisions in the future. Why did I pick that class in the first place?

The real reason is beginning to bust out. I want to boost my high school stats. That's all it was. Nothing more. Nothing less. It's telling me something else though. I have to understand what it is I want most. What do I want to do with my life?

Beth, I'm sorry this letter turned into me analyzing me. But sometimes things don't quite end up the way you want them to."

December '93

AP Bio When You Really Want To Sleep

If science could only

Stop thinking

Relax

Listen

To the motionless cell

Before trying to dissect and stain

Sing the morning song of the willow tree

Before cutting off the harmony

Taste the sudden rain

Before feeling the sunny shower

Of yellow bumblebees in spring

Or geese who head east instead of south for the winter

I'm afraid it would become too vain

In absolute awe of its benevolent force and complex   simplicity

And eating lotus leaves all day

Wither away

There was one way to live life: do it full force. Outside the classroom, I had been doing more my junior and senior years, so I was living more. But with college on the horizon and teachers reminding me every day, I had to re-evaluate my commitment to school.

Outside of Gateway I lacked the commitment to persevere when those around me were not as focused as I needed to be. I didn't have that drive successful people talked about, that energy black leaders noted when they said we had to work twice as hard to get half as much as the white man. I lacked that energy but I had something else though: faith. I had faith that something was going on in me that was good. I had faith that my failure was going to be a good one.

Part of that faith was the assurance that I was a quality student and the best soccer player in Brooklyn. I was getting a full scholarship to college.

After joining the Brooklyn Italians soccer team in fall 1993 and soon taking part in a soccer showcase event for college coaches, my faith grew.

The week after the showcase, Coach Joe told me he fielded inquiries from UCONN, St. Johns, Hofstra, Fordham, St. Francis, Long Island University, Columbia, Dartmouth, Princeton, Cornell, North Carolina State and others. Joe knew the main reason I played for him was because he had the connections to get me a scholarship. And it had to be a full scholarship. So when I learned that Ivy League schools did not give out full rides, Columbia, Princeton and the rest were out. I wanted to go the Ivy League route but couldn't be saddled with loans the rest of my life.

Both North Carolina State and St. Johns made it clear in the phone calls and letters that I was being offered a full scholarship. The two schools became my top options. I visited Raleigh, North Carolina first, flying down on Saturday morning, October 23, 1993. Asst. Coach David Allred met me at the airport and we drove to campus to watch the team train. He and I had been talking for about an hour each week. Allred knew I was interested in the school so there was no need to go through the maneuvering on the phone. Instead, we spent the time talking about Notre Dame football.

That Saturday, I went to my first football game: NC State vs. Georgia Tech. That night, I went to my first party and had my first beer. I thought the can of Budweiser would go to my head so I sipped it for a full hour. I remember my student host, Alberto, leaving me so he could talk to girls all night. I remember dancing with some college girl. It was the night Joe Carter hit his ninth-inning homer off Mitch Williams to give the Blue Jays a World Series Championship over the Phillies. I remember feeling good about the scene.

The next morning, the team met for breakfast at the athletic dining hall. In her Southern drawl, a lady behind the counter asked, "And what's your name, baby?" It took her a few tries to pronounce my

218

name but she eventually got it. The lady smiled the whole time. When I left the dining hall, she said, "Hope to see you here, Oh-RON-day."

NC State beat Duke 3-2 that day in a very exciting soccer game. On the plane ride back to New York City I thought about that lady in the dining hall. She cared about my name. A complete stranger showed this black boy warmth in the South. What if I went to NC State and actually got to know that lady? Wouldn't I receive more of that feeling? I could stay in New York and go to St. Johns but would I feel the same? In winter, would New Yorkers be as warm?

When I was young, the dream was to get on a bus and leave Brooklyn. If I left, I'd surely miss the City's variety, its energy, miss my brothers and sisters. I'd have to begin fresh; Tabla Rasa. Rebirth. Reinvention. Reincarnation. I'd leave my history and become a new man, a better man. I could become my self.

As the plane touched down in Queens, I realized that if I stayed in New York I'd be close to all the things I knew. I could be happy finding a cafe in Greenwich Village sipping coffee with a few friends, pretending to be an intellectual. Hundreds of people did that. But would I be true?

In Raleigh, North Carolina, I'd have to search long and wide just to get started. That work didn't bother me. I was ready for it. In a new city, I'd seek out people, go through people, talk to people, hang out with people. People were waiting for me at NC State. Warm people were there.

When I got to practice that week Joe told me not to make a decision yet, to keep my options open. He knew NC State was probably a good fit but why close my options off so early?

When Coach Dave Masur at St. Johns came to visit my mother the following week, we all sat down on the couch in 3R and talked. My mother had little to say. She and I had not discussed my trip to NC State or all the other schools calling each day. College was my decision. My mother didn't have to worry about paying for it so she had no say. I'd worked for my reward.

In early December, I took the train to Jamaica, Queens to visit St. Johns. At a station in Manhattan, there was a man playing his violin and commuters gathered around to listen. The man played Christmas tunes along with a spate of classical favorites. The crowd around him was black, white, Asian, Hispanic, men, women, old and young children. Would I ever see that variety in Raleigh? The man may have

218

played at the Bolshoi in Moscow or the Philharmonic. And he wasn't alone on the subway platform.

At the other end of the station was a Rastafarian panning Christmas music on a steel drum. The mix was something I knew I'd never find anywhere else in the world. In Raleigh there were no subway walls to echo this fusion. Where else would I hear this life?

After touring the academic buildings, the dorms, the Astroturf soccer field, speaking to the players at St. Johns, I made up my mind.

"Are you sure this is what you want to do?" Coach Joe asked. "So I can tell all these other guys to stop calling?"

"Yeah."

I had labored through the weekly conversations with assistant coaches, not having the heart to disappoint any of them. They each had the same thing to say. The talks went the way I once saw male-female relationships.

The woman knew what the man wanted so what was the point in playing the game? I knew what the coaches wanted, they knew what they had to say to get me to commit, so why play the game, especially if my mind was already made up.

"So that's where you going, huh," Nigel said.

"That's where I'm going. Full ride, good school, the best competition in college soccer."

"They paying you too?"

"What?"

"Are they giving you money? You're a big time athlete, kid. That's what they do, right? Naked white girls in your dorm room and all that."

"Soccer ain't like that."

"Just don't marry a white chick. You can date 'em. You already had sex with one of 'em. Just please, please don't marry one. Don't be no sellout negro."

"I'll try."

"Show those suckers what Brooklyn is all about."

"Word."

"Me? I don't know where I'm'a end up next fall?"

"What about Howard [University]?" I asked.

"I got in, but the financial aid ain't enough. Some of us can't be good athletes and get shit paid for."

"You're so lucky you're an athlete," Julius told me one day. I was an athlete but I was a student first and foremost. I didn't want to hear that excuse or the hint of any affirmative action backwash. In 1993, there was a lot of that nonsense in the media. Was it fair? Was it right? I wasn't an affirmative action baby nor was I lucky. If anything, I'd created my own luck.

I once heard Joe say, "Luck is the point where preparation meets opportunity." I had been prepared for college since my early days in Scotch Plains. Uncle Rudy told me I used to practice alone is his backyard no matter what the weather was like outside.

On E. 52 Street, the schoolyard across the street was two hundred square yards of asphalt for me to hone my talents. I fell, got bruised, bloody, but I dribbled, shot and passed a soccer ball against the wall for hours, for days. I had worked for my full ride.

It took a while, but I asked my self, what were the disappointed white kids doing on the weekends? Were they showcasing their talents? Were they advertising themselves? That's what I had been doing since I was nine years old on the Spirit of '76. I had worked to bring attention to my talents and did the best to convince the trained eyes of college scouts and coaches that I was worth their investment. Wasn't that what the guidance counselor was telling seniors to do? Make their application stand out, include all the best things about themselves in their essay.

My essay was action on the field and in class. I'd been writing it for years. It was good. I deserved my reward.

When the signing date approached in February 1994, I inked my future with the North Carolina State University and waited to mail the National Letter of Intent, formally accepting their offer of financial aid. A lot of worries were over.

1-29-94

"I've signed the forms. It's over. No more calls from schools I don't want to go to. Nerve wrecking asking a kid to choose between great options. But that's my fate. At least I have options. Princeton, Columbia, St. Johns, NC State. Great options. But I've chosen.

Haven't thought about or written much in months. Didn't realize how much this college stuff consumed me. Freedom now. Ideas should be coming my way. I want to get in that creative zone again. I miss being a channel from the Creator. I miss *The Wonder Child*. Where has he been these past months? I am acutely aware of this SENIORITIS. It has been a year now. I am failing AP Bio, Social Science Research and Law Studies. What if I don't graduate? What if I have to go to summer school? What if I have to become a super senior and stay another semester? I don't hear any voice screaming at me to stop my present course. What an embarrassment to stay at Tech another year. I'd never live it down. Can't do it. 'Get to work, Oronde...'"

"... I remember when I did school work because I did the work and not much else. Now I know what it takes to be a good student. It takes an ethic. You have to figure out what you want to do and work at it. Even if you have to do things you don't want to, you have to do them if they will aid your dream. You have to figure out a way to tackle yourself. You have to expose yourself to yourself. Just by completing the difficult thing you didn't want to, you're growing. Westinghouse projects, AP Bio tests, Law Studies reports aren't what I do best, but I have to do them. I am worse off than I was a year ago. At least then I knew the person I was running away from. I want to study, do my schoolwork and watch less TV. I want to bond with someone. Again, I am at the point of birth. The slate is blank. My pen is ready to create my history."

American Studies. Ms. Desiano. Another 8:05 class my last semester at Tech. We read documents written by the first settlers at Jamestown, Virginia. I cut class once each week, stopped listening to Ms. Desiano and cried. No one saw the tears but I wept when I understood the logic in the decisions of gentrified, English aristocrats. Slavery made so much sense when I read their journals and manifestos.

The first settlers seldom worked the land in England, so why work it in America? When more land became available, they ordered more horses, more oxen, more human chattel to toil beneath the blazing sun. The damn thing was so rational.

It tore me up when, for one split second, I reasoned that slavery was inevitable and, furthermore, it made sense at that time in America's history. In that split second, I cursed my brain for having thoughts, for skillfully mastering the process of divorcing my black boy anger about slavery from the detached, objective way the subject matter had to be presented in class.

Ms. Desiano had to know how damaging the truth was to me but I couldn't blame her for carrying on with her lessons. She had no time to stop and talk to me about what I must have been feeling. I skipped many days, so maybe the fault lay in me. I had cracked.

Perhaps Ms. Desiano could have helped me put the pieces together but breakfast in the cafeteria was better than listening to historical ignominy or tackling my own personal ignominy... In me there was *Emptiness*.

In March 1994, the NY Times was delivering blow-by-blow accounts of the genocide in Rwanda. The black and white images struck me hard. Machete-wielding children in Kigali, Ruhengeri, Byumba, swayed by the misguided whims of pathological genocidaires, killed indiscriminately. Black people, my people; how could we?

As the details grew grimmer, I wanted action from the US government, wanted my peers talking about the human tragedy before us. No one did.

Strife over ethnicity is not borne in human nature. Man does not emerge from the womb wielding a machete. Man must learn to hold the machete; to hold onto lies about a contrived enemy; to hold onto hate so long, that letting the machete fly into the flesh of another man has a healing effect on the hole a man's hate has in him.

I was a victim of the Times. I thought I knew what was happening in Kigali but I was misinformed. Rwanda was no "civil war", no "tribal warfare" as the papers described. It was genocide. I was as duped as the conscripted, young masses acting on the directives of Radio Mille Collines. *Inyenzi*. I was a cockroach, scurrying from the truth foretold in black and white. More should have been done. More should have been done. Black people, my people... In me there was *Madness*.

I had to get away. Thankfully, the Brooklyn Italians had planned a ten-day trip to Italy in late March. Ms. Desiano had reservations about me missing more classes but since I was going to Italy and she was Italian, I promised to bring her back the most delectable prosciutto I could find.

Joe had gathered the best high school soccer players in and around New York City to compete in the Torneo Enzo Ferrari just north of Milan. Ten days before our departure, my right ankle got caught on the turf while practicing at Brooklyn College and I went down. The swelling was immediate. The doctors at Kings County hospital put me on crutches the next day. I knew I wouldn't be playing in Italy. In the back of my mind, I thought my skills would have certainly earned a tryout with a professional Italian club. And then puff, dream deferred.

"Why God? What's the new plan?"

My mother sensed my disappointment. I was looking forward to the trip. I hadn't left America since we arrived in August 1985. I couldn't. Except for Randi and Keri, both Americans, no one in our apartment had papers to travel. For years, my mother had been filing for a green card for her, Annie and me but nothing ever happened. I understood the waiting game. It had taken Grandma thirteen years to get her green card. I understood the thousands of dollars my mother's lawyer asked from her over the years. I understood Ma didn't want to see more disappointment on my face. I had just made her proud and earned a full scholarship to college. I was her first child and I was doing well despite the connections we never made, despite all the men who screwed her over, despite all that could have gone wrong for both of us in Brooklyn. Moreover, I'd done it on my own… In me there was *Self-Reliance*.

When my mother said, "You should go to Italy, go for the fun of it, enjoy yourself," maybe she wanted the best for me. When she took me to see a Vincentian *nointer* to massage my ankle and held my hand as the lady put pressure on the balls of my grapefruit-sized ankle, maybe Ma was looking out for me?

When my mother doused an ace bandage in vinegar and wrapped it tight around my ankle every night, promising the vinegar would reduce the swelling, maybe she was helping? Every morning, she would look at my ankle, smile and say, "I think its getting better. Run on it. You'll be fine."

And so I left for Italy with my mother's positive energy, knowing there was little chance of me actually playing in a game. "Enjoy yourself," she said.

When the team returned to Kennedy Airport ten days later and a big, black customs agent in a high chair told me, "We're putting you on a plane to St. Vincent, young man. You will never see your family again. You're leaving this country. Your mama isn't going to help you. You're gone tonight." When the customs agent said that, I understood that my mother had screwed me over again.

Before I left for Italy, I asked Ma if it was okay for me to leave the country even though I didn't have a green card. "You'll be fine. They can't do anything to you. If anybody asks you, just tell then you're in the system." Ma didn't think I believed her so she had Uncle Rudy tell me the same thing.

"You have an alien number," she kept saying. "You're okay." An alien number meant everything to my mother. As long as some computer in the Immigration and Naturalization Service registered that the green card process had begun, there wasn't much airport officials could do. It was a waiting game until the number came up.

I waited in line for one customs official after another to inspect my passport. "Where's you I-94? Show me your visa. What's your name?"

"I'm in the system."

"What's your alien number?"

"I don't know."

"Let me see your passport again?"

After about five minutes and the line behind me getting restless, the customs official took me to an adjacent room. I was embarrassed. My teammates were going out to the City to meet their families. Most of them were in front of me and had no idea of the commotion I was causing. The same thing happened at the Milan International Airport. There, customs officers didn't want to let me in because I didn't have an Italian visa. They looked my St. Vincent passport up and down wondering where it was. I was taken to a room and had to point out my homeland on a world map.

In New York, the Brooklyn Italian team officials never bothered to ask me if I had a green card or an alien number. They knew I'd been in the country since I was nine years old and assumed I'd gotten a green card. The majority of the managers, treasurers, and team chaperones had come to America from Italy and they all had green cards or were citizens. Why wasn't I?

After waiting two hours in the Milan airport, I think some money was exchanged and a stamp appeared in my passport. The visitor's visa was something that could have been taken care of in New York weeks before the trip. All I had to do was present my passport to the Italian Consulate in Manhattan and the stamp would have been there.

At Kennedy Airport, Coach Joe and the team officials all showed concern but I told them my mother was on her way to straighten everything out and they should go home. In the ninety minutes it took my mother to leave her job in Manhattan and reach me, I saw Chinese, Arabs, Indians, Russians and other huddled masses either not ready to enter the country or being sent back home. When my mother arrived, she ran over and hugged me tight. She was crying... In me there was *Anger*.

"I told you this was a mistake," I said, trying to hold back my own tears.

"Trust me, they can't do anything to you. They're just trying to scare you. You're in the system. You have a number."

"That doesn't mean anything to him," I pointed to the big, black man who had threatened me. "He says I'm going back to St. Vincent tonight."

"That's not going to happen," my mother assured me. "These people don't know anything. You have a number. The have to let you in."

My mother tried her best to offer comfort but I wanted nothing from her. A part of me saw the situation as her attempt to coddle favor from me. She must have seen it as a shining moment to do something significant for me. She could be the hero in my life for once.

My mother saw how terrified I was. I had my friends, my dreams, my scholarship was riding on whatever number or whatever confidence she tried showing me. When the big, black man called my name, Ma walked with me and repeated, "He doesn't know shit. You'll be okay."

At the counter, my mother pleaded with the man to look into his computer. She even shed a few crocodile tears and winked at me when the man's eyes turned to his monitor.

The man began asking questions about our life. How long had we been in Brooklyn? Where did my mother work? What was her tax ID number? Who was her spouse? Did she have more kids? Was she married?

Ma was clever. She had been since the days waiting on line at the US Embassy in Barbados. *God helps those...* She kept her mouth shut and only answered the questions she had to. "Never tell anyone more than they ask," she once told me. Years of dealing with crooked lawyers and the INS had made her hip to the game. Speak when spoken to; Short sentences; To the point. She did.

Ma showed the customs officer she would not budge, that she and I had every right to walk out of the airport and back to our lives in Brooklyn. When the man finally punched Ma's info into the computer, our numbers came up. Bingo!

With confidence, my mother said to the officer, "I told you." The guy knew he had no further reason to intimidate my mother and me.

"Go sit over there," he commanded bitterly. "Someone will come get you soon."

Ma gave the man the evil eye she reserved for Mudd after one of their fights. She had won.

We waited another ninety minutes in the INS room. Ma told me she had called Annie, Teri, Randi and Keri and told them what was happening. She said they were all balling their eyes out at the thought of me getting deported. That made me feel better. My brothers and sisters genuinely loved me.

Another INS official came by, walked us to yet another room and entered our number into his computer. My mother's name came up. She answered the man's questions and told him it was only a matter of time until she got her green card and could sponsor me. The officer agreed that would happen but said I still had to go through a deportation hearing.

Between April and June 1994, Ma and I visited her lawyer's office five or six times to discuss my deportation. By then, I'd received my letter of acceptance from NC State. My I-20 and student visa soon came. I had applied as an international student. I had to.

"Then, you will get a student visa," my mother said. "You'll be legal here." Since I was eighteen, I would've had to start the green card process all over again on my own; too much time. A student visa was the solution.

I'd have to leave America, get a stamp from an American Embassy abroad and then reenter the country as an international student. I'd be in the system with a valid entry visa and alien number. As far as the government was concerned, all my years in America would be wiped clean. Tabla Rasa. It was all legal. My lawyer agreed. He said it helped that I'd earned a scholarship, had not committed any crimes and was already a model citizen.

"Nobody wants to ruin your life," he said. "You're gonna come back to the US on your student visa anyway." The judge said the same thing.

At the hearing, my lawyer spent three minutes explaining my case. I never had to say a word. The judge spoke some legalese and I was formally deported. Actually, my petition to enter the US --which is what the official term is for what happened at Kennedy Airport-- was denied and I was told to leave the country by July 11, 1994. It was mid June. I had three and a half weeks... In me there was *Uncertainty*.

Late June. I passed my NY State Regents exams, dressed up in costume each day of senior pride week, took pictures with classmates, smiled, signed yearbooks. I told no one in school I might never see them again. Instead, I enjoyed my last days in America.

I didn't buy my own copy of The Blueprint --Brooklyn Tech's yearbook. I had my memories scribed in a five-subject notebook at home and a little red book I kept in my backpack.

My four years of high school were in me. Gateway, CTY, Alex, Social Science Research, Sarah, OFFestival '93, Anna, Roxanne, Dr. Weinberger, Bekim, Nigel, Nadine, Julius, Ms. Floyd, Ms. Sigelakis, Mr. Ruzich, Ms. Cohen, blackness, consciousness, dread, locks, mirrored shades, air, breath, life. Brooklyn Tech was in me. It was the best thing I'd ever done. That knowledge was my blueprint. I had been building on it for years. Why waste money on a keepsake my classmates would eventually consign to the dust in their closets?

In the end, no one said anything about me going to summer school for failing three senior year classes. The principal called me into his office one day and gave me a stern talking to. "You know you should have done better," he said. "You have friends here pulling for you."

The principal was an assistant my freshman year and accompanied the Gateway kids to Comsett State Park. Maybe I threw him a touchdown or two that day and he was repaying me. Just like my lawyer said, no one wanted to ruin it for a kid who had done the right things and earned a full ride to college. I would still finish Brooklyn Tech with a four-year overall average of 82%. Thank God for my first two years of straight A's. My yearly average had dropped ten percent every year since then. Freshman year: 95%. Senior year: 65%. But I was a better person with my 65%. I took great comfort in that immeasurable factor.

"How much are the graduation tickets?" my mother asked one day. "Grandma wants to come too."

"I'm not going."

"Why not?" she asked.

"I don't want to," I stated. My mother had no follow up questions. She knew I was still heated about the whole deportation thing. For all I knew, I'd leave the country in three weeks and never be back. That was her fault.

I thought Italy was not a good idea. While there, I tried to play soccer but my ankle was too weak. I watched the team tie the first game against a local squad called Sassuolo, saw us beat the tournament favorite, Sampdoria FC --a youth professional team-- 2-1. That was the biggest upset --an American team from Brooklyn beating Italian players training with a professional club. Sampdoria was a big name in the Italian professional league. We had beaten their U-19 youth team -- the kids who would be playing on the professional level in two or three more years.

After the upset vs. Sampdoria, the local people began following our progress in the tournament. We received a standing ovation as we left the grandstands the day of the finals. That day, *il paisan* knew we should have been playing for a trophy instead of watching.

What happened was the local team, Sassuolo, was tied with us on points. To make it to the finals versus Russian powerhouse Dynamo Kiev, they had to win their last game by four goals. Their opponent was another local team. And wouldn't you know it, Sassuolo won their game by four goals and advanced to the finals ahead of us. We got hosed but the people knew the truth... In me there was a call for *Fairness*.

When the fellas snuck out to a club the last night and got drunk, I stayed in my room nursing my injury. I had gone to Italy and spent most days in bed icing my ankle. And then I got the life scared out of me at JFK. You could say I had a little issue with my mother. No graduation ceremony for her.

And the auditorium would be hot as hell anyway. Brooklyn Tech had the second largest auditorium in the city but it had no air conditioning. With eleven hundred students walking, all their parents, friends and relatives, the room would be stifling. I didn't see the point of that.

If truth be told, I didn't want a repeat of my joyless eighth grade graduation; didn't want to see kids and families smiling, laughing, crying. It would remind me of what I may have missed out on at Tech.

Unlike eighth grade, I knew more of what I had in me. I had graduated from emptiness. I had seen myself be my self. I had a sense of my place in the universe; had faith in my internal compass and took pride in where it was pointing me. No keynote speaker needed to tell me to go out and conquer the world. That was my own directive. What pomp or circumstance could explain what that knowledge of self meant to me?

The Wonder Child had channeled something profound through me. The movement began around Christmas '92 during the Anna-Roxanne affair.

I sat down to start a journal entry one night and for three hours, the pen never came off the page. I wasn't thinking, I wasn't eating, drinking, wasn't breathing. I was writing and couldn't stop. It wasn't putting thought to paper, more like dictation from the universe.

I penned what had been in me for days, months, maybe years. Bits and pieces had fleshed out in poems, stories, plays, but never like this. That day I bled onto the notebook page. When it was done, I had the bare bones of some philosophy I wanted to call my own. It was my will to power.

My heroes had their manifestos, their treatises, their great works. I felt what I'd written was mine. In the months to follow, I refined the skeleton of that essay. Little had to be done to the key points. They were as they should be. The book *17 to Life* began as what it would be.

And why not an adolescent philosophy? Why not an adolescent philosopher? What was wrong with our scope on life? I was at the apex of my innocence. What was wrong with feeling and speaking from the heights of childhood? From the mouth of babes, they say… In me there was *Hope*.

I wondered if the rest of the graduating class realized that someday soon a narrowing, a winding down, a cutting off from innocence was coming for them. Maybe their signatures in The Blueprint were future odes to halcyon days? But yearbooks would be shadow boxes in closets and attics. Tech's days would wither to dust themselves and reunions would be excuses to drink, flaunt individual success and try to sex up the old girlfriend. I had no plans to come back in ten, twenty or thirty years. I wanted my reunion documented, preserved, now and forever.

And so I wrote and wrote and rewrote. Those days in June when seniors didn't have to come to the building, I wrote. On prom night, when my classmates were at Tavern of the Green in Central Park dancing and drinking, I wrote. Maybe I should have gone to prom or to graduation? Perhaps I should have done it for my mother and grandmother? Maybe it was selfish of me? But adolescence is selfless and selfish all the same. I was what I was.

Following the prom, I got a letter from Cynthia, a player I coached on the girl's soccer team for three years. I'd tried a thing or two with her but I was rough then, our conversations altogether awkward. She was as randy and untamed as me. She felt the same uncertainty. Cynthia was an itty, bitty, Korean chick with her own rivers to cross. The more I got to know her, the more I realized she was going through the same family nonsense, the same academic pressure, the same fears about the future.

Reading Cynthia's letter, I realized her words were my yearbook signature. Unknowingly --or perhaps *knowing without knowing*-- she had encapsulated my high school days.

"Hey Big O,

I can't believe you stayed up to write that beautiful letter. That was really sweet. I didn't even know I was "worthy" enough to be on your priority list. About your cold 'goodbyes'" I've gotten used to it. It's just one of those Oronde things--it comes with the whole package. I don't understand [when you ask] how do you finish a relationship? Relationships can fade or deteriorate, but you can't finish a relationship. However, I think I understand what you're saying. Oronde, you worry too much. You're a beautiful person. Maybe a little too skinny but that's OK.I miss our maybe-it-could've/should've been relationship.

I really miss those erotic, spazzy, horny-assed conversations also. Whatever happened to it all? I think we're both suffering from I've-had-enough-of-this-school-and-everyone-in-it-and-I-can't-wait-to-get-out-of-here syndrome. Hey, open yourself up! You have so much spazz to share with the universe. And if you really miss writing something in the middle of the night, then please write to me.

It's too bad you won't be taking part in our corny graduation festivities. I seriously considered asking you to the prom, but I didn't think you'd care to go with me. Think of this as a compliment :) Hey bud, don't be so negative. I'll probably remember you for a long time --maybe too long. You were the first dude who's ever been bold and brave enough to tell me you liked me. Guy's usually aren't stupid or they're too smart to do that. Of course, me being the psycho-bitch that I am, I haven't had many relationships. And believe me --you bring out my decent side. Scary, isn't it?

I've seen many views of Oronde Ash. I've seen you w/ hair, w/o hair, with little locks, with big locks, w/ clothes, w/out a shirt, in a swimsuit. I think the thing I'll remember about you is you carrying me up seven flights of stairs when I was hurt. Wow! That totally amazed me. As small as I am, I'm heavy. You're my hero.

Anyway, I'll always remember 'the kiss'. I'll remember going to 47th/50th Street and sitting on the cold, wooden bench and the mice at our feet. (I miss talking dirty to you, by the way. You were the only guy I can be dirty with.) I'll remember playing soccer with you (not that I can play.) I'll remember Teresa chasing you with a broken bottle.

Before I say goodbye, a little reminder: Stay in touch!

Lovingly, The Midget,

Cynthia"

All along, from Scotch Plains to Brooklyn Tech, I had probably been more than I gave my self credit for. I'd come into adolescence enclosed, fearful, unaware. But at seventeen, I was going on about sex and turning tiny Korean chicks on. Not bad.

I had more chances to do things if I'd only asked more questions, put forth a bit more effort or simply had more faith in and less fear of other people. Cynthia would have gone to prom with me. Maybe other girls would have gone too? Who knows what may have been? No one ever will.

On the night of July 10th, 1994, my mother and I rode the subway to Port Authority bus terminal in midtown Manhattan. My brothers and sisters wanted to come but I talked them out of it. Ma and I reassured them I was coming back. They took that comfort to bed with them. I boarded a Greyhound bus bound for Toronto, Canada. I was to stay with my uncle Kenneth, take my I-20 student visa from NC

State to the American Embassy in Toronto, get my passport stamped and return to NY in two weeks to complete preparations for my freshman year of college. At least that was the plan.

As the bus drove upstate pass Ithaca, NY, I saw Cornell University on a nearby hill and thought about the Gateway program. Five or six of those kids got into Cornell. A lot of Brooklyn Tech kids got into Cornell.

I thought about the black and Latino college students who visited Mary McLeod Bethune in the sixth grade to talk to us about the State University of New York (SUNY) and the possibility of higher education for us. After six weeks, we each got a navy blue sweatshirt with the SUNY seal on the front and the words, **I'M GOING TO COLLEGE** written on the back in bold letters.

After six years, I still had the shirt. Like me, it had gone through some alterations. By my senior year, the shirt was too small so I cut off the sleeves and turned it into a workout jersey to use when I ran or played soccer that spring, readying my body for NC State.

I thought about CTY in 1991, about Alex, Sarah, Annie, my mother. What had I gotten from each woman? Had I given them anything in return?

My life had always been about women, even when I didn't know it. They were teachers who praised me --even the males, because the ones I admired, like Mr. Matthews and Mr. Cacheiro, were as nurturing as any woman. Women raised me, fed my body, my intellect, my loins. I got up for and lay down with women. I read, I wrote. Somehow, sharing thoughts and giving life to dreams on paper seemed more a female trait. I mean, how many boys keep diaries… I mean, journals.

I thought about Richard Wright's *Black Boy*, Claude McKay's *Manchild in the Promised Land*, James Baldwin's *Notes of a Native Son*, Mark Mathabane's *Kaffir Boy*. I thought about the different selves in them and in me. I thought about the slaves too, running north to Canada and freedom, thought about my childhood fantasy of escaping the apartment, getting on a bus, starting new. But mostly, I thought about the writers.

I thought about the hours spent in quiet contemplation over the right image, the correct degree, the perfect sentiment to convey the Creator's vision. Separate, disparate lives, miles and decades apart, joined and sustained by words and truth; their stories were my American history foretold and retold.

Those black men nurtured my philosophy, kept alive my destiny. I was alight in their words and they were kept alive in my actions. And my progeny? My brothers and sisters? They were on one side of the Peace Bridge separating Buffalo, NY and Fort Erie, Ontario. Or were they on the other side of the Peace Bridge connecting the US and Canada --my past, my present and my future.

Alone, on a Greyhound bus and hundreds of miles to roam, I thought about my own story and marveled at the threads that kept the tale spinning. My neighbor Jerry in St. Vincent; my cousin Gerry in Scotch Plains; Mrs. Cohen in fifth grade and Ms. Cohen at Brooklyn Tech; Alexandra in middle school, Alex at CTY, Alex, the scary vision from *A Clockwork Orange* I was afraid to become; the Spirit of '76, The American Revolution, the same spirit in me wanting to change the world, do more, be more.

I thought about the star on my forehead. My father swore he saw that star in a photo taken when I was four or five. He said Jah had blessed me. Perhaps Jah had. Perhaps there was the promise of better days for me. More than likely that star was the camera flash or the sunlight bouncing off the petroleum jelly my mother liked to dab on my face when taking pictures.

That photo and the ideas surrounding it symbolized my vision from seventeen to life. The road ahead was not about the vista or even what happened along the way. My life would be defined by what I chose to believe and do with those events, those people, in whatever place and time I chose to inhabit. The story of my life was waiting to be told. I was the author. I had always been the author. It was time to write. I could do it. I had always done it.

Speaking at such a young age, reading at such a young age, book reports, stories, essays, journal entries, poems, acting off-Broadway, a commitment to learning had armed me with the tools to shape my experiences and stamp them with meaning. And that meaning had always been and would always be alive in the spaces between my thoughts, between actions, between people, between the ways I dealt with it all. Intelligence and awareness fill in the silent, troubling spaces where fear, anxiety, dread and doubt can run havoc on a life.

I had used school and teachers and books and words to shape my thoughts along the same lines as the great men of the world. I wanted to be a great man. Perhaps I was being a big grandiose but that

234

fantasy, that striving for a higher order had awaken me out of bed many mornings. I accepted what I had done and was ready for what I would do.

My story was my life. I knew it better than anyone. That's a power beyond measure.

Now what would I do with my story? Would I even make it back to America to continue living and writing it?

Alone of a Greyhound bus heading north, the question was my own, as was the freedom to search for the answers I needed to find.

THE BEGINNING...

Going to Church, Fall 1985

Author, Skinny Legs, Fall 1985

First Trophy, Fall 1985

Author, 5th Grade, Fall1986

The Spirit of '76, Spring 1986

i

8th Grade Valedictorian, June 1990   Randy, Keri and the Infamous Door Panel   Kaffir Boy

8th Grade Class Photo

Author and Friend Patrick, Mirrored Shades, Trophy Collection

i

Article on Author, 1994

Alex, CTY, 1991

Ma, Teri, Keri, Randi

Tech's Ash : The Complete Package

Oronde Ash takes care of business on the soccer field and at home as well

James Baldwin

Author, 1994

Barrouallie Anglican Church, Bell

St Vincent

Barrouallie

Tech Lunchroom Table, Nigel, 1993

Deportation Papers, 1994

17 to Life: The Soundtrack

Disc 1

1. Living in America, James Brown
2. The Message, Grandmaster Flash
3. Living For the City, Stevie Wonder
4. Theme to Video Music Box
5. Right Here Right Now, Jesus Jones
6. It Takes Two, Rob Bass and DJ EZ Rock
7. Everything I Do, Bryan Adams
8. Take Five, Grover Washington Jr.
9. Down on the Corner, Credence Clearwater Revival
10. Holding Back The Years, Simply Red
11. Feels Good, Tony! Tony! Tone!
12. Redemption Song, Bob Marley

Disc 2

Wake Up and Live, Bob Marley

Pride, Living Colour

The Choice Is Yours, Black Sheep

Tennessee, Arrested Development

360, Grand Puba

Scenario, Leaders of the New School

In The Name of love, U2

Juice (Know the Ledge), Eric B & Rakim

Fight The Power, Public Enemy

Cool Like That, Digable Planets

Fragile, Sting

America the Beautiful, Ray Charles

Your Life, Age 9-17: The Soundtrack

(Write your favorite songs from those years. Email the list to bygINCpresents@live.com or post your playlist at http://www.youtube.com/17tolife)

Disc 1

1. _____
2. _____
3. _____
4. _____
5. _____
6. _____
7. _____
8. _____
9. _____
10. _____

Disc 2

TO THE READER

Thank you for taking the time to read the book. It has gone through countless revisions since I began writing it in high school nearly twenty years ago. I finally came to a point where it was time to let it go, warts and all.

If you've found errors, omissions, issues that need correcting, let me know. Like life, my memoir is a work in progress. Help me make the next edition better.

Offer an evaluation, review, critique or suggestion. All comments welcomed. Email bygINCpresents@live.com or visit www.orondeash.com to book a reading/talk with your school, group, club or organization.

Thank you.

bygINCpresents
Oronde Ash   *Author, Educator, Speaker*
The Black Box And Your Flight To Life ™

Oronde Ash *at a Glance*

Teacher, Former Division I College Coach, College Recruiter, World Cup Soccer Player,
Scholar-Athlete, Filmmaker, Actor, Radio DJ, Youth Organizer, Mentor, Husband, Father

Oronde Ash is an author and speaker on motivation,
achievement, empowerment and change.

His topics include
- The Black Box And Your Flight to Life ™
- Life in the Constancy of Change ™
- Identity Formation in Adolescence and Beyond
- The Person You Want To Be Has Been In You All Along
- How to *Right* The Story of Your Life
- From Black Boy to Black Man in America

Oronde works with
- College-age Students and Groups
- High Schools, Middle Schools, Elementary Schools
- Teachers, Parents, Administrators
- Youth Development Programs and Professionals
- Churches, Camps, Retreats, Sports Clubs

Presentation style
- Speeches --Face-to-Face, Conference, Video
- PowerPoint
- Workshops
- Seminars

Some Clients
- North Carolina State University
- The Tupac Amaru Shakur Center for the Arts
- The NFL Player's Assoc. High School Player
  Development Forum
- DC Lutheran Social Services Teen Haven AIDS Retreat
- The St. Vincent U-20 National Soccer Program
- NC State Univ. English Dept. Teen Writing Workshop

In the end Oronde's message is about creating positive CHANGE
1. **Live** the *process* – Life is all about Change
2. **Learn** the *function* – Finding Value in the Midst of Change
3. **Love** the *outcome* – The Change in You

Past Speeches
(All talks can be tailored to your specific theme
with advanced notice.)

1. 9 Years Old and I HATE YOU ALL!
2. School Was My Home: Teachers My Parents
3. I Loved To Learn When I Learned To Love
4. Young, Gifted, Black and Still Hating Myself
5. I'm Doing Exactly What I Envisioned at 17
6. From Moments to Memoir: How Keeping A
   Journal Wrote the Story of My Life

For Bookings and Inquiries
Contact
bygINCpresents
Oronde Ash
PO Box 33332
Raleigh, NC 27636
919-600-3210 (w)
bygINCpresents@live.com
www.orondeash.com

Character, Leadership, Greatness, Wisdom
Creativity and the Complexities of Life.

www.ingramcontent.com/pod-product-compliance
Lightning Source LLC
Chambersburg PA
CBHW022014090426
42739CB00006BA/135